3rd Australia

Getting
Started in
Shares

FOR

DUMMIES®

A Wiley Brand

by James Dunn

FOR

DUMMIES®

A Wiley Brand

Getting Started in Shares For Dummies®, 3rd Australian Edition

Published by
Wiley Publishing Australia Pty Ltd
42 McDougall Street
Milton, Qld 4064
www.dummies.com

Copyright © 2016 Wiley Publishing Australia Pty Ltd

The moral rights of the author have been asserted.

National Library of Australia
Cataloguing-in-Publication data:

Author:	Dunn, James, 1962-
Title:	Getting Started in Shares For Dummies / James Dunn
Edition:	3rd Australian Edition
ISBN:	9780730320623 (pbk.)
	9780730320630 (ebook)
Notes:	Includes index
Series:	For Dummies
Subjects:	Stock exchanges — Australia
	Investments — Australia
	Stocks — Australia
Dewey Number:	332.63220994

Cover image: © adrian825 / iStockphoto

Typeset by diacriTech, Chennai, India

Printed in Singapore by
C.O.S. Printers Pte Ltd

10 9 8 7 6 5 4 3 2 1

Contents at a Glance

Table of Contents

Introduction

. . . .

Thanks for choosing the third edition of this compact edition, *Getting Started in Shares For Dummies*. This smaller-sized edition is what's called a *portable* edition, full of information but small enough to carry on the tram, train or bus or to take with you on holidays for easy reading. This edition brings you up to date with the many exciting developments in the Australian stock market. If you're a first-time investor, this book has advice on where to start, the pitfalls to avoid and tips on how to have fun (and not take too many risks) while your money goes to work for you.

The global financial crisis (GFC) and the market slump that ensued — which has become one of the longest-lived the sharemarket has seen — has dented many investors' faith in shares as an investment, but despite the scary headlines and the ever-present possibility of a market fall, profitable companies continue to generate capital growth for their shareholders over the long term. The great paradox of the sharemarket is that while it's the most volatile of the asset classes, it's also the one most capable of reliably building wealth over the long term for the individual investor; I show you how in this book.

Australia has grown and developed in many directions since the first edition of *Getting Started in Shares For Dummies* welcomed investors taking their first steps into the sharemarket. If you followed the first edition (or indeed the second), you're hopefully now managing a portfolio, researching stocks that interest you, keeping abreast of the daily market play and boosting your initial investment to something that'll at least pay for your dream holiday and at best see you comfortably through the years.

In many of the speeches that I've made around the country in 28 years as a finance journalist, I've tried to present the sharemarket as a hugely interesting institution. Because it is! And, moreover, this market, which touches every one of our lives in one way or another, doesn't have to be daunting. The sharemarket isn't a hard concept to understand. When people say to me that I make the idea of buying and selling shares understandable for them, I curse whatever it was they'd been reading or hearing that made it appear the opposite.

About This Book

Getting Started in Shares For Dummies explains the sharemarket's intricacies in terms that anyone can understand. Although the sharemarket looks like a high-tech computer game with its flashing lights and scrolling letters and numbers on the trading screens, the sharemarket is actually based on a very simple concept. Companies divide their capital into tiny units called shares, and anyone can buy or sell these units in a free market at any time. Companies use the sharemarket to raise funds from the public, and the public — meaning you — invests in the companies' shares. You invest your money in shares because you expect to get a better return in earnings than with other investments.

Most of the time the sharemarket is profitable for investors. Despite the occasional spectacular market fall, such as the great 'bear market' of 2007 to 2009 — or even the odd collapse of one of its constituent companies — the sharemarket generally plods along making money for its investors. The sharemarket revolves around money, but is also very much a human institution. The sharemarket is sometimes described as a living entity (for which we finance journalists are often mocked). Oddly, the sharemarket does have human moods because it reflects the greed or fear of its users, who are sometimes *very* human.

Greed is a powerful influence on the sharemarket, and so is fear. A saying on Wall Street suggests that these two emotions are the only influences at work on the sharemarket, and they fight a daily battle for supremacy. On a day-to-day basis, the sharemarket wavers between the two. The 2000s began with the fear of the 'tech bust', and then switched firmly to greed for the middle part of the decade, only for fear to come roaring back into the spotlight in late 2007, and again in 2015. The two will always have their days on top.

The sheer range of activities of the companies listed on the Australian Securities Exchange (formerly the Australian Stock Exchange) makes it a very interesting place — if a trading system that you can see only on computer screens all over the nation can be called a place. The number of different types of shares you can invest in is mind-boggling — perhaps there is too much choice. As an individual investor, you can't own every type of share, so the solution is for you to come up with a share investment strategy.

As you will discover, of the 2,200 or so stocks listed on the
Australian Securities Exchange (ASX), most investment
professionals confine their activity to about one-sixth of them.
Even in the 500 stocks that comprise the All Ordinaries Index
(one of the Australian sharemarket's main indicators), the last
200 or so don't hold much interest to Australian fund managers.
This is where a self-reliant investor like you can find some
undiscovered gems caught in that bind of being too small to
attract the fund managers' and brokers' attention, and then
remaining small because they can't get this attention. Some of
the sharemarket's acorns really do become great oaks. As a self-
reliant investor, with the knowledge and the time to thoroughly
research potential stock purchases, you can really steal a march
on the pros.

It gets harder and potentially more rewarding the deeper you
delve into the sharemarket. In the bottom 1,900 or so stocks, you
may find some real dogs that should not be listed (and probably
won't be for very much longer), but you can also discover
wonderful companies that are just about to flourish. This kind of
investing is called bottom-fishing. You need to be wary and know
how to back up your discoveries with solid research. At these
depths of the market, you can make some very wrong moves.

You have to own some of the 2,200 stocks in order to experience
the ups and downs of the sharemarket. The tools that enable
you to get into the market intelligently are right here in
this book. The sharemarket should be an essential part of
everybody's investment strategy. Sharemarket participation in
Australia is among the highest in the world, but too many people
still don't understand its benefits. As the nation's population
ages and superannuation grows in importance, the amount of
Australians' investment assets (and retirement nest eggs) going
into Australian shares is set to rise dramatically. My aim in this
book is to help you understand the sharemarket so that you can
control your future financial security.

Foolish Assumptions

I don't assume a lot about you as a reader and budding share
investor, but I do make these brief assumptions before I
encourage you to get started:

- ✔ You are interested in knowing more about the sharemarket.
- ✔ You know some of the basics, but you'd like to flesh out
  this knowledge.

> ✔ You know that even if people don't think they're involved in the sharemarket, a big chunk of their superannuation certainly is!

Icons Used in This Book

Throughout this book you see friendly and useful icons to enhance your reading pleasure and highlight special kinds of information. The icons give added emphasis to the details that I think are extra important. Although the icons are self-explanatory, here are their basic messages.

Take extra special notice of this piece of information. I mean it, too — this detail is really something to store away for future use.

It's not vital that you read this stuff as you'll get a good understanding of the subject matter anyway. But it's often interesting and sometimes an entertaining diversion.

This is information I think you can profit from, so I've pre-highlighted it for you (I'm trying to save you from getting highlighter ink on the opposite page when you close the book).

Uh-oh! Wealth hazard ahead! Manoeuvre carefully around this obstacle, and mark it down in the memory bank.

Beyond the Book

This book also comes with a free access-anywhere Cheat Sheet that provides plenty of helpful share investing tips. To get this Cheat Sheet, simply go to www.dummies.com and search for 'Getting Started in Shares For Dummies Cheat Sheet' in the Search box.

Where to Go from Here

You don't need to read this book cover to cover, but if you're a beginner in terms of the sharemarket, starting at Chapter 1 is a good way to go. In fact, I hope you do. If you're not a beginner, then each chapter is written as a self-contained read, with plenty of cross-references to other chapters scattered throughout the book. If you want to know more about a particular topic, don't hesitate to follow the cross-references and gain a broader, fuller understanding of that particular topic.

I hope that after you go through this book — if you haven't already dipped your toe in the sharemarket waters — you'll want to take the steps to starting your first portfolio of shares. If you're already an investor — great! Now you'll want to become a better-informed and more effective investor. Work out for yourself what financial security means to you, sit down with a financial adviser (or not, if you prefer; but it is advisable) and decide how shares can help you achieve your goals. Then, get started. Today!

Part I
Putting the Share in Sharemarket

In this part . . .

- See how the sharemarket builds wealth.
- Figure out the two functions of the sharemarket.

Chapter 1

So, You Want to Invest in Shares

*I*f you've been hearing about the sharemarket for a long time, but you're only now taking the plunge, welcome aboard. There simply isn't a better place to invest money.

You're probably already familiar with shares and how they generate long-term wealth. In that case, you may want to skim through Chapter 1 and Chapter 2 quickly and then move on to Chapter 3 for an in-depth view of investment strategies. If that isn't the case, you're in the right spot to get started.

Investing Is All about Timing

Australians are among the world's most avid share investors, with 33 per cent of the adult population, or 5.9 million people, owning shares directly. This figure has fallen since 2004, when 55 per cent of Australians (or 8 million people) owned shares, but Australia is still equal-second in the world (with Hong Kong) when it comes to share-owning (the US is first with 52 per cent of Americans owning shares). The proportion of the Australian population owning international shares is also now 13 per cent, up from 10 per cent in 2012. Given that 19 per cent of Australian adults have owned shares in the past, chances are you've dipped your toes in the sharemarket pond before picking up this book.

Figure 1-1 shows share investing trends in Australia from 2000 to 2014.

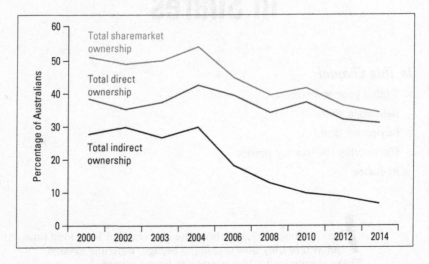

Figure 1-1: Share investing in Australia 2000–2014.

Source: 2014 Australian Share Ownership Study, Australian Securities Exchange

'Hang on,' you say, 'doesn't the sharemarket crash and correct regularly? What about the headlines that talk of billions of dollars of investors' savings being wiped off the value of the sharemarket in a day?' (See the sidebars 'What happened? The GFC at a glance', 'GFC economic recovery: Quick to lose, slow to come back' and 'Bouncing back from the GFC: Sharemarket recovery', later in this chapter.)

Occasionally, that happens. No one who goes into the sharemarket can afford to ignore the fact that, from time to time, share prices can suddenly move in an extreme fashion: Sometimes up, sometimes down. When share prices move down, they attract media headlines. However, what the headlines don't tell you is that on most other days, the sharemarket is quietly adding billions — or even just millions — of dollars in value to investors' savings.

The unique qualities of shares or stocks (the terms mean the same thing in Australia) as financial assets make the sharemarket the best and most reliable long-term generator of personal wealth available to investors.

Since 1900, according to AMP Capital, Australian shares have earned a return of approximately 11.9 per cent a year, split fairly evenly between capital growth and dividend income, for a real (after-inflation) return of 7.8 per cent a year (which is almost double the return from bonds). Since 1950, according to research house Andex Charts, the All Ordinaries Accumulation Index (which assumes all dividends are reinvested) has delivered an average return of 12.0 per cent a year, for a real return of 6.9 per cent a year. In the 30 years to 30 June 2015, says Andex Charts, the same index has earned 10.8 per cent a year, for a real return of 7.3 per cent a year.

In 1985, according to the Australian Securities Exchange (ASX), the Australian stock market was valued at $76 billion, about one-third of Australia's Gross Domestic Product (*GDP:* The amount of goods and services produced in the Australian economy). In mid-2015, the stock market was valued at $1,700 billion, while GDP was about $2,000 billion. Although the nation's economic output has grown almost nine times since 1985, the value of the stock market has grown by more than 22 times.

Investing is about building wealth for yourself so that you can have the lifestyle you want, educate and give your children a good start in life, and ensure that you have a well-funded, carefree retirement.

When you invest in shares, you get a number of advantages, such as:

- The opportunity to buy a part of a company for a small outlay of cash.
- A share of the company's profits through the payment of dividends (a portion of company profits distributed to investors).
- The company's retained earnings working for you as well.
- The possibility of capital gains as the price rises over time.
- An easy way to buy and sell assets.

The sharemarket is unbeatable as a place for individuals to build long-term wealth. Shares can provide long-term capital growth as well as an income through dividends: More than half of the long-term return from the sharemarket comes from dividends.

The GFC dents Australians' love of the sharemarket

Australia is second only to the US as the world's leading share-owning democracy. But with the global financial crisis (GFC) souring many investors' experiences with shares, ownership had fallen to 36 per cent (33 per cent direct) by late 2014. According to the 2014 ASX Share Ownership Study, total share ownership (including retail managed funds) in Australia now stands at 36 per cent of the adult population, meaning that about 6.5 million people own shares. About 5.9 million Australians — 33 per cent of the adult population — own shares in their own right. According to the ASX's numbers, retail investors (as in households) own 13 per cent of the Australian sharemarket by value — about $220 billion worth of shares — and account for 14 per cent of trade by value, 51 per cent of trade by volume of shares and 12 per cent of the number of trades. In addition, in 2014, investment bank Credit Suisse estimated that self-managed super funds (SMSFs) own 16 per cent of the sharemarket.

The 2014 ASX Share Ownership Study also points out that 13 per cent of Australian share owners own shares listed on other exchanges (up from 7 per cent in 2002, but down from a peak of 19 per cent in 2006).

Australian share ownership rose dramatically between 1991 and 2004; in 1991, only 9.9 per cent of the adult population owned shares and total Australian share ownership (including retail managed funds) stood at only 21.8 per cent. Perhaps the memories of the 1987 sharemarket crash and the 1990–1991 recession were too vivid for Australians to trust the sharemarket back then. But two major factors sent the Australian shareholder population booming in the 1990s.

The first was a wave of privatisations, in which government-owned businesses were sold through the sharemarket. Prominent among these were Telstra, the Commonwealth Bank, Qantas, CSL and the former Totalisator Agency Boards of New South Wales, Victoria and Queensland.

The second was a succession of demutualisations, in which mutually owned insurers and cooperatives converted their structure to share-based companies and listed on the sharemarket. In this way, AMP, National Mutual (which then became AXA Asia–Pacific, which merged its Australian business with AMP in March 2011 and sold its Asian business to the French parent, AXA), the NRMA (now Insurance Australia Group) and even the ASX itself joined the sharemarket. Both AMP and Telstra brought more than one million first-time investors to the sharemarket.

By 1999, 54 per cent of Australian adults owned shares (41 per cent direct), but this fell to 50 per cent (37 per cent direct) by 2002, in the aftermath of the 2000 'tech crash'. The recovery from that slump saw share ownership rise again, to 55 per cent (44 per cent direct) by 2004, making Australia then the world leader.

Thirty-eight per cent of adult males were direct share owners in 2014, down from 40 per cent in 2008. But the proportion of women who were direct share owners fell from 30 per cent in 2008 to 27 per cent in 2014.

The likelihood of share ownership increases with age: The peak level of share ownership is the 75+ age group. People with higher incomes are also more likely to own shares; almost half those earning more than $100,000 a year own shares.

The sharemarket has an exaggerated reputation as a sort of Wild West for money and therefore it can be a daunting place for a new investor. The sharemarket is a huge and impersonal financial institution; yet paradoxically, it's also a market that's alive with every human emotion — greed and fear, hope and defeat, elation and despair. The sharemarket can be a trap for fools or a place to create enormous wealth. Those who work in the industry see daily the best and worst of human behaviour. And you thought the sharemarket was simply a market in which shares were bought and sold!

The sharemarket is precisely that: A place for buying and selling shares. Approximately $4.4 billion worth of shares change hands every trading day. Shares are revalued in price every minute, reacting to supply, demand, news and sentiment, or the way that investors collectively feel about the likely direction of the market. The sharemarket also works to mobilise your money and channel your hard-earned funds to the companies that put those funds at risk for the possibility of gain. That ever-present element of risk, which can't be neutralised, makes the sharemarket a dangerous place for the unwary. Although you take a risk with any kind of investment, being forearmed with sound knowledge of what you're getting into and forewarned about potential traps are absolutely essential for your survival in the market.

Finding Out What a Share Is

Companies divide their capital into millions (sometimes billions) of units known as shares. Each share is a unit of ownership in the company, in its assets and in its profits. Companies issue shares through the sharemarket to raise funds for their operating needs; investors buy those shares, expecting capital gains and dividends. If the company fails, a share is also an entitlement to a portion of whatever assets remain after all the company's liabilities are paid. The following is a partial list of share definitions.

A *share* is

- Technically a loan to a company, although the loan is never repaid. The loan is borrowed permanently — like the car keys, if you have teenagers.

- A financial asset that the shareholders of a company own, as opposed to the real assets of the company — its land, buildings and the machines and equipment that its workers use to produce goods and services. Tangible assets generate income; financial assets allocate that income. When you buy a share, what you're really buying is a share of a future flow of profits.

- A right to part ownership, proportional to the amount of shares owned. In law, the part of the assets of a company owned by shareholders is called equity (the shareholders' funds). Shares are sometimes called equities. They are also called securities because they signify ownership with certain rights.

Now you know what you're getting when you buy shares. You become a part-owner of the company. As a shareholder, you have the right to vote on the company's major decisions. Saying 'I'm a part-owner of Qantas' sounds so much more impressive than 'I'm a Qantas Frequent Flyer member'. Just remember not to insist on sitting in with the pilots; as a shareholder, your ownership of Qantas is a bit more arm's-length than that. That's what shares were invented to do: Separate the ownership of the company from those who manage and run it.

Sharing the profit, not the loss

When you're a shareholder in a company, you can sit back and watch as the company earns, hopefully, a profit on its activities. After paying the costs of doing business — raw materials, wages, interest on any loans and other items — the company distributes a portion of the profit to you and other shareholders; the rest is retained for reinvestment. This profit share is called a dividend, which is a specified amount paid every six months on each share issued by the company. Shareholders receive a dividend cheque for the total amount earned on their shareholding.

If the company makes a loss, shareholders are not required to make up the difference. All this means is they won't receive a dividend cheque that year, unless the company dips into its reserves to pay (for more on dividends, see the section 'Dividend income' later in this chapter). However, if a company has too many non-profitable years it can go under, taking both its original investment and its chances of capital growth with it.

Companies that offer shares to the public are traded on the sharemarket as limited companies, which means the liability of the shareholders is limited to their original investment. This original investment is all they can lose. Suits for damages come out of shareholders' equity, which may lower profits, but individual investors aren't liable. Again, shareholders won't be happy if the company continues to lose money this way.

Understanding the share in sharemarket

Shares aren't much good to you without a market in which to trade them. The sharemarket brings together everybody who owns shares — or would like to own shares — and lets them trade among themselves. At any time, anybody with money can buy some shares.

The sharemarket is a matchmaker for money and shares. If you want to buy some shares, you place a buying order on the market and wait for someone to sell you the amount you want. If you want to sell, you put your shares up for sale and wait for interested buyers to beat a path to your door.

The trouble with the matchmaker analogy is that some people really do fall in love with their shares. (I talk about this more in Chapter 7.) Just as in real love, their feelings can blind them to the imperfections of the loved one.

Investors are wise to remember that their shares are assets that are meant to do a job: To make money for the investors and their families. Making money is what the right shares do, given time.

Because shares are revalued constantly, the total value of a portfolio of shares, which is a collection of shares in different companies, fluctuates from day to day. Some days the portfolio loses value. But over time, a good share portfolio shrugs off the volatility in prices and begins to create wealth for its owner. The more time you give the sharemarket to perform this task, the more wealth the sharemarket can create.

Buying Shares to Get a Return

Shares create wealth. As companies issue shares and prosper, their profits increase and so does the value of their shares. Because the price of a share is tied to a company's profitability, the value of the share is expected to rise when the company is successful. In other words, higher quality shares usually cost more.

Earning a profit

Successful companies have successful shares because investors want them. In the sharemarket, buyers of sought-after shares pay higher prices to tempt the people who own the shares to part with them. Increasing prices is the main way in which shares create wealth. The other way is by paying an income or dividend, although not all shares do this. A share can be a successful wealth creator without paying an income.

As a company earns a profit, some of the profit is paid to the company's owners in the form of dividends. The company also retains some of the profit. Assuming that the company's earnings grow, the principle of compound interest starts to apply (see Chapter 3 for more on how compound interest works). The retained earnings grow and the return on the invested capital grows as well. That's how companies grow in value.

Ideally, you buy a share because you believe that share is going to rise in price. If the share does rise in price, and you sell the share for more than you paid, you have made a capital gain. Of course, the opposite situation, a capital loss, can and does occur — if you've chosen badly, or had bad luck. These bad-luck shares, in the technical jargon of the sharemarket, are known as dogs. The simple trick to succeeding on the sharemarket is to make sure that you have more of the former experience than the latter!

When creating wealth, shares consistently outperform many other investments. Occasionally you may see comparisons with esoteric assets, such as thoroughbreds, or art, or wine, which imply that these assets are better earners than shares. However, these are not mainstream assets, and the comparison is usually misleading. The original investment was probably extremely hard to secure and not as accessible, and not as *liquid* (easily bought and sold) as shares. Of the mainstream asset classes, in terms of creating wealth over the long term, shares usually outdo property and outperform bonds (loan investments bearing a fixed rate of interest); however, in more recent comparisons, shares have been weighed down by the GFC slump. The latest 20-year comparison — which incorporates this slump — is shown in Figure 1-2. Australian shares generated a gross return of 9.5 per cent a year over 20 years, which was beaten by residential property, which earned 9.8 per cent a year — but when tax was taken into account, the impact of franking credits helped push shares to best-performing status.

Investing carefully to avoid a loss

Shares offer a higher return compared to other investments, but they also have a correspondingly higher risk. Risk and return always go together — an inescapable fact of investment, as I discuss in Chapter 4. The prices of shares fluctuate much more than those of property, while bonds are relatively stable in price. The major risk with shares is that, if you have to sell your shares for whatever reason, they may, at that time, be selling for less than you bought them. Or they may be selling for a lot more. This is the gamble you take.

Everybody who has money faces the decision of what to do with it. The unavoidable fact is that anywhere you place money, you face a risk that all or part of that money may be lost, either physically or hypothetically, in terms of its value. The simplest strategy is to deposit your money in a bank and leave it there. However, when you take the money out in the future, inflation (the rate of change in prices of everyday items) may decrease its buying power.

Risk is merely the other side of performance. You can't have high returns without running some risk. You can lower risk through the use of *diversification* — the spreading of your invested funds across a range of assets, as explained in Chapter 5.

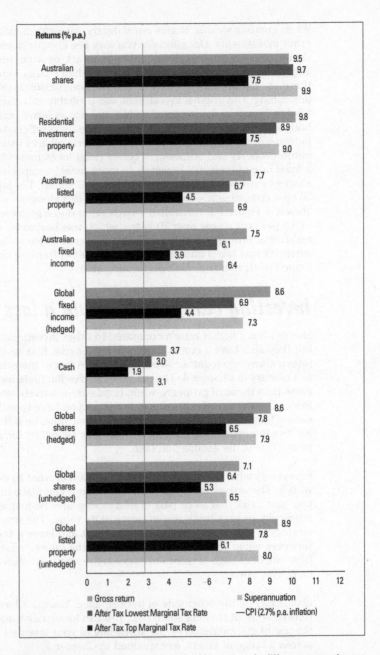

Figure 1-2: A comparison of the growth of investment in different asset classes over the past 20 years.

Source: Australian Securities Exchange/Russell Investments

Trying to avoid risk is self-defeating because you're passing up the chance of any return, which is why you invest in the first place. So accept risk, manage your level of risk and don't lose any sleep.

Making the Most of Share Investing

Investing in shares offers five big pluses. The first two pluses that I discuss in this section are the most critically important. The other three pluses are bonuses, one literally so.

Capital growth

As a company's revenue, profits and the value of its assets rise, so does the market price of its shares. Subjective factors, such as the market's perception of the company's prospects, also play a part in this process. After you've looked through this book, you'll know how to put together a share portfolio that makes the most of this crucial ingredient — capital growth.

Shares are the undisputed champion of capital growth (which I talk about further in Chapter 3). As the magic of compounding interest gets to work on the higher returns generated by shares, your portfolio starts to build wealth at an unmatched rate. The longer you hold your sharemarket investment, the better its performance over any other investment. By following a few basic rules (see the strategies for investment, also in Chapter 3), you can be confident your investment keeps on growing.

Dividend income

Shares may generate for their owners an income, which is called a *dividend* (a portion of company profits distributed to investors). The dividend is another important method for generating investor wealth. The dividend is paid in two portions: An interim dividend for the first six months of the financial year; and a final dividend for the second half. The two amounts make up the annual dividend. Not every company pays a dividend, but the paying of dividends is a vital part of becoming a member of that elite group of shares known as blue chips.

Franking credits are not dividends paid directly to an investor but arise through the system of dividend imputation, in which shareholders receive a rebate for the tax the company has already paid on its profit. The flow of franking credits from a share portfolio can reduce, and in some cases abolish, your tax liability. (I look at dividend imputation in detail in Chapter 10.)

Shareholder discounts

Recently another reason for owning shares — or more correctly, a bonus for shareholders — has emerged in the form of the discounts companies offer to shareholders on their goods and services. Many companies offer some form of discount, and the number of companies making these offers is growing. These businesses realise that any inducement they can give people to buy their shares makes good marketing sense. Shareholder perks range from holiday deals to wine, shopping and banking discounts. For example, gaming and wagering company Tabcorp offers shareholders free entry into certain horseracing meetings, plus accommodation and food and beverage discounts at the company's hotels and casinos.

Liquidity

A major attraction of shares as an asset class is that they are extremely liquid, meaning that you can easily buy and sell them. The stock exchange's trading system, ASX Trade, can match virtually any number of shares put on the market by a seller, with a buyer for that amount of shares. Some shares are less liquid than others; therefore, if you buy unpopular shares, they may be hard to sell.

Divisibility

A share portfolio is easily divisible. If you, the shareholder, need to raise money by selling some shares, you can sell any number to raise any amount. Divisibility is a major attraction of shares as compared to property. You can't saw off your lounge room to sell it, but you can sell 500 Telstra shares with one phone call — or at the click of a mouse.

Guarding Against Risk

Shares are the most risky of the major asset classes because no guarantees exist as to the likelihood of capital gains. Any investor approaching the sharemarket must accept this higher degree of risk.

Share prices fluctuate continually and can move in a downward direction for extended periods of time. You can't get a signed, sealed and delivered guarantee that a share's price will rise at all after you buy it.

You can minimise but never avoid the risk that accompanies investing in shares. Share investment is riskier than alternative investments, but after you discover how to keep that risk under control, you can use this knowledge to build wealth for you and your family. I discuss the possible risks you can encounter and how to minimise their effects in Chapter 4.

What happened? The GFC at a glance

Sharemarket slumps are an occupational hazard to investors, but the great global sharemarket slump of 2007–09 was a doozy. Very quickly it went from being a crash to a bear market, with the Australian stock market losing 52 per cent of its value — or $690 billion — between November 2007 and February 2009. The Australian market was not alone:

- In the US, the S&P 500 Index fell 57 per cent from its all-time high in October 2007 to a low in March 2009.

- In the UK, the FTSE 100 Index fell 48 per cent from its all-time high in June 2007 to a low in March 2009.

- In Japan, the Nikkei 225 Index fell 61 per cent from its high in July 2007 to a low in March 2009.

- In Hong Kong, the Hang Seng Index fell 65 per cent from its all-time high in October 2007 to a low in October 2008.

According to the World Federation of Exchanges, its 53 member markets lost US$34.4 trillion in value between November 2007 and February 2009; a fall of 54.5 per cent.

The bluest of blue chip Australian stocks were hammered in the GFC slump: Rio Tinto lost 80 per cent; BHP, 41 per cent; ANZ Bank fell 63 per cent; Commonwealth Bank slumped

(continued)

(continued)

by 61 per cent; National Australia Bank lost 60 per cent and Westpac plunged 53 per cent. Wesfarmers lost 63 per cent, Telstra lost 40 per cent. The best-performing blue chip, Woolworths, managed to limit its loss to 30 per cent.

The slump had its roots in the early part of the 2000s, when the US economy struggled to deal with recession and the shock of the September 11 terrorist attacks. To stimulate the economy, the Federal Reserve Board cut US interest rates, all the way to a 46-year low of 1 per cent, in 2003.

The monetary treatment worked on the economy, but a side effect of the historically low rates was to kick off both a debt binge and the biggest housing boom in US history. Both individuals and companies simply took on far too much debt.

As people scrambled to get into the US housing market, banks and non-bank lenders adopted a market-share-at-all-costs attitude, with lending standards going out the window.

House prices were pushed higher as more people got home loans, making lenders even more eager to lend. Subprime lending (to borrowers with poor credit histories and limited capacity to service their loans) grew to account for 25 per cent of total US home loans. Many of these loans were packaged by investment banks into mortgage-backed securities and sold around the world. But when US house prices began to fall in 2006, the bubble burst.

Faced with falling house prices, subprime borrowers simply walked away from their loans, because many owed more than their houses were worth. Because the mortgages weren't being

paid, the cash flows on the mortgage-backed securities collapsed, which led to the prices of those securities plunging. No one wanted to buy them. Falling prices meant margin calls for many hedge funds and investment banks that held these securities: Suddenly unable to sell what had become illiquid assets, investors found they had to sell higher-quality, more liquid assets to raise money — thus spreading the contagion into other credit markets around the world, even areas that had no exposure to subprime mortgages at all.

The low-interest-rates policy of the Federal Reserve had also allowed institutional investors to borrow heavily, and invest in mortgage-backed securities. Much of the mortgage-backed derivatives house of cards was kept off the banks' balance sheets, in a variety of investment vehicles. But the banks were forced to bring their exposures back on to the balance sheets, even though they had not set aside enough capital to back them. This resulted in massive write-downs, a river of red ink flowing through the books of some of the biggest names in global finance.

By June 2007, Wall Street investment bank Bear Stearns was in financial difficulty, having leveraged its balance sheet 35 to 1: For every dollar of equity, Bear Stearns had $35 of borrowings. Because many of the assets (securities) that had been bought with this borrowing were now worthless, both lenders and investors lost confidence in Bear Stearns. In March 2008 it was sold to JP Morgan Chase in a bail-out organised by the Federal Reserve.

The financial industry was in disarray: No one knew which bank was holding which liability, and who was a counterparty of whom. The availability of credit virtually ceased. If portfolios such as those held by Bear Stearns were to be liquidated, no one knew which other banks or investors could collapse. Confidence evaporated.

The GFC peaked following the collapse of Wall Street investment bank Lehman Brothers and the bail-out of global insurance giant AIG by the US Federal Reserve in September 2008. The following six months saw unprecedented stress in global capital markets. By now investors were questioning the very solvency of banks, and global stock markets were slumping. By this stage short-sellers were attacking stocks like sharks around a sinking cruise ship, magnifying the share price falls.

What no one could have foreseen was how what had essentially been a financial industry problem affected the real economy when Lehman Brothers collapsed. Bank-lending to businesses, the life blood of the economy, shut down; banks were unwilling to lend to each other, let alone businesses. Letters of credit — which finance 90 per cent of global trade — were starting to be dishonoured.

Because businesses could not get letters of credit, world trade ground to a halt. The Baltic Dry Index (a proxy for the cost of world shipping, and thus an indicator of world trade) fell 85 per cent between May and October in 2008. With goods unable to leave the docks, factories cut their activity and industrial production slumped. By late 2008/early 2009, the fear was no longer whether the world had a functioning financial system, it was whether the global economy still functioned.

In the first quarter of 2009, at annualised rates, the US economy shrank by 6.1 per cent, while Japan's economy contracted by 15.2 per cent, Germany's by 14.4 per cent, the UK's by 7.4 per cent and the Eurozone by 9.8 per cent. With demand slumping, world trade fell by 12 per cent in 2009, according to the World Trade Organization (WTO).

By 2010 the focus of the GFC had spread to the debt held by governments. The European sovereign (government) debt crisis mainly hit the so-called PIIGS countries — Portugal, Ireland, Italy, Greece and Spain — which typically run huge budget deficits. In 2010, Greece and Ireland had to be bailed out by the European Union (EU) and the International Monetary Fund (IMF). In July 2011 even the US (considered to be the world's best credit risk), went close to technically defaulting on its debt.

Slowly the banking system has repaired its balance sheets, after US$2.8 trillion worth of write-downs (slashed asset values). In 2008 the Federal Reserve began pumping trillions of dollars into the US financial system through its *quantitative easing* policy, by which it increased the quantity of available money by buying assets such as government bonds and mortgage-backed securities, and creating new money to pay for them. In this way, the Federal Reserve pumped about $US3.7 trillion into the global financial market.

The European Central Bank and the Bank of Japan conducted similar programs — with the Japanese mounting a quantitative easing programme even larger than that of the US, relative to the size of the economy.

GFC economic recovery: Quick to lose, slow to come back

Post-GFC, the major issues for the world economy — and thus, the sharemarkets — have been continued economic weakness in Europe, Japan and North America; a slow-down from the locomotive of world economic growth, China; and an amassed mountain of debt. The McKinsey Global Institute calculates that global debt has increased by nearly 20 per cent since 2007, growing by US$57 trillion.

Initially, China's economic growth provided support to the world economy: China grew its economy by 10.3 per cent in 2009. But China's growth rate has slowed as the country transitions to what Beijing considers more sustainable growth — that is, growth generated more by domestic consumption than growth driven by massive infrastructure investment. This well-advertised process saw China's official 2015 second-quarter annual growth rate come in at 7 per cent, the slowest pace since the GFC in 2009, and the World Bank expects the growth rate to start with a 6 by 2017.

Economic growth in the Eurozone has struggled, with the bloc slipping back into recession in 2012 — for the second time since the GFC — and narrowly avoiding a 'triple-dip' recession in 2014 with the escalating crisis in Greece. In mid-2015, Greece became the first developed country to default on a payment to the IMF, and investment markets were once again plunged into turmoil by the possibility of Greece leaving the eurozone, with unknown ramifications for the single European currency.

With many major European economies forced to use public funds to bail out banks, the debt/GDP ratio in European economies boomed. As holders of European debt became increasingly nervous about the ability of the PIIGS to meet their debt obligations, bond premiums spiked, and the risk of European economies being unable to meet their debt repayment schedule led to a secondary, highly damaging European economic crisis from 2011 to 2013. In June 2015 the Greek electorate voted to reject the terms of an extended EU bailout (effectively a second bailout), causing stock markets around the world to tumble. In July 2015 Eurozone leaders reached a deal on a third bailout package, which started to flow in August 2015. But Greece's problems are definitely not solved — there are still concerns about its bailout and arguments with its creditors raging at the moment — but it seems the markets moved on to worry about other, bigger things (like China).

In 2012, a new Japanese government tried economic shock therapy in the form of an all-out assault to jolt the long-moribund Japanese economy out of recession, based on creating massive fiscal and monetary stimulus, making company tax cuts and weakening the yen to increase the competitiveness of Japan's exporters. There was some initial success for the 'Abenomics' program — named after Prime Minister Shinzō Abe — but by mid-2015, Japan was back to its familiar state of zero growth.

In the US, the years 2008 to 2012 were the worst four consecutive growth years since the 1930s. The US economy had been trying to mount a recovery, with GDP growth reaching 2.4 per cent in 2014, but America's economy was reported to have shrunk in the first quarter of 2015 — the first contraction since the second quarter of 2009. The Congressional Budget Office now says the US economy grew by 2 per cent in 2015, however it projects stronger growth (2.7 per cent) in 2016 before dropping again (2.5 per cent) in 2017. The US has now held interest rates near zero for nearly a decade, and in mid-2015 the IMF, for the first time, urged the Federal Reserve to hold off raising rates to avoid potentially stalling the US economy and wreaking havoc in global markets.

The IMF expected global economic growth to slow in 2015 to its weakest rate since the GFC, as China and other emerging markets decelerate and advanced economies continue to struggle to shrug off the legacies of the crisis. The final IMF figure for world economic growth in 2015 came in at 3.1 per cent, the weakest since the global economy contracted in 2009. More positively, however, the IMF expects global growth to rise to 3.5 per cent in 2017.

Bouncing back from the GFC: Sharemarket recovery

The GFC was the greatest crash of them all, but slowly, painfully, share-markets began to recover:

- The US market was the first of the major markets to recover fully from the GFC. It took just over four years for the S&P 500 and Dow Jones Industrial Average to get back to their October 2007 levels, but now they've left that pre-crisis mark well behind on their way to record highs — the S&P 500 is now 36 per cent above the level from which it fell in October 2007, while the Dow Jones is 27 per cent higher.

- The Financial Times Stock Exchange 100 (FTSE 100, or the *Footsie*) in London finally recovered all its lost ground by December 2013 — but has since slipped back below its 2007 peak.

- The Japanese Nikkei 225 got back to its 2007 peak in February 2015, and is 13 per cent higher than its 2007 peak (but still a long way short — 47 per cent short, in fact — of its all-time high, reached in December 1989).

- The Hang Seng in Hong Kong has mounted a strong recovery from its 2009 low-point. It's up 90 per cent from there, but it remains 22 per cent lower than its 2007 peak.

In Australia, the recovery has seen similar challenges to many global

(continued)

(continued)

markets. The S&P/ASX 200 Index is still 16 per cent shy of its 2007 peak, despite having risen 60 per cent from its 2009 trough. The same divergence of performance can be seen in stocks. Commonwealth Bank was the first of the Australian banks to regain its pre-crash peak, which it did in October 2012; it now trades 47 per cent above its 2007 peak. Westpac followed in January 2013, and has now risen to 20 per cent above its 2007 peak. ANZ Bank got into clear water in April 2013, and has subsequently added an additional 7 per cent. But National Australia Bank has not yet recovered its pre-GFC high, and remains 19 per cent short of it.

BHP briefly regained its 2007 high-water mark in March 2011, but then lost value in the iron ore slowdown of 2011 to 2014; BHP now trades at 37 per cent below its 2007 peak. Rio Tinto has never recovered its pre-GFC peak, and is still 55 per cent lower. Telstra was back at its 2007 peak by March 2013, and has moved 33 per cent higher. Wesfarmers and Woolworths both got back to clear water on their share price in February 2013, but have diverged since then, as Wesfarmers' Coles operation has consistently beaten Woolworths on sales growth: Wesfarmers trades 6 per cent above its pre-GFC peak, while Woolworths has slipped back to fall 16 per cent short (having lost 29 per cent from mid-2014 to mid-2015).

These companies are all strong businesses, but they can never be considered to be immune to a general market slump — which, thankfully, is a rare event! That's one of the risks of share investment, but this risk is why stocks generally perform better than other investments over the long term.

Individual company share prices are fluctuating all the time, and can suffer big falls, as well as spectacular rises. This can be due to company-specific factors, as well as events and sentiment changes that affect the market as a whole. The GFC and the crash it inspired is an extreme example of what causes sharemarkets to fall, but it's also an example of how — although it can take a long time — the best stocks, and markets in general, do recover.

Chapter 2

Watching the Market Operate

● ●

In This Chapter

▶ Obtaining shares through a float

▶ Perusing a prospectus

▶ Trading, buying and selling

▶ Meeting the major markets

▶ Introducing the futures market

● ●

This chapter is about the two different types of market that make up the Australian sharemarket. The primary market is where companies, new or old, offer their shares to investors for the first time. This offer is called a *float*. Primary refers to the initial issuing of shares, not whether this particular type of market is more important. The secondary market is the day-to-day trading of all shares listed. Both of these markets make up the activity of the Australian stock market.

Floating of new companies is an important part of sharemarket activity, but small in terms of dollar value. Although floats of companies that are worth more than $1 billion are still rare on the sharemarket, the secondary market turns over on average about $4.7 billion worth of shares every day.

Floating: The Primary Market

The primary market is where companies raise money to fund their enterprises. Companies offer shares for sale through a prospectus (see more on the function of a prospectus in the later section 'Planning the Prospectus'). A *prospectus* is a legal document that invites the public to subscribe to a share issue, or *initial public offering* (IPO). As the name suggests, an IPO signifies the first public offering of shares. Investors provide capital for a company by buying shares in the IPO. A company *floats* on the sharemarket when it lists or quotes its shares for trade. As soon as the first trade takes place, the shares join the secondary market, which is where listed shares are bought and sold, all day on every trading day.

Actually, describing all new companies that come to the sharemarket as floats isn't strictly accurate because some sink like a stone and don't get back to the surface without a pretty exhaustive salvage effort.

Understanding why companies float

Companies float to raise money from investors. Like anybody selling anything, companies try to convince you that buying their shares is the greatest thing since sliced bread.

Occasionally you hear a lot of noble-sounding guff about the primary market being the great engine of the capitalist economy, mobilising the funds of the savers in the economy and channelling the funds to the enterprises that can make best use of them. All that may be true, but it's still guff. Vendors still want your money. However, you can make their need for funds work for you.

A company that floats is seeking private investment capital, whether from ordinary individual investors or professional investors such as *fund managers* — the people who manage the big investment companies. The company uses the money raised from the float in its commercial ventures, literally putting the money at risk. The risk is high because you have no guarantee the company is going to be successful. Some companies fail. For this higher risk, investors expect their capital to earn more than it can with less risky investments. In many cases, they also expect an ongoing income from the company in the form of dividends (for more on dividends, refer to Chapter 1).

Raising money

Suppose you want to start a business making furniture. To do this, you employ managers to buy raw materials and you put together a workforce to make and sell the furniture.

Who invented the sharemarket?

In post-Renaissance Europe, economic activity moved from feudalism to mercantilism, and the burgeoning of trade that accompanied this shift required an infusion of capital that traditional banking sources couldn't supply. The great breakthrough came with the invention in London in the 16th century of the joint stock company.

Formed as trading companies, the first joint stock ventures were the Muscovy (1555), Levant (1581), East India (1600) and the Dutch East India (1602). These early trading companies were the ancestors of today's public companies. For the first time, individuals were able to invest their capital in an entity that transacted business on their behalf, and the investors shared in the profits. More importantly, investors were able to buy and sell their interest in these ventures.

The joint stock company concept was further refined with the legal definition of *limited liability*, which restricts the liability of the members for the company's debts.

When the Muscovy Company — or the Mystery and Company of Merchant Adventurers for the Discovery of Regions, Dominions, Islands and Places Unknown — was formed, each of its investors received an individual deed of title, considered to be the first share certificates.

The trading companies grew in number with colonisation and expansion, and consequently the means to trade the shares had to grow

as well. Intermediaries, the first stockbrokers, sprang up. In 1760, after being kicked out of the Royal Exchange because of their rowdiness, a group of 150 brokers formed a club at Jonathan's Coffee House where they met to buy and to sell shares. In 1773, the members of this club voted to change the name of Jonathan's to the Stock Exchange. By the 1790s, securities dealers were also operating in New York, again from a coffee house. In 1817, the New York Stock Exchange (NYSE) was formed.

In Australia, share trading sprang up in the 1850s, following the big gold discoveries. Virtually all of the major goldfields had their own stock exchanges. Ballarat, Bendigo, Gympie, Charters Towers, Zeehan, Queenstown, Kalgoorlie, Coolgardie and Cobar had their own exchanges. Even Broad Arrow — a gold boom town that is now nothing more than a pub in the desert north of Kalgoorlie — had a stock exchange.

The unofficial trading spread to Melbourne and Sydney, where formal exchanges were set up in the 1860s and 1870s, respectively. The Hobart exchange was formed in 1882, followed by Brisbane (1884), Adelaide (1887) and Perth (1889). In 1937, the six exchanges formed the Australian Associated Stock Exchanges.

The Australian Stock Exchange (ASX) was formed in 1987, and computerised screen trading took over from the trading floors soon after. In 1998

(continued)

(continued)

the ASX completed a remarkable 150 years when it transformed itself from a member-owned cooperative to a company limited by shares and listed on its own exchange, only the second stock exchange (after Stockholm) to do so. Most major exchanges are listed companies in their own right, including NYSE Euronext, Deutsche Boerse AG, Nasdaq OMX Group and the Hong Kong Stock Exchange.

In July 2006, the Sydney Futures Exchange (SFE Corporation Limited) merged with the ASX. Later that year, the Australian Stock Exchange changed its name to become the Australian Securities Exchange (which is also known as the ASX).

Unless you already have capital set aside to fund the business, you need to find a way to finance your business. Your investment, allowing you to buy the raw materials and to pay the people who make and sell your furniture, probably has to be made with borrowed capital; for example, a normal commercial loan. As you sell the furniture that your company makes, you generate cash, which pays the cost of those sales — your wages, factory rental, marketing and advertising sales. Then, you must pay off the loans that enabled you to get started. Any money left after that is your *profit*.

The profit that your firm generates is the basis of wealth creation. How this wealth is shared depends on what corporate structure you choose for your furniture-making company. You can be a *sole proprietor* (own your own business); you can form a *partnership* (own a business with others); or you can form a *company* (own a formal legal entity). If your company decides that it wants to tap the private capital market, it may offer shares in itself and float on the stock exchange.

Offering shares to the investing public is a straight swap of capital for the privileges of ownership. Obviously, you, as the company's owner/founder, are giving up some control, allowing others to have a say in the running of your company. The shareholders of a company limited by shares own the company by law. Some shareholders aren't shy in expressing this fact. The dilution of control can be disconcerting to the owners of private businesses that have floated, because management's aims are often different from those of the shareholders — who want to see returns, and pronto!

Often the owners of a business float the company to sell some (or all) of their holding. The instant *liquidity* of the sharemarket — that is, the ability to sell shares when a company needs money — is attractive to owners. Selling a stake in a business or a partnership can be as time-consuming as selling a house — offers are made, haggled over and refused. However, on the sharemarket, the business is priced to the cent at any second.

Planning the Prospectus

The document that invites the public to invest in a company is called the *prospectus*. A prospectus sets out in great detail the company's background, business, financial accounts, management, and prospects. You can make an application for the shares only through the application form contained in the prospectus. The prospectus is a legal document and may read like the very worst of that breed, but the prospectus also contains all the necessary facts to inform and persuade a buyer.

Under the Corporations Law, the requirements of what to include in a prospectus are strict. Unfortunately, this means that a prospectus is a very bulky document, with many pages of material in small, closely packed type. For investors who aren't also accountants, a prospectus can be a daunting read. However, it's a vital document. You can find everything you need to know about a company inside the prospectus. Too many investors don't read it. Don't make that mistake.

A South Sea dream — then the bubble burst

Promoters of companies listing on the sharemarket have never been guilty of overestimating the avidity with which the investing public scours every paragraph of a prospectus. No one has ever done it as blatantly as the chap who, at the height of the South Sea Bubble investment mania of the 1720s, hawked a prospectus around London seeking subscriptions to 'an undertaking of great advantage, but nobody to know what it is'.

He decamped to the Continent with several thousand pounds. Obviously, no one read his brief prospectus.

Nowadays the Australian Securities and Investments Commission (ASIC), which regulates the fairness of the securities markets, wouldn't let anything as crass as that happen. Unfortunately, floats that rely more on the gullibility of investors than the intrinsic merits of the company still occur.

For companies listing on the sharemarket, the prospectus is a marketing document too. The design, artwork and photography are all part of the effect. Many prospectuses resemble an edition of *National Geographic*. Visually impressive documents they may be, but don't let that distract you from reading the difficult bits because the difficult bits are where you find the nitty-gritty that tells you whether the shares are worth buying.

Trading: The Secondary Market

The Australian Securities Exchange is the operator of the main Australian sharemarket. The 2,200 companies listed on the Australian market have a total value of $1,700 billion, which makes Australia one of the top ten world sharemarkets.

After a company floats, it joins the secondary market of the Australian Securities Exchange (which is abbreviated to and known colloquially as the ASX). Every day on the exchange, about $4.7 billion worth of these shares are bought and sold. No restriction exists on the amount of shares that can change hands during trading hours. *Stockbrokers*, who are employees of stockbroking firms that are participants of the ASX, do the buying and selling of transactions.

You can also find several other stock exchanges in Australia:

- **Chi-X Australia:** The second-largest Australian stock exchange, Chi-X Australia was established in 2011. Owned by several institutions and big users of its services, Chi-X offers trading of all of the ASX-listed companies, and is an alternative trading venue to ASX Trade (see the following section for more on ASX Trade). Brokers connected to Chi-X can send all or part of an order to Chi-X to be executed, allowing them to seek the best possible price.

    ASX and Chi-X compete for trades. Chi-X charges different fees depending on whether an order provides or takes liquidity from the market. Many of the trades struck on Chi-X are from algorithm-driven *high-frequency traders* (HFTs; high-frequency trading is an automated trading platform that uses powerful computers and trading algorithms to transact a large number of orders at high speeds), but institutional and retail trades also use it. Chi-X commonly handles about 10 per cent of equity trades in Australia, but it has had days where it has struck 27 per cent.

- ✔ **The National Stock Exchange of Australia (NSX):** The NSX — formerly the Stock Exchange of Newcastle — re-opened in March 2000. The NSX has 90 listings, 22 of which are debentures, with a market capitalisation of $1.6 billion. The company that operates this exchange, NSX Limited, is listed on the ASX.

- ✔ **Asia Pacific Stock Exchange (APX):** Australia's fourth stock exchange, the Sydney-based APX, was launched in 2014 with the specific aim of offering Chinese companies an alternative listing venue to the Shanghai and Shenzhen stock exchanges in China. APX currently has three listed companies.

Finding the action at ASX Trade

All transactions in shares are conducted on the trading screens of the ASX's trading system, *ASX Trade*, to which only authorised stockbroking firms are permitted access. The ASX introduced ASX Trade in November 2010, to replace the Integrated Trading System (ITS) in use since 2006.

ASX Trade retains the public openness of the original trading system. It does this by placing all *bids* (the prices that buyers are prepared to pay) and *offers* (the prices that sellers are prepared to accept) on the brokers' computer screens. However, ASX Trade also allows instant access for brokers around Australia, which was impossible in the original system, where bids and offers were shouted by operators working on the six trading floors.

Brokers access ASX Trade through a range of interfaces. The ASX's own trading terminal software is *ASX Best*, which was introduced in 2011. It's an order router that connects into the ASX through the exchange's electronic 'pipe', called *ASX Net*. Many brokers now have their own alternative interface to the ASX and other markets: IRESS Trader (provided by ASX-listed company IRESS Limited) is a major one, while some brokers have their own proprietary interfaces.

Through these interfaces, brokers get access to the ASX Trade order books (an *order book* is an electronic list of buy and sell orders for a specific stock or for other financial securities, organised by price level) and potentially other non-ASX order books too: The ASX order books are TradeMatch, which is the main ASX market, and CentrePoint, which offers anonymous execution at the prevailing mid-point of the national best bid and offer.

Investors don't see or interact with ASX Trade — only brokers do. Through whatever interface they're using, any broker can see the market's transactions in an instant. Clients of online brokers see a re-presented version of ASX Trade on their screens. I discuss the operation of the ASX Trade screen in detail in Chapter 6.

Buying and selling for everyone

Two kinds of investors use the sharemarket: Institutional and private investors. Institutions, such as superannuation and pension funds, insurance companies, fund managers and investment companies, trustee companies, banks, and other financial institutions, buy shares with other people's money. Private investors are individuals, like you and me, who buy shares with their own money.

Anyone who has insurance cover, a superannuation plan or a managed investment portfolio is indirectly a sharemarket investor. This means that institutional investors dominate the ownership of the Australian sharemarket and, within that category, the superannuation funds and life insurance companies dominate the institutional investment industry. Because of this, even those people who shun the sharemarket are likely to be involved in share trading indirectly.

When you buy shares as a private investor, you don't know the identity of the person selling them to you. It may be an institution selling the shares you're buying, or the wife of a cane farmer in Queensland. Your bid (buying) and offer (selling) prices are matched, but you don't have any contact with the person on the other side of the transaction.

Institutions occasionally trade shares among themselves in transactions called *specials*, but even these transactions must be struck through a stockbroking firm. The stockbrokers have a monopoly, which so far has avoided the scrutiny of the Australian Competition and Consumer Commission (ACCC).

Working with a go-between

Every transaction on the stock exchange must be conducted by a stockbroking firm that is a corporate member of the ASX. About 70 firms are registered as stockbrokers in Australia, although some of those deal only with institutional or professional investors.

Open outcry — at the top of your lungs

If your mental image of the share-market is a big group of adults shouting, gesticulating and waving paper while children run around with chalk and dusters, alternatively marking hieroglyphics on large blackboards and rubbing them out, get with the times. That scene is from the old days of the trading floor, when open outcry was the trading system. Open outcry was the term used because traders had to shout out their buy and sell offers for the 'chalkies' to record them.

The open outcry system was considered the perfect means of discovering a fair value for a market price. *Price discovery* — that is, the ability to trade large amounts of shares quickly and easily — is the key to liquidity, which is what a market needs most. The pushy individuals who worked as floor traders were able to shout the buy and sell prices at deafeningly loud levels and prices tended to get discovered pretty damn quickly.

These days, the ASX Trade platform matches buyers and sellers automatically. ASX Trade is efficient and easy, but the downside is that a physical market no longer exists. The market exists only on the ASX Trade platform, and on the brokers' screens linked to it, wherever they are. You can't be a spectator on the trading floor and watch adults behaving like pre-schoolers running amok. They still do that, but now they're out of the sight of the investing public.

Before you walk into a stockbroking firm with that $4,000 you saved to start your investing career, check with the ASX whether your broker deals with the retail, or private investor, market.

Stockbroking is now a buyers' market and brokers are engaged in a price war over fees, helped by the easy access the internet provides. What was regarded as the model stockbroker/client relationship, where the broker advised the client and provided research and access to floats, is under increasing pressure from the discount brokers. These brokers perform transactions without any extras. Discount brokers, using the internet to attract clients, have lowered transaction fees considerably. You can get more details on stockbroking and the price war in Chapter 9.

Using the Index

Every sharemarket has a major *index*, a notional portfolio designed to reflect the wider sharemarket as accurately as possible. The index gives investors a means of tracking market performance. The index is also a shorthand way of assessing the performance of the sharemarket on a given day. However, an index is only an indicative number. The index may not tell you whether a share you own has risen or fallen, but only the general trend in the market. Sometimes, some shares rise in price although the index itself has fallen, or vice versa.

In June 2015, the ASX was the twelfth-largest sharemarket in the world but accounted for only about 1.8 per cent of the total value of world sharemarkets. To put the size of the Australian market in perspective, the largest US stock, Apple, is worth 54 per cent of the Australian market on its own; add the second- and third-largest US stocks by value, Exxon Mobil and Microsoft, and the big three US stocks are worth 19 per cent more — that's US$236 billion more — than the entire Australian sharemarket. Table 2-1 shows the world's top 20 sharemarkets by value as at June 2015.

Table 2-1	The Top 20 Sharemarkets by Value
Sharemarket	*Market Value (US$ billion)*
1. USA	26,480
2. China	9,601
3. Japan	4,944
4. UK^	4,176
5. Euronext*	3,751
6. Hong Kong	3,414
7. India	3,152
8. Canada	2,046
9. Germany	1,752
10. Switzerland	1,545
11. South Korea	1,334
12. Australia	1,239

Sharemarket	Market Value (US$ billion)
13. Nasdaq OMX Nordic[#]	1,237
14. Taiwan	967
15. Spain	961
16. South Africa	929
17. Brazil	760
18. Singapore	749
19. Saudi Arabia	537
20. Russia	492

[^]London and Milan stock exchanges
[*]Paris, Brussels and Amsterdam stock exchanges
[#]Copenhagen, Helsinki, Stockholm, Iceland, Tallinn, Riga, Vilnius and Armenia stock exchanges
Source: International Federation of Stock Exchanges

The All Ordinaries Index

The best known indicator of the Australian Securities Exchange is the S&P/ASX All Ordinaries Index, which contains the 500 largest companies by market capitalisation, or value. The All Ordinaries Index covers more than 95 per cent of the value of the Australian market, making it relatively broad in scope when compared to its international peers. You can follow the ups and downs of the All Ordinaries Index in newspapers and media reports.

As a junior market, the ASX barely cracks a mention in the world's financial press, but its international peers make headlines over here. The global indices are the equivalents of the All Ordinaries in the overseas markets. However, not many international indices have market coverage that is as broad as the Australian index, which gives you, as an Australian investor, a decided leg-up.

The S&P/ASX 200 Index

In 2000, the S&P/ASX 200 Index was introduced as a replacement benchmark index for the Australian market. It comprises the 200 largest companies by market value, and is used by investment managers as a proxy for the Australian market, to build portfolios and compare performance. The S&P/ASX 200 Index is a subset of the All Ordinaries, and covers about 80 per cent of the Australian market by value. While the S&P/ASX 200 is more important to professional investors, the All Ordinaries is still widely followed as an indicator of the Australian sharemarket.

The Dow Jones

The venerable Dow Jones Industrial Average has been tracking the industrial heavyweights of the New York Stock Exchange (NYSE) since Charles Dow first calculated it in May 1896. Since then, the index has chopped and changed 53 times, with only one constant — General Electric, now the ninth-largest US stock by value.

The Dow Jones is unfortunately an unrepresentative index, comprising only 30 industrial stocks at any time. It was criticised in the late 1990s for not adequately reflecting the technology-based new economy. The only technology-related companies in the Dow Jones were Hewlett-Packard and IBM because they were the only tech stocks old enough to qualify. In the famous 'new economy' shake-up of November 1999, stalwarts Goodyear, Sears Roebuck, Union Carbide and Chevron were ditched and Microsoft, Intel, SBC Communications and Home Depot added.

Apart from name changes, the most recent major shake-up to the Dow Jones was in September 2013, when Goldman Sachs, Nike and Visa replaced Alcoa, Bank of America and Hewlett-Packard. Three companies in the Dow Jones — Cisco Systems, Microsoft and Intel — actually trade on the Nasdaq (see the following section), not the NYSE. The largest US stock by market value, Apple (worth US$670 billion), is not a Dow Jones member.

The Nasdaq

The *Nasdaq* is the acronym for the National Association of Securities Dealers Automated Quotation, the other US sharemarket. Today it's known as the Nasdaq Stock Market.

The Nasdaq was formed in 1971 to provide a screen-based marketplace for shares that didn't meet the listing requirements of the NYSE but were widely owned and had outgrown the smaller, local markets on which they traded.

From the beginning, the Nasdaq hosted the technology start-ups that have gone on to become well known and larger, in some cases, than the industrial giants that make up the Dow Jones. The fourth-largest US stock — Microsoft — is a Nasdaq stock. Valued at US$7 trillion, the Nasdaq has become known as the technology market, and its major index, the Nasdaq Composite, as the prime technology indicator.

Based at Times Square in New York, the Nasdaq Stock Market regularly trades more dollar value in shares than its larger (US$19.3 trillion) cross-town rival, the NYSE — about US$65 billion a day, versus US$37 billion — and also trades more shares, at 1.8 billion shares a day to 934 million for the NYSE. Although it has lost some of the lustre that it had in 1999–2000 as the flagship of the 'new economy', the Nasdaq Composite Index remains the most widely followed indicator of the 'other' US stock market. The largest US stock by market value, Apple, is a Nasdaq stock, as is the third-largest, Microsoft, and the fourth-largest, Google.

The S&P

The S&P 500 Index, calculated using the value of the top 500 US stocks by market value, is the broadest of the big three US indices but somehow lacks the star quality of the Dow Jones and the Nasdaq. The S&P is rarely in the headlines, but is widely used by fund managers as a proxy for the US sharemarket when they need a benchmark against which to compare the performance of their portfolios. Calculated by the 155-year-old financial data and analysis firm, Standard & Poor's, the S&P 500 was introduced in 1957. Only 66 of the original companies still remain in the index, which actually contains 502 stocks.

The Footsie and the rest

The Financial Times Stock Exchange 100 (FTSE 100), better known as the Footsie, is the major indicator of the London Stock Exchange. The Footsie, which comprises the 100 largest British stocks by market value, was introduced in 1984. When the index celebrated its 30th birthday in 2014, only 19 of the original 100 had been constant constituents. Along the way, 250 companies have left the index for various reasons.

All sharemarkets have a major index. Here are some of the other global heavyweights:

- ✔ Shanghai Composite for the Shanghai Stock Exchange
- ✔ EURO STOXX 50 for Euronext (the French, Dutch, Belgian and Portuguese stock market)
- ✔ Nikkei Index for the Tokyo Stock Exchange
- ✔ Hang Seng Index for the Hong Kong Stock Exchange

These indices operate the same as the All Ordinaries. Anywhere a stock market exists, somebody has developed an index to track it.

The mighty MSCI

Now that you have the basics of the market covered, you can move on to how to use it. Before the rise of index funds, which put together portfolios to follow or track a particular index and mirror its performance faithfully, the major indices were merely indicators of the sharemarket. Now these indices represent guaranteed buying on the part of the index funds. If a company is included in one of the major indices, its shares will find instant buyers. If they leave that index, the index funds will sell them. For smaller companies, graduation into the major indices is a rite of passage and exclusion sends their share price plunging.

In Australia, we think of our own benchmark index, the All Ordinaries, as the ultimate in status, but it's not. Global fund managers want to know whether an Australian stock is part of the Morgan Stanley Capital International (MSCI) World Index, which is market capitalisation weighted, meaning bigger companies have more clout. The MSCI World Index comprises the largest companies in the world's most developed economies.

More than 2,400 institutional investors worldwide use the MSCI benchmarks, which track more than 14,000 stocks in more than 70 countries. In North America and Asia alone, more than 90 per cent of institutions' international shareholdings are benchmarked to MSCI indices. MSCI estimates that more than US$9.5 trillion is benchmarked to its indices on a worldwide basis.

Stepping into the Futures Market

The sharemarket has a double that exists in future time, although this sharemarket, the futures market, trades in the present. *Futures markets* are a long-established and legal way to buy or sell a specified commodity at a fixed time in the future. Futures markets began in the agricultural commodities markets of mediaeval Europe and have grown in sophistication since then.

Futures markets allow producers and consumers of commodities to lock in their prices. Producers like to know what price they will get for their product in six months' time. Users like to know what they will have to pay for that product in six months' time in order to plan their budget accordingly. Speculators want to make money either way, by picking which way the price will go. These three players are the essential oil that lubricates the futures market.

Late last century, the technique of trading commodities was applied to the sharemarket. In this situation, a certain value of shares becomes the commodity being traded. This value is the notional value of a market index, multiplied by a certain dollar value per point on the index. In the US, the main index on which futures contracts are traded is the S&P 500. In Australia, it's the Share Price Index 200, or SPI 200, which is the S&P/ASX 200 Index's futures market twin. The actual sharemarket represents the *spot market*, the term used in the commodity markets to denote today's price. The futures market anticipates what that spot value will be in the future. If investors expect the spot price of the S&P/ASX 200 to rise, they will pay a premium for the future value. If, on the other hand, they expect the S&P/ASX 200 to fall, the SPI will trade at a discount to its actual twin.

The futures market is a specialised area and you need a lot of experience and information before you venture into it. The futures market is a *leveraged investment*, meaning that losses as well as profits are magnified and you can lose more than you invest.

Keeping up with the sharemarket menagerie

The sharemarket also contains some forms of animal life — the descriptions given to different kinds of investors.

First come the bulls, who are hoping that share prices will charge upward and are trying to propel them that way. The bulls are as impetuous as their namesake and charge through the market as though they're being run through the streets of Pamplona. However, if these sharemarket creatures lose their nerve, they can just as likely resemble the tourists running from the bulls at Pamplona.

Then come the bears, who are expecting prices to bear downward. The bears are not as swift as the bulls, being a more lumbering type of animal. Although habitually slow and ponderous, bears can occasionally act with frightening speed, tearing at share prices with their sharp claws.

The battle between the bulls and the bears for influence over the sharemarket doesn't really faze the third member of the menagerie, the stag. Stags are concerned solely with how new floats perform on debut. Sometimes the stags are allied with the bulls because they're looking to sell out of a float as soon as the shares list, banking on a good reception for the shares and a nice instant capital gain. Stags aren't happy to see the bears take over the market because it limits their opportunities severely.

After any sharemarket boom, a fourth member of the menagerie appears — the dogs. Dogs sit accusingly in an investor's portfolio at prices far below what was paid for them. A dog is a stark reminder of what happens when you leave the sharemarket to animal instincts.

Part II
Investing Strategies for Success

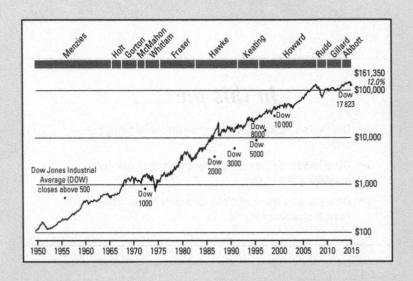

In this part...

- ✔ Develop a strategy for building wealth while riding out volatility.

- ✔ Get a handle on assessing different types of risk and identifying dud shares.

- ✔ Diversify your share portfolio as widely as possible for a smooth sharemarket ride.

Chapter 3

Developing an Investment Strategy

. . . .

In This Chapter

▶ Enjoying the luxury of time

▶ Defining your investment goals

▶ Timing your trading

. . . .

Devising a sharemarket investment strategy means asking a basic question: 'Why am I buying this share?' If the answer to the question is 'My brother-in-law told me at a barbecue on the weekend that this share was about to go through the roof' ... then you're gambling.

But if the answer to the question is

✔ I've researched this unloved stock pretty thoroughly and I think the company is making a good product that doesn't have much competition.

✔ I'm fairly confident the company has solved the problems that caused the share price to fall and I believe its earnings are going to grow.

✔ This share fits all my criteria for buying and I'm happy to buy it at this price ...

... then you're investing, and developing your investment strategy is what this chapter is about.

Investing is a simple concept. You store buying power in the form of money today for future use. What you're trying to do when you invest is to conserve the capital that you've earned and saved, and to make it grow. To invest successfully, you need to put your money where your investment can generate a return ahead of inflation (the rate of change in the cost of living), so that the purchasing power of your capital is at least conserved. Naturally, you want to earn a return above the inflation rate so that your invested money is actually growing in value.

Getting Rich Slowly

Investing in shares requires patience. If you attempt to compress the wealth-creating power of the sharemarket into weeks or even days, you're asking for trouble. Occasionally — for example, amid the technology boom of 1999 to 2000 — Australians forget this rule and try to participate in the spectacular short-term capital gains available on the sharemarket.

Only after one of these periodic bouts of insanity do investors remember how the sharemarket really creates wealth — slowly, over years. Since 1900, according to AMP Capital Investors, the All Ordinaries Accumulation Index has delivered a total return of 11.9 per cent a year; if you'd had an astute investor in your family tree who'd put $100 in the sharemarket on your behalf in 1900 (in the equivalent of the All Ordinaries Index) and left it to accumulate, with all dividends reinvested, that investment would have grown to almost $40 million ($39.8 million) by now.

Since 1950, says research house Andex Charts, the S&P/ASX All Ordinaries Accumulation Index (which counts dividends reinvested as well as capital gain) has delivered a return of 12.0 per cent a year, enough to turn an investment of $100 in 1950 into $161,350 (see Figure 3-1).

Not many people have an investment term of 100 years, or even 50 years. Most investors are active for 20 or 30 years. The good news is that in the past three decades, shares have actually outpaced their century-long average return because of economic growth and falling inflation. Over the 30 years to the end of 2014, says Andex Charts, the S&P/ASX All Ordinaries Accumulation Index has earned investors 11.4 per cent a year. This steady rise in share price is the key to sharemarket investing. Although share prices are extremely volatile, share dividends are far less so. When you buy a share, you're buying a portion of the future earnings of that company, part of which comes to you as a dividend, and part of which goes into retained earnings. Over time, this process of building equity also results in capital gain.

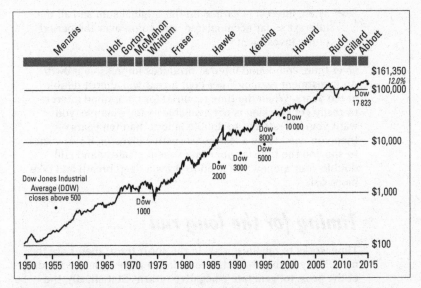

Figure 3-1: The growth of a $100 investment in the sharemarket over 65 years.

Source: Andex Charts Pty Ltd

You can't expect a return of 12.0 per cent on your share portfolio next year or the year after that, but the pattern of growth should remain similar even though the market may lose value during any given year. Those downward blips on the graph represent risk.

Compounding magic

You're taught about compound interest at secondary school, but you probably didn't pay too much attention to it. Einstein is quoted (probably apocryphally) as describing compound interest as 'the greatest mathematical discovery of all time'.

The longer you maintain an investment, the greater will be your financial gain. This gain happens because of the magic of compound interest, which is the investor's major ally in achieving all financial goals.

Here's how compound interest works:

- ✔ Interest is earned on the original sum invested.

- ✔ Next, interest is earned on both the original sum invested plus the first round of interest.

> ✔ Then, interest is earned on the original sum and all the interest so far accumulated, and so on over the period of the investment.

Over time, compound interest produces impressive growth. An investment earning 7 per cent a year will almost double in ten years. When the time required for compound interest to really get cracking is not available — for example, you want your investment to double in less than ten years — then you need to be a less conservative investor. If you want to shorten the time for your investment strategy and still double your money, you need to draw a deep breath and take more risk.

Timing for the long run

Time works to minimise risk. In the short term, shares are the most likely of the asset classes to fall in price — in the words of the pros, to 'generate a negative return'. Statistically, the sharemarket is more likely to record a negative return than any other asset class. In the longer term, however, shares are the most likely to generate a positive return.

Investing in the sharemarket requires patience. You need to give your share portfolio investment at least five years to see positive growth. That's enough time to smooth out the volatility of the sharemarket and allow you to get the kind of returns that a balanced and diversified portfolio of shares can achieve. Andex Charts has calculated the risk and return from the Australian sharemarket (as measured by the S&P/ ASX All Ordinaries Accumulation Index) over the period 1 January 1950 to 31 December 2014, measured over one, three, five, ten and 20 years, with investments made at month ends. Andex measured 769 one-year periods, 745 three-year periods, 721 five-year periods, 661 ten-year periods and 541 20-year periods (see Figure 3-2).

The one-year investments showed great volatility, with a best return of 86.1 per cent and a worst performance of minus 41.7 per cent. The average gain was 13.9 per cent, but nearly one in five of the short-term investments showed a loss.

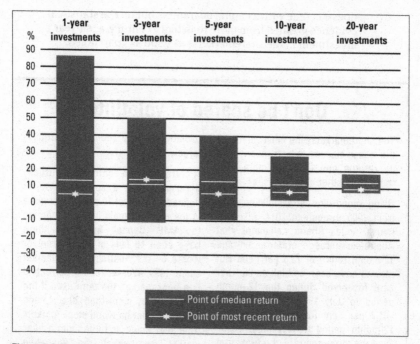

Figure 3-2: How time tempers the risk and return on shares.

Source: Andex Charts Pty Ltd

When the investment period was extended to three years, the probability of success rose to 90 per cent. The best return was 50.3 per cent a year, while the worst performance was minus 10.9 per cent a year. The average gain was 12.5 per cent a year.

The average return over five years was 12.5 per cent a year, with a best return of 40.4 per cent a year and the worst performance being a loss of 9.2 per cent a year. The risk of loss in the five-year periods was still present, though, with a handful of the periods (4.7 per cent) failing to make a positive return.

By the time the investment term was extended to ten years, all investment periods showed a positive return. The best result was 28.7 per cent a year, the worst was 2.9 per cent a year and the average gain was 12.7 per cent a year.

Over 20 years, the average investment in the sharemarket showed a gain of 12.8 per cent a year. The best was 18.9 per cent a year, while the worst came in at 8.4 per cent a year. The sharemarket doesn't come with a capital guarantee, but on the statistical evidence gleaned from more than half a century, a ten-year investment in the sharemarket is as good as guaranteed.

Don't be scared of volatility

The sharemarket is the most volatile of the asset classes, which means that its returns can fluctuate more than those from other asset classes.

Using month-end accumulation data from 1900 through to 2014, research house Andex Charts calculates that Australian shares generated an average 12-month return of 13.3 per cent. But returns have been as high as 86.1 per cent (observed during the 12-month period to July 1987) and as low as −41.7 per cent (observed during the 12-month period to November 2008). Even the three-quarters of returns that fell within just one standard deviation of the average (17.2 per cent either side of the average) still fell within a very broad range, from 30.4 per cent to −3.9 per cent.

The average return from shares since 1900 has been far higher than for bonds or cash, but investors often had to endure years of negative returns (one in five 12-month periods, on average), and periods of great volatility. Those willing and able to ride out the bad times have been rewarded. During the greatest market downturn — the period between 1 November 2007 and 6 March 2009, when the ASX All Ordinaries Accumulation Index lost 52 per cent of its value — many investors discovered that they didn't have the nerve, or the resources, to stay in the game, but those who were able

to hang on have seen their portfolios largely recover.

A correction in a sharemarket (usually a reversal after a sustained rise) is defined as a fall of 10 per cent or more in the market's main index. According to AMP Capital Investors, there have been 16 falls of 10 per cent or worse on the Australian sharemarket since 1989. Worse than a correction is a bear market, the term used if the index falls by more than 20 per cent. The crash that hit world stock markets from 2007 onwards turned into a bear market, from which the Australian market is still recovering.

A sustained bear market can last years. The sharemarket has shown that it always regains and exceeds its previous peak after a fall — refer to Figure 3-1 — but the big question is how long that takes.

According to AMP Capital Investors, there have been 12 major bear markets in the Australian sharemarket since World War II, including the 2007–2010 bear market. Of these 12 bear markets, the average decline in the All Ordinaries index had been 35 per cent, over an average period of 15 months to the trough. From that trough, the market had taken an average of 41 months to make a new high. It may take a while, but it does get there in the end!

Share prices can and do fluctuate alarmingly. In the crash of 2007–09, when the market slumped more than 50 per cent, many Australian stocks fell by 95 per cent or more, while even the best blue chip stocks fell by 30–40 per cent (see Chapters 1 and 4). In that kind of heightened volatility and extreme nervousness, shares can go into freefall. In January 2008, struggling property group MFS lost two-thirds of its value during a two-hour conference call with analysts!

On the plus side, news of a takeover bid, or a mineral discovery, or a successful drug test result can send a share rocketing. Any share that you own can jump by 10 per cent tomorrow, but it can just as easily suffer a drop of the same proportion.

Successful investing on the sharemarket isn't easy — but it is straightforward. All that an investor has to do is to find well-run and profitable companies, and wait for the dividend flow and the compounding of retained earnings to create wealth.

If you get in on the ground floor, the rewards can be spectacular. For example, the former Commonwealth Serum Laboratories (now CSL Limited) is one of the great stories of the Australian stock market. When the Australian government floated CSL on the stock market in June 1994, it clearly had no idea what it owned.

CSL was floated at $2.30, raising $300 million. After a three-for-one share split in 2007, the float price was effectively 77 cents a share. Each of those shares now trades at $96.35. Add in the $10.21 that has been paid in dividends and the original shareholders have made almost 140 times their investment.

Since 1996, pathology and radiology group Sonic Healthcare has burgeoned from a market value of $144 million to $9.5 billion, global share registry operator Computershare (the world's largest) has grown from $130 million to be worth $6.8 billion and hearing aid maker Cochlear has swelled from $125 million to $5.2 billion.

But sadly, some companies are also going the other way. In 2002, paper merchant Paperlinx, which had been demerged from Amcor in 2000, was valued at $1.9 billion. Once the largest paper merchant in Europe, Paperlinx is now worth a paltry $15 million. The stock slid from $5.66 to 2.3 cents — and remember, that high point exists because someone paid $5.66 a share for Paperlinx.

At least Paperlinx can say that it still exists. Investors could have bought any of the over-debted groups that the crash of 2007–09 sent to the corporate knackery (see Chapter 4).

Clearly, investors want the stocks in their portfolios to be heading in the direction of up rather than down.

Starting with Strategy

Self-knowledge is the key to setting up your investment strategy. You have to know where you're going before you set out on the journey. You already know that time, patience and diversification load the dice in your favour when approaching sharemarket investment.

Before you start, you need to determine what kind of investor you are:

- ✔ **Income investor:** Someone looking for share investments that can pay a wage
- ✔ **Retiree:** The most conservative and risk-averse income investor
- ✔ **Straight investor:** A wealth builder
- ✔ **Speculator:** An impatient wealth builder willing to take risks
- ✔ **Trader:** An impatient wealth builder, prepared to spend a lot of time watching the market for opportunities

Each of these types of investor faces different challenges. You can determine which type of investor you are and then choose the strategy that serves your needs. Retirees invest their money conservatively in order to guarantee returns. Gamblers — speculators — take very risky short-term bets to make a quick capital gain. Straight investors stick to the higher-quality industrial stocks, the blue chips, for long-term growth.

Spreading the risk

Diversification, which you can read more about in Chapter 5, is a popular investment strategy. The idea is to spread the funds you have available for investment among different assets in order to distribute and hopefully contain the risk.

Although diversification is a fundamental law of investment, the concept of diversification can easily be misunderstood. Spreading invested funds across a number of different assets reduces the overall risk for your portfolio because you're not relying on only one asset as your investment.

The other side of diversification is that it can lower performance because it introduces more elements; but for many investors, containing the risk of sharemarket investment is more important.

Diversification isn't just a protective measure; it also allows you to generate a higher rate of return for a given level of risk. You can achieve reasonable diversification of a share portfolio with as few as ten stocks. Buying up to 15 different stocks adds to the diversification, but beyond that number, monitoring your portfolio of stocks properly is difficult. A good diversification strategy for ten stocks means not having more than 15 per cent of your portfolio by value in any one stock.

A share portfolio can be spread around and still not be properly diversified. You need to buy shares from market sectors that balance each other, so if one part of the portfolio is performing poorly, other shares will be doing better. For example, an investor who bought shares in Telstra and subsequently in National Australia Bank balanced banking with an investment in telecommunications. If the same investor bought Woodside Petroleum, it would give the portfolio an interest in an industry unrelated to the other two.

Generally, buying shares in similar companies isn't a good idea. If one of the big four banks has done well for you, don't buy the other three as well. You'll find that your portfolio is too heavily weighted to banks. Be comfortable in the choice you've made and stick with your choice unless circumstances change and you find you have to sell shares.

Diversification within a share portfolio isn't much use if a major correction (or worse, a bear market) hits the market. In that case, you hope to have a diversified portfolio of investments, not just a diversified share portfolio.

Setting your goals

What are you hoping to do with your share investments? Are you saving for a deposit on a house? Your children's school fees? Retirement income? Or, are you simply trying to maximise capital growth? All these goals pose different time constraints and risks. After you've settled on the type of return you're after — a decision that also helps you decide what type of investor you are — you can decide which shares can deliver the results and which shares you can rule out. If you're a straight investor, look for companies that promise long-term capital growth. If you're a retiree, you may be interested in good dividend returns.

Setting your time frame

How long can you give the investment? The longer you give your investments, the better. However, if you need short-term income, you have to be more aggressive in your wealth creation strategy. You may have to take on some speculative shares that carry more risk but promise greater return. This means, unfortunately, that you're in for some scary periods because you're unable to use the great risk minimiser — time. Deciding how much time you have helps you determine what type of investment strategy, and therefore shares, you require.

Setting your risk tolerance

After you know your goal and your time period for investing, you can begin to understand your risk profile. What is the maximum level of risk that's acceptable? How comfortable will you be if your investment loses 20 per cent of its value? If you can't handle that sort of volatility, you may need to adjust your goals and the time frame. Unfortunately, risk comes with the territory. If you want to invest in the sharemarket, as opposed to other asset classes, it pays to be realistic about the level of risk that you can tolerate.

If you want your share investments to fund your children's education, or your own retirement, you have to be reasonably risk-averse. That doesn't mean sticking to government bonds because that wouldn't create the capital growth that you need.

Being risk-averse as a share investor means concentrating on those companies with the most reliable long-term track record of earnings and dividend growth, rather than speculating in a minerals explorer or drug-development hopeful that has not yet made a profit. Those kind of stocks *may* make a lot of money, but as a risk-averse investor you can't afford to take that bet. You need to be in stocks where the compounding of a growing earnings stream is a much surer driver of capital growth.

Setting your financial needs

Do you have tax and liquidity issues? If you have short-term financial needs, you may have to face the prospect of unravelling your strategy. If the money you plan to invest in the sharemarket is money that you really can't afford to lose, maybe you need to rethink what you're doing in the first place.

Although the sharemarket offers a better prospect of capital growth than a term deposit in a bank or a government bond, it's not as safe a place to put money that you can't afford to lose. The sharemarket is much better suited as a place to invest money that you can afford to lose — and leave for a long time — to give your investment the best possible chance to make money for you.

Buying and Holding

A straightforward strategy for share investment is to buy and hold. You buy a portfolio of stocks and hold on to them for the long term.

If you stay in the market long enough, you minimise the risk that your portfolio may lose its value and you allow the value of your portfolio to increase through compound interest. You also pay transaction costs only once.

One more element to the buy-and-hold strategy exists and that is 'sell' (although the strategy would then become buy, hold and sell). If you never sell a stock, the wealth the stock creates exists only on paper.

Philip Fisher, in his classic book *Common Stocks and Uncommon Profits*, states: 'If the job has been done correctly when a common stock is purchased, the time to sell it is — almost never.' This approach is fine if you want the value of your shares to be part of your estate, to be passed on to your heirs, but plenty of people look at successful buy-and-hold share investing as a way to fund a happy and fulfilling retirement, free of financial worry. If that's what you've decided, selling shares to raise money is fine if you plan carefully.

For the buy-and-hold strategy to work, you have to choose your stocks carefully. Obviously, you want more stocks in your portfolio to be like Westfield or CSL. (If you manage to pick the next Westfield or CSL, you don't have to worry about the rest of your portfolio. See the sidebar 'The miracle of Westfield' for more information on this stock, and the earlier section 'Timing for the long run' for more on CSL.) Buy and hold doesn't work with every stock. For example, it doesn't make sense to buy shares in building materials companies, such as CSR, Boral, James Hardie Industries and Fletcher Building, and just put them in your bottom drawer. The Australian building industry is highly cyclical because it's based on the ups and downs of the economic cycle. The industry has taken steps to rectify this, by moving into other countries, but it remains vulnerable to Australian construction cycles.

A range of shares exists that's too volatile to be part of a stable portfolio that doesn't change over a long period. For example, property developers and contractors don't really suit this purpose because their activities depend on interest rates, which can fluctuate. The same used to be said for the big mining shares, such as Rio Tinto, BHP Billiton, Alumina and Newcrest, because they are linked to the ups and downs of commodity prices, which are linked to the economic cycle of the major Western economies. (However, this perception prevailed before the China-driven commodities boom kicked off, making profitable investment in these stocks a no-brainer for most of the 2000s — until the global financial crisis came along. See Chapter 8 for more.)

The miracle of Westfield

If you'd invested the equivalent of $1,000 in the float of Westfield Holdings in September 1960 — an amount that inflation has turned into about $13,400 — and reinvested every dividend and bonus that Westfield paid, your investment in the Westfield Group (as it's now known) at October 2011 would have been valued at about $242 million. (The company has since been split into Scentre Group, which holds the group's Australian and New Zealand shopping centre assets, and Westfield Corporation, which holds its portfolio of shopping centres in the US, UK and Europe, as well as any development activity in those regions.)

The Australian Securities Exchange believes the Westfield experience is the best example of long-term wealth creation of any stock. Forty-five consecutive increases in Westfield's overall profit have gone towards generating this amazing record. Sure, this figure is a gross calculation and doesn't take into account how much money has been reinvested. However, the point is that no other money was needed. That amount of $242 million — almost enough to gain you a place in the BRW Rich List — was all generated by that fortunate original investment. Companies older than Westfield can't match this performance. The original investment in Westfield has grown at a compound annual rate of return of 21.2 per cent a year for 51 years. Certainly, compounding looks like magic in the case of Westfield. A rate of return such as Westfield's, with more than 50 years of upward growth, results in what the Americans call a *hockey stick graph* of earnings. It goes virtually straight up.

Not every stock does what Westfield has done. Many companies fail and their stocks disappear from the market and take their investors' money as well. Plucking one exceptional stock out of 2,200 may distort what is possible. But the beauty of ordinary equity is that while losses are limited to 100 per cent, the gains that can be made in a successful stock — such as Westfield — are not.

 With a buy-and-hold strategy, you're buying growth, such as shares in the banking and finance sectors. You're also buying compounding interest and you're also buying time. If done well, buy and hold is as close as you can get to worry-free investing on the sharemarket. But as investors saw in 2007–09, when a major bear market hits, you may have to hold your buy-and-hold investment a bit longer than you thought!

Timing your strategies

With the right timing, you can make money on the sharemarket. You can buy a share, sell it for a gain, watch it fall all the way back and buy it again, and then begin the whole process over. However, this sort of transaction is hard to do because it involves forecasting. Predicting the points in the sharemarket at which a top or a bottom is reached is virtually impossible.

Nobody rings a bell at the top, or the bottom, of the market; these highs and lows can usually only be seen in hindsight. For example, in March 2009 when the Australian market finally found a bottom after 15 months of falling, going back into the market seemed the worst thing to do, because the headlines were uniformly gloomy and the prevailing sentiment was terrible. Studies from the USA, Canada and Australia show that professional investors and fund managers don't always make money from attempting to correctly time their moves. In fact, some of these experts can make big mistakes. Knowing when to time risk can be a big problem for market timers; they often fail to predict a turning point. An example is when market timers pull their investments out of the market, believing that the market will fall, and then a sudden rally leaves them little time to get back in. The problem for aspiring market timers is that very few investors, even professional ones, can accurately predict the behaviour of the market.

A further problem is that if you buy and sell an investment several times, you have to take this activity into account when adding up your profit. Your profit can be eroded by transaction costs: If you sell the shares and remake the initial investment several times, your capital gain may not be as good as that made by the investor who buys once, holds and sells.

Trading on your portfolio

Even if you invest with a long-term view, you can also act in the short term. You may think that, having chosen 10 to 12 stocks for a portfolio, you'll still be holding them at the end of your predetermined investment period. But, sometimes you have to change your strategy.

If some of the shares in your portfolio are performing poorly, or if you change your view on the quality of the business, don't hesitate to turf them. The shares in your portfolio are there to do a job, which is to make money for you. If circumstances change and they can't do the job, cut them loose. Set a level of loss beyond which you're not prepared to follow, say 15 per cent. Set a profit limit, too, beyond which you're not prepared to follow. Be ruthless with yourself and don't regret the profits you didn't get. As the saying goes, you don't go broke taking a profit. Of course, long-term investors may choose to use a short-term price fall to buy more shares.

 If you're lucky enough to double your investment in a stock, consider selling half the holding. You keep the rest for free. You've eliminated your downside but kept the upside open.

Whatever strategy you choose, stick to it. If you adopt the buy-and-hold approach, don't allow yourself to be panicked out of a shareholding. If your strategy is to maximise your returns through active trading, make sure you have your ground rules in place on when to buy and sell. Don't be seduced by emotion — whether it be fear or greed!

Chapter 4

Assessing Your Risk

. . . .

In This Chapter

▶ Being honest with yourself

▶ Exposing your investments to risk

▶ Picking the danger signals

. . . .

I once studied English literature and language and thought myself a traditionalist, particularly when watching Shakespeare's plays. That perception changed when I saw the Bell Shakespeare Company's version of *The Merchant of Venice*, with the characters dressed in snappy suits and sunglasses with mobile telephones glued to their ears. Antonio and his friends looked like stockbrokers — the Venetian equivalent. I was hooked on this modern interpretation. I found out that Antonio, like any finance professional, understood that diversification helps to spread the risk.

> *My ventures are not in one bottom trusted*
> *Nor to one place; nor is my whole estate*
> *Upon the fortune of this present year:*
> *Therefore my merchandise makes me not sad.*

Well, he thought he was protected by diversification, until all his ships hit bad weather and were wrecked. The problem for Antonio was that, although his ventures were all seemingly well diversified and his ships sailed from different places, his investments were all the same asset class: Trading ships. In this chapter, I discuss how many investors think they've covered their risk through diversification or hedging until some unforeseen event changes everything.

Gambling or Investing?

Risk is the chance of an unexpected event happening or a particular objective or outcome not being attained; its basis is the unpredictability of the future. Risk is a relative concept that alters with circumstances and personalities. In the context of finance, risk means the possibility of losing invested capital. However, an investment doesn't have to be unprofitable to be an unacceptable risk; the major aim of investing is to generate a financial return above inflation.

The highest risks bring the highest rewards. If you place your money on a single number at the roulette table, you have a 1 in 36 chance of your number coming up. That's why the table pays $35 for every dollar you put on it. As anyone who plays roulette can tell you, the 35 to 1 payout is a wonderful win to have early in the night. However, if the hour is late and you're chasing a win to get out of trouble, your odds may seem more like a 1 in 360 chance.

Like successful roulette players — if such people exist — successful investors understand that risk is merely the other side of gain and you can't have gain without risk. An experienced investor knows that the promise of high percentage returns usually means increased risk. Sometimes, people new to investing don't make the proper connection between risk and return.

Measuring risk mathematically is possible. The statistical terms of variance and standard deviation measure the volatility of a security's actual return from its expected return, but that's a discussion that belongs in another book. However, in discussing the risk of a particular stock, standard deviation of return is a useful concept. The *standard deviation* measures the spread of a sample of numbers and the extent to which each of the numbers in the sample varies from the average. A *low standard deviation* of return in a stock means that it's a relatively less risky investment.

Another way of measuring risk uses the *beta factor*, a statistical measure of a share's volatility (see the sidebar 'Measuring volatility' later in this chapter) compared with the overall market. The beta factor measures a share price's movement against that of the market as a whole (for example, the S&P/All Ordinaries Index). The index has a beta factor of 1.0. If the share has a beta factor of less than 1.0, you can expect its price to move proportionally less than the index. If the share has a beta factor greater than 1.0, you can expect the share price to rise or fall to a greater extent than the index. The higher the beta factor, the more volatile is a share's price.

Measuring volatility

Don't confuse volatility with risk because volatility is only one measure of risk. Volatility is the statistical term for the extent to which any series of numbers (such as a share price history) fluctuates. The higher the volatility of the price of an asset, the less certain is the return from that asset.

For example, research firm Andex Charts looked at 1,369 twelve-month investments in the S&P/ASX All Ordinaries Accumulation Index (with dividends included), and its forebears, from January 1900 to December 2014 (that is, investments made at each month-end, and held for 12 months). The average 12-month return was 13.3 per cent and the standard deviation was 17.2 per cent. Of the 1,369 12-month periods examined, 75.2 per cent fell within one standard deviation of the average.

In other words, approximately three-quarters of the 12-month returns measured between 1900 and 2014 fell within a range of plus 30.5 per cent to minus 3.9 per cent. So, in a given 12-month period, an investor could reasonably expect a range of returns from 30.5 per cent to minus 3.9 per cent. The remaining quarter of the 12-month returns fell outside this range.

The good news is that, over the long term, returns tend towards the market average, and volatility is greatly reduced over longer periods.

The most famous volatility measure is the Market Volatility Index (VIX) of the Chicago Board Options Exchange (CBOE). Introduced in 1993, the VIX measures the implied volatility of options contracts traded over the value of the S&P 500 Index, on the CBOE. It has become the benchmark for short-term (30 days) expectations of stock market volatility, and goes by the nickname of the 'Fear Index'.

When the VIX is at high levels, the market expects a large change over the next 30 days. A low VIX implies a market expectation of very little change. Up until 2008, US investors believed that any time the VIX approached 48, it was a time to buy stocks. It was this kind of thinking that had investors buying back into the US market in mid-2008, because accepted VIX wisdom told them that was the right thing to do. But what nobody had envisaged was the sheer turmoil of the global financial crisis (GFC): When the VIX peaked at 89.53 in October 2008, in the wake of the collapse of Lehman Brothers, the fear was no longer whether the US stock market was going to recover — it was whether the global economy financial system still functioned. The VIX has

(continued)

(continued)

returned to the low 20s, trading as low as 10.3 in mid-2014, before spiking back toward 20 in June 2015 as the prospect of a Greek exit from the euro roiled markets.

In September 2010 the Australian Securities Exchange (ASX) introduced the S&P/ASX 200 VIX, constructed using the same methodology as the US VIX. Like its US counterpart, ASX back-testing shows that the Australian VIX surged to a high of 66.72 points when Lehman Brothers collapsed, but an improved outlook saw it fall to as low as 9.3 points in mid-2014, before following its US counterpart higher, to trade at over 20 points in mid-2015.

The beta factor can provide a guide to expected returns when the market moves in a predictable pattern. Investors must remember that the beta factor, although handy, is an historical and not a prospective figure. In other words, because the future is unpredictable, using the beta factor in making investment decisions carries a risk.

The bad news: Risk is inescapable

All investors store money for future use. What most concerns you is the possibility of losing the money you're saving. Now you're talking risk! However, some professional investors set even higher risk levels than the average individual investor. For example, a fund manager may decide that her fund will outperform the S&P/All Ordinaries Index. The manager's main risk is not achieving this goal. Even if the fund's investments make money, if they don't exceed the return of the index, the portfolio has had a bad year. Investors know the fund failed to reach its benchmark, which can cause some fund investors to take their money elsewhere.

Wary investors associate risk with cataclysmic events, such as the great sharemarket crashes of 1929, 1987 and 2007–09, the bond market downturn in 1994 and the tech wreck of 2000. These events spark memories of collapsing companies, bankruptcies and share certificates made worthless overnight.

All assets offer a different reward and a different level of risk. They range from government bonds, which are considered a risk-free asset because they're guaranteed by the government, to futures contracts and options, where you can easily lose all of your money. With futures assets, you're taking on higher risk than if you buy an Australian Government ten-year Treasury bond, but you're entitled to expect a far greater return. Successful investing means balancing the return against the risk.

The good news: Risk is manageable

You can offset risk either by hedging or diversification. *Hedging* is investing in one asset to offset the risk to another. *Diversification* is the spreading of funds across a variety of investments to soften the impact on your portfolio return if one investment performs badly. You can also include a few individual risk shares in a portfolio that's otherwise well balanced. Because returns from different assets aren't perfectly correlated, by diversifying your portfolio you decrease your overall risk. But you can't eliminate all risk. A well-diversified portfolio gives the best risk–return trade-off over the longer term.

The elusive risk-free asset

In every market an investment considered a risk-free asset exists, against which all other investment returns are compared. In Australia, it's the Australian Government ten-year Treasury bond because the Australian Government guarantees to pay the holder of that bond the interest payment on the due dates, and the amount of the bond in full on maturity. You can't lend money to a better or more reliable debtor.

The ten-year bond is risk free only if the buyer holds it to maturity. You can buy and sell bonds, just like shares, on the market, five business days a week. Bond prices move up or down based on how the market assesses the likely movement in interest rates. If interest rates rise, bonds issued at lower interest rates aren't as attractive as higher-yielding newer bonds.

Naturally, the opposite is true if interest rates fall. When you're unable to hold the bond to maturity and have to sell it, you may have to sell it at a loss. The world bond markets fell dramatically in 1994 when interest rates spiked upward and caused the prices of lower-yielding bonds to slump.

The difference between the risk-free return and the much riskier return on shares is called the equity risk premium, or ERP. Share investors demand a risk premium over bonds and they generally get it: Over the period 1900–2012, according to the Credit Suisse Global Investment Returns Yearbook 2015, the Australian stock market generated the highest equity risk premium in the world — a 5.6 per cent gap in the annualised returns between shares and bonds. This compares to 4.5 per cent for the US,

(continued)

(continued)

3.7 per cent for the UK and 3.3 per cent for the world.

But the ERP does have one major drawback: It's not valid for any and all time periods. Someone who bought shares in October 2007 has struggled to achieve a premium. Circumstances can exist when the premium disappears for long periods.

But generally speaking, because of the equity risk premium, low-risk assets such as the Australian Government ten-year Treasury bond, which generates low returns, may actually be too risky in the context of building capital wealth because the bond doesn't generate the returns of a long-term equity investment.

Hedging is a form of insurance in which you try to make two opposite investments, so that if one goes wrong, the other can nullify or lessen the blow. When buying or selling shares, you can use the derivatives markets (exchange-traded options or warrants) to take the opposite position to an investment in the sharemarket. You may own shares in National Australia Bank (NAB), but also own a *put option* (the right to sell the shares at a predetermined price) in NAB that will increase in value if the share price falls.

Time also manages risk, by minimising it psychologically. As you come to understand the returns a share portfolio can generate over time, you begin to relax about short-term fluctuations.

Spreading the news: Risk increases your return

The mathematics involved in *risk-and-return* theory are mind-boggling. In taking your first steps into share investing, you may come across terms like 'Modern Portfolio Theory' and the 'Capital-Asset Pricing Model'. These are complicated theories for money nerds to play around with and are far beyond the scope of this book — and far beyond your humble author, too! Simpler ways exist to understand how risk increases your return. For example, when you have an asset that earns a rate of return every year, you end up with a sample of yearly returns. When you've owned the asset for two years, you can calculate the average return that the asset has earned. However, the share return at any given time may fluctuate a good deal more than your calculated average. The wider the variance of the extremes, the more volatile the asset and the higher its standard deviation.

To reduce the standard deviation of your portfolio and increase its return, you can increase the proportion of more risky assets. Adding a new asset to the portfolio acts as a hedge to the other shares. With careful portfolio selection, you can achieve such a result, but it's necessary for you to bring in assets other than shares.

Assessing Your Risk

As an investor, you have to deal with different kinds of risk. In some instances you may be able to lessen the risk, but in other situations, the degree of risk may be unchangeable. Some investments are like a cocktail of several kinds of risk. Understanding how each type operates helps you put together a balanced portfolio.

Market risk

Market risk is the risk you take by being in the sharemarket. As the market fluctuates, the price of a company's shares varies too, independent of factors specific to the company. The higher prices rise and the more the market moves away from its long-term trendline, the more likely a correction will take place (when a share price or market index falls by 10 per cent or more).

The crash of 1987 stripped 25 per cent from the value of the All Ordinaries Index in one day. The slump knocked the very best stocks off their perch for a year to 18 months. Many others in the Top 100 took three years to get above their pre-crash highs and some stocks never recovered.

More recently, the massive bear market of November 2007 to February 2009 stripped 54 per cent from the value of the Australian sharemarket. That is the impact of market risk. It didn't matter how well diversified your share portfolio was; all stocks fell. In 2015, most of the market's top stocks have not only recovered their 2007 peaks, but have moved higher — most, but not all. NAB and Woodside Petroleum have not yet regained their 2007 peak prices, while Woolworths — which did at one point recover — has slumped back below its 2007 pre-crash high.

Economic data, such as inflation, interest rates and gross domestic product, all contribute to the risk of being part of the market. If the market falls by a marked amount, most shares fall as well. You can't lessen market risk by diversifying within your share portfolio. To offset the systemic risk of the sharemarket, your portfolio needs to contain other asset classes, such as property or bonds. Ideally, your portfolio features overseas assets as well, to lessen the reliance on the Australian economy. Even then, in 2008 and 2009, you needed to own bonds to have any part of your portfolio doing well, because everything else fell.

Financial risk

Every company has *financial risk*, that is, the possibility of the company getting into financial difficulties. Managing the finances of a publicly listed company isn't an easy task. The company may have borrowed too heavily and exposed itself to danger from rising interest rates, a recession or worst of all, a *credit crunch* — when banks stop lending. That's what happened in the GFC, particularly after Lehman Brothers collapsed and the global banking system temporarily froze. Suddenly, after years of cheap credit, debt was a dirty word. Over-borrowed companies' share prices simply sank like stones on the sharemarket, when they couldn't roll over their debt.

Investment bank Babcock & Brown, which floated at $5 in 2004 and reached a peak of $33.90 in mid-2007 (when it was valued at $10 billion on the ASX), fell 99.6 per cent — 45 per cent of that in two days in June 2008 — before it limped into administration in March 2009. Structured finance specialist Allco Finance Group, which was valued at $5 billion at its peak in February 2007 — shortly before it was the key player in a consortium that tried to take over Qantas — fell 98.9 per cent on the way to administration in November 2008, owing more than $1 billion.

Shopping centre owner Centro Properties lost 99.4 per cent between February 2007 and April 2009; 84.5 per cent of that value was lost in two trading days, in December 2007, after it revealed that it couldn't roll over $4 billion in short-term debt. (Centro did not go into administration, in fact it never missed an interest payment: Its banks sold the debt to the bondholders, who ultimately swapped the debt for equity in a new company, Federation Centres, which in 2015 merged with Novion Property Group to form Vicinity.) In January 2008, financial services and property group MFS lost almost 70 per cent of its value during a phone call: A conference call with analysts in which chief executive Michael King revealed a shock $550 million capital raising, almost three times larger than the analysts were expecting. MFS changed its name to Octaviar, but went into liquidation in July 2009. Property developer City Pacific's shares plunged 58 per cent in a day in March 2008 after it revealed difficulty in repaying

$500 million in short-term debt to Commonwealth Bank; from a peak of $5.95 in October 2006, City Pacific shares fell 99.4 per cent on its way into receivership in 2009.

Garden products maker Nylex slumped 97 per cent on its way into administration; managed agribusiness investment companies Timbercorp and Great Southern fell 97 per cent and 96 per cent respectively as they collapsed; and childcare centre operator ABC Learning plunged 92 per cent on its way into receivership. Infrastructure operator Asciano fell 96.5 per cent, from $11.64 in June 2007 to 40.8 cents in February 2009 (Asciano recovered to $6.50 in mid-2015). The end of the road in share price terms for Allco Finance Group, Babcock & Brown, MFS/Octaviar, Centro Properties and ABC Learning is shown in Figure 4-1.

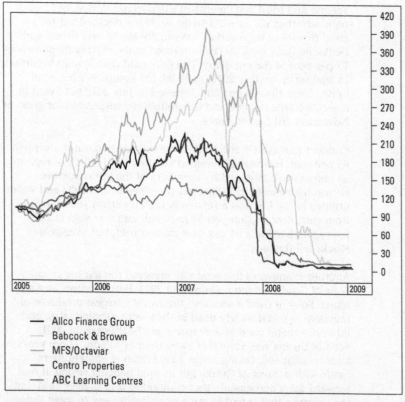

Figure 4-1: Allco Finance Group, Babcock & Brown, MFS, Centro Properties and ABC Learning share prices, 2005–09.

Data source: © IRESS Market Technology

Real estate investment trusts (REITs) with high debt levels were hammered just as badly. FKP Property, Goodman Group and ING Industrial Fund all fell more than 95 per cent; GPT lost just less than that. Abacus Property and Australand both lost 91 per cent. Anywhere the market saw short-term refinancing risk, or simply too much debt, it was much the same.

The worst slump of all was toll road company BrisConnections, which was floated by Macquarie Group and Deutsche Bank with awful timing — in August 2008, when over-geared infrastructure stocks were badly on the nose. BrisConnections' $1 partly paid units fell 59 per cent on their first day of trading, and by May 2009 they were trading at 0.1 cent (the lowest tradeable price on the ASX), for a fall of 99.9 per cent.

At the time, holders of the units were still obliged to pay the second and third instalments of the purchase price, of $1 each; naturally, they didn't want to do so. Many decided not to, amid threats of legal action. Eventually Macquarie Group and Deutsche Bank took up the unwanted units, leaving them owning 79 per cent of the company. The fully paid (to $3) units returned to trading in January 2010, at $1.30; the company's toll road in Brisbane, the Airport Link, opened in July 2012 but failed to meet its traffic targets, and the units were suspended for good in November 2012, at 40 cents.

Connect East (CEU), the Melbourne toll road operator, dropped 85 per cent. Hastings Diversified Utilities Fund (HDF) — regarded as one of the higher-quality members of the infrastructure sector, with assets including gas pipelines in Australia and water utilities in the UK, and a relatively high dividend yield funded from cash flow — slumped 93 per cent, and was sold in 2011. Every stock fell in a 54 per cent market rout, but over-geared stocks fell the most.

Another example of financial risk involved the mining group Sons of Gwalia, which collapsed in 2004. Better known as a gold miner, Sons of Gwalia was also the world's largest producer of tantalum, a metal widely used in the electronics industry, and lithium, a metal used in aerospace and healthcare. In 2001, Sons of Gwalia was valued at more than $1 billion. Three years later it collapsed, taking about $250 billion of shareholders' funds with it. Sons of Gwalia got its gold hedging wrong. It had forward sales agreements that committed it to deliver gold, but the reserves that it had to mine were insufficient to meet those commitments. A $500 million liability on its gold and foreign exchange hedging 'book' brought it down.

Mining is a risky business, but the financial engineering that the miners' treasuries indulge in can be even riskier. Sons of Gwalia's fall (see Figure 4-2) came only four years after zinc and lead miner Pasminco imploded after getting its foreign exchange hedging wrong. Pasminco was refinanced in 2002 and returned to the sharemarket in April 2004 as Zinifex, which in 2008 merged with Oxiana in an $11.6 billion merger that created Australia's fourth-largest miner, called Oz Minerals. Bad timing: The credit crunch hit, and Oz had to make massive write-downs and sell its refinery and smelting operations, on the way to a $509 million loss in 2008–09. The share price fell 80 per cent, and at mid-2015 was still 90 per cent below its pre-GFC peak. Two of that company's three incarnations have given shareholders a tough time!

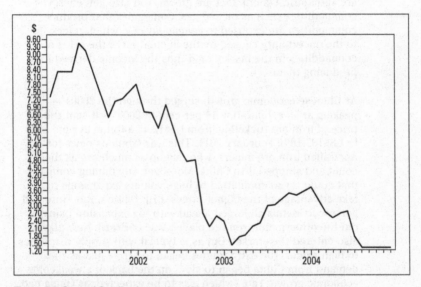

Figure 4-2: Sons of Gwalia share price, 2001–04.

Data source: © IRESS Market Technology

Another kind of financial risk is when the price of a company's product drops for reasons beyond its control. Agrichemical company Nufarm encountered this problem between 2008 and 2010 when prices for its main weedkiller product, glyphosate, slumped as cheaper Chinese products and weak demand hit the market. Nufarm's margins more than halved over the period, forcing the company into a loss in the 2009–10 financial year, its first loss in more than a decade. Nufarm was forced to slash its earnings forecasts in half in July 2010, triggering breaches of debt covenants (agreements between a company and its bankers that the company should operate within certain limits) that left it at the mercy of its banks. Nufarm shares slumped by 70 per cent in 2010, and by mid-2015, the share price had not yet fully recovered.

Commodity risk

A *commodity* is a tradeable good; the word is generally used in the context of physical commodities — basic resources and agricultural products — that are bought and sold all over the world, and have actively traded markets. 'Hard' commodities are those extracted by mining, while 'soft' commodities are agricultural goods that are grown. You also get 'energy' commodities, such as oil and gas. Companies that produce commodities are exposed to *commodity risk,* which refers to the uncertainty caused by the fluctuation of the price of commodities in the market, and thus the income derived from producing them.

As Chinese economic growth surged through the 2000s — peaking at an exhilarating 14 per cent in 2007 — it sent the price of iron ore rocketing, from US$12.45 a tonne in June 2000 to US$187.18 in February 2011. This was fabulous news for Australian iron ore miners, who dug up as much ore as they could and shipped it to China. Moreover, any mining company that could do so committed to huge volume expansions to take advantage of the higher prices. BHP Billiton, Rio Tinto and Fortescue Metals all forged ahead with big expansion plans, as did the other major iron ore player, Valé of Brazil. New players also entered the market. But as is typical with supply responses to high prices, the extra tonnes began to arrive just as the demand from China began to slow, on the back of a weakening economic growth rate (which was to be expected, as China had moved slowly towards a more consumer-spending and services-oriented economy, and relied less on massive infrastructure projects to boost its growth).

By 2015, China's GDP growth rate had fallen to 7 per cent a year, and although this is still massive growth, given the sheer size of the Chinese economy, it meant that iron ore was less in demand. Sure enough, by mid-2015, the iron ore price was under US$50 a tonne.

This was bad enough for the major producers, BHP Billiton and Rio Tinto, but at least they were diversified commodity producers. For the miners that only produced iron ore, however, it was a disaster, as the sagging iron ore price threatened to fall below their cost of production.

The largest of the single-focus iron ore miners, Fortescue Metals, dropped 71 per cent on the ASX. The smaller iron ore 'juniors' fared even worse: Gindalbie Metals slumped 98.5 per cent; Atlas Iron lost 99 per cent; BC Iron plunged 94.5 per cent; and Mount Gibson Iron fell 91 per cent. Gindalbie and Atlas Iron bit the bullet, and stopped mining temporarily.

Liquidity risk

Liquidity risk is the possibility that you'll be unable to get out of an investment because no one will buy your shares. Holders of internet stocks after the April 2000 tech wreck know all about liquidity risk, as do owners of small company stocks during the GFC. You can't sell shares if no one wants to buy them. If liquidity risk bothers you, don't stray out of the Top 100 stocks.

Business risk

Each share carries *business risk*, that is, the possibility that the company will make a mistake in its business. Business risk is part and parcel of the capitalist system. But business risk can very soon become financial risk — a very good reason to have a well-diversified share portfolio.

Company collapses do happen — and they come in all shapes and sizes. Australian company ABC Learning was once the world's largest provider of early childhood education services. First established in 1988, and owning only 18 childcare centres in 1997, it grew to own 1,200 centres in Australia and expanded into the US. The company was floated on the ASX in 2001 at $2 a share; by December 2006, ABC's share price hit its peak of $8.62, valuing the company at $4.1 billion, and giving founder Eddy Groves a personal fortune of about $300 million. But the attempted expansion in the US exposed the company's flaws, and ABC Learning collapsed in November 2008 with reported debts of up to $2.7 billion, and a share price at 54 cents.

It was discovered that the company's accountants had used some highly dubious practices. Payments from developers that subsidised loss-making centres were included as normal revenue — which hid the fact that as much as one-quarter of the company's centres were losing money. The company also had billions of dollars' worth of intangible assets, which made up most of ABC's balance sheet; therefore, company valuations were ultimately discredited. ABC also made a large number of related-party transactions involving family members. In the end, ABC Learning's chief financial officer pled guilty to making available false or misleading information about the affairs of ABC.

Groves also declared bankruptcy — and the auditor who signed off on ABC Learning's last financial report before its collapse (for 2006–07) was suspended from practice for five years. Shareholders at least got a loss declaration in 2009–10 from the Australian Tax Office, enabling them to claim a usable capital loss (see Chapter 10).

Shareholders can also suffer from business risk issues before a company actually collapses. Transport company McAleese Limited floated at $1.47 a share in November 2013, after buying the Cootes Transport business from Champ Private Equity in 2012. But the stock has been on a one-way slide virtually ever since, to a share price of 12.5 cents in mid-2015.

McAleese's problems started just before the float, when one of its Cootes Transport fuel tankers was involved in a deadly crash on Sydney's northern beaches. The company didn't make sufficient provision for the financial impact of the accident, and ongoing unresolved maintenance issues dogged its fleet. Subsequently McAleese lost a string of lucrative contracts, lost its chief executive officer and chief financial officer, and cut 680 jobs in a drastic restructure. In April 2015, one of its major clients, Atlas Iron, stopped mining iron ore — which McAleese had hauled to port for it. Shortly after that shock, a McAleese subsidiary went into administration. Long-suffering shareholders have seen 92 per cent of the value of their investment wiped out.

Product risk

Similar to business risk, some companies carry *product risk*, that is, the possibility that their products may fail. This is a particular concern for biotech shareholders, because a failed clinical trial can make a major dent in their investment.

Just ask the shareholders of Alchemia, who saw their share price fall by 94 per cent over 2014–15 after the Phase III trial of its cancer treatment candidate showed no benefit over the placebo (after the news was reported in October 2014, the shares opened the trading day 80 per cent down on the previous day's close). The shareholders of Prana Biotechnology had a similar experience, when Prana's shares fell by more than 70 per cent in 2014 after a failure with its Phase II Alzheimer's disease trial. As did the shareholders of QRxPharma, who watched their shares drop by 98 per cent in 2014 after the US Food and Drug Administration knocked back its pain combination therapy — for the third time. A bitter pill to swallow indeed.

Not even Australia's world-leading medical device makers — hearing aid maker Cochlear and sleep-breathing product developer ResMed — have been immune from this kind of issue. In September 2011, Cochlear issued a global recall of its best-selling product line after noticing a mysterious rise in the number of its hearing implants that had suddenly stopped working: The share price fell 25 per cent in a morning. In May 2015, ResMed shocked the market with the results of a clinical trial that they'd hoped would show that its sleep therapy products protected heart attack victims; instead, the trial result showed that a group of patients were put at increased risk of dying. The sharemarket reacted by dropping 27 per cent of ResMed's share price.

Legislative risk

Another form of specific risk is *legislative risk*, which is the possibility that a change in legislation may adversely affect a company whose shares you own. (This is also known as *regulatory risk*.) A good example is Telstra, which, until the Telstra 3 sale in 2006, was 51.8 per cent-owned by the Australian Government.

Telstra has three 'levers' to its business:

- ✔ Costs
- ✔ Revenue
- ✔ The regulatory framework in which Telstra operates

The company has some control over the first two, but not the third. The Telstra regulatory regime effectively became a political football during the parliamentary horse-trading required to pass the legislation for full sale, and Telstra's earnings were seen as being overly influenced by parts of its service obligation, as well as the setting of its wholesale rental charges and call charge rates.

Telstra has always been a politically sensitive stock because of its status as the incumbent monopoly with a universal service obligation, but this sensitivity kicked into overdrive when the Rudd Labor Government took office in November 2007. The new government made no secret that it wanted Telstra to separate its wholesale and retail businesses, and open its networks to promote greater competition. The government had proposed a National Broadband Network (NBN) in the 2007 election campaign and, in 2008, called for proposals to build the network. Telstra made a proposal, but the government rejected it; in December 2008, the government announced that it would build the NBN.

In June 2010 Telstra announced a deal with the government by which it would share its infrastructure with the NBN Company and move its fixed-line customers to the government's new fibre network in return for $11 billion from the government. The deal was seen as a win–win, removing the risk that Telstra and the NBN Company would compete head to head. Telstra shares had lost 38 per cent between the accession of the Labor Government and the signing of the deal. Much of that was ascribed to the legislative risk element, although to the long-suffering shareholders, it was simply a continuation of Telstra's downward trend through the 2000s (see Chapter 8). However, the benefit of the NBN deal can be seen in Telstra's share price recovery since then — which arguably represents the flipside of legislative risk. The effect of these events on Telstra's share price can be seen in Figure 4-3.

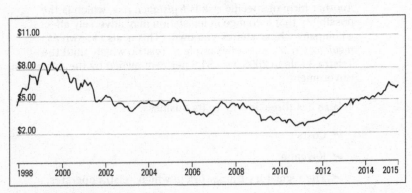

Figure 4-3: Telstra share price, 2007–15.

Data source: © IRESS Market Technology

Another celebrated case of legislative risk was that of salary packaging and fleet management services company McMillan Shakespeare, in July 2013. McMillan Shakespeare was blindsided by the Labor Government's proposed changes to fringe benefits tax (FBT) laws in relation to car use for business. As a major player in the car-leasing market, McMillan Shakespeare immediately stood to lose up to 40 per cent of its earnings. The shares promptly fell 55 per cent.

Up until then, McMillan Shakespeare had been a market darling, rising from its post-GFC low of $2 to $18. What most angered McMillan Shakespeare and its fellow car-leasing companies was the lack of consultation — the change was sprung on the industry by the government, out of the blue. Hence the dramatic share price fall.

Even though a new Coalition government overturned Labor's changes later that year, the shares remain 31 per cent lower than they were before Labor's FBT changes.

A more collective example of legislative risk is the effect on mining companies' share prices in May 2010, after the Australian Government announced a proposed resource super profits tax (RSPT), which would take 40 per cent of mining companies' 'super profits'. The super profits were defined as profit (revenue minus costs) above the ten-year government bond rate, which at the time was about 5 per cent. The savage reaction to the proposal, which affected about 2,500 companies, was one of the reasons why the Labor Government replaced Prime Minister Kevin Rudd with his deputy, Julia Gillard, shortly before the August 2010 federal election. On taking over, Prime Minister Gillard announced a modified proposal, called the mineral resource rent tax (MRRT), which applied only to producers of iron ore and coal, and was levied at 30 per cent on the mining companies' profits above their cost of capital, reckoned at 12 per cent. The MRRT was scrapped by the Coalition Government in 2014.

What was most interesting about the announcement of the RSPT was not only that mining stocks fell in price and the Australian dollar fell against the US dollar, but that the dollar also fell against its fellow resources currencies — the Canadian dollar, the South African rand and the Brazilian real — showing that the global market's initial reaction to the RSPT was effectively to downgrade Australia as a *sovereign risk;* that is, as a jurisdiction in which they felt comfortable investing. ('Sovereign' risk refers to the trustworthiness of a sovereign government in terms of paying interest and debt, and making decisions out of the blue that affect agreements and contracts into which outside investors have entered in good faith.) Local investors feared the impact on the Australian economy of a capital flight from the resources industry.

Technical risk

Occasionally companies developing ambitious new projects using new technology can come unstuck on *technical risk*, when the technology proves difficult to bed down or simply doesn't work.

Anaconda Nickel was a Western Australian nickel company that saw, in the mid-1990s, the potential of large, already-discovered laterite deposits in the northern goldfields of WA. These deposits were discovered in the nickel boom of the early 1970s but were left untouched because they were considered to be uneconomic. But with the development of a new process called pressure-acid-leach, suddenly these deposits became viable.

Anaconda embarked on an ambitious $1 billion world-scale 45,000 tonnes-a-year nickel plant at Murrin Murrin, near Leonora in Western Australia. Anaconda had no difficulty raising the money, with mining giant Anglo American and Swiss metal trader Glencore among the project backers. The plan was to expand production at Murrin Murrin to 100,000 tonnes of nickel and become one of the biggest producers in the world. In 1999, Anaconda was a Top 100 company, valued at $1.5 billion. However, the cracks in the plan were emerging.

Anaconda was in a hurry to get into production, so it skipped the demonstration plant stage and went straight from the laboratory to full-scale production. The plant couldn't handle it. The ore proved more difficult to process than first thought, and construction design flaws and engineering problems rose aplenty. In March 2002, Anaconda — now out of the Top 100 — defaulted on its debt, and in September 2002 the company posted a net loss of $919 million, the largest loss from a company ranked outside the Top 100.

Closely related to technical risk is *engineering risk*. In December 2000, Australian Magnesium Corporation (at $2.36 and a market capitalisation of $262 million) joined the S&P/ASX 200 Index. The company was seeking funding for a 90,000 tonnes-a-year Stanwell Magnesium project in central Queensland. Australian Magnesium had the support of car giant Ford, which invested US$30 million — its first investment in a metal supplier — and signed on to take delivery of 45,000 tonnes a year for ten years, underwriting $2.5 billion in revenue from the project.

Australian Magnesium was a $1.7 billion project that employed 120 people, and projected 1,350 jobs during the engineering and construction phase and a permanent workforce of 350. But over 2001–03, costs blew out as funding fell short. With the market becoming increasingly sceptical, the federal and Queensland governments tipped in more than $300 million to keep the project alive.

The Queensland Government put up $100 million to guarantee dividend payments to investors for three years. In November 2001, Australian Magnesium raised $525 million through the issue of 'distribution entitled securities' at 80 cents each — the dividends on which were effectively being paid by Queensland taxpayers. But the market dumped the shares, as shown in Figure 4-4.

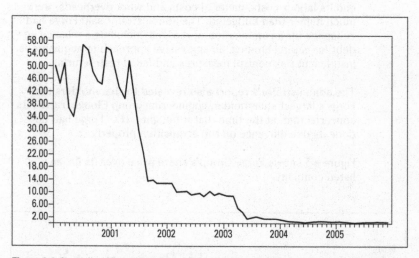

Figure 4-4: Australian Magnesium Corporation/Advanced Magnesium share price, 2000–05.

Data source: © IRESS Market Technology

Australian Magnesium had done a great deal of establishment work on its technology, had a major automotive company as a supporter and a customer, had a demonstration plant that worked well and did not have significant scale-up risk, but it blew up on the capital cost of building the project, which escalated out of control.

Project risk

Similar to technical and engineering risk is *project risk*, when a project runs into problems that end up being terminal.

Mining services company Forge Group floated in 2007 at 64 cents a share, and peaked at $6.80 in 2011. But the company collapsed in March 2014, with the shares back down to 82 cents and under the weight of more than $500 million in debt.

Forge's problems began when it bought power station builder CTEC in 2012. Two power stations that CTEC was building ran into construction problems and cost blow-outs, and Forge Group had to make major write-downs. The power station issues couldn't be solved and the company had to go into administration.

The administrator's report was not enjoyable reading for Forge shareholders. It found that Forge's under-estimated income, and its labour costs, material costs and work overheads, were much higher than budgeted. The administrator said Forge had collapsed for a combination of reasons, including a reliance on debt for capital funding, an aggressive approach to acquisitions, insufficient risk control measures and failed restructuring.

The administrator's report also revealed to shareholders that Forge's largest shareholder, engineering group Clough, raised its concerns that, at the time that it bought CTEC, Forge had not done its due diligence on the acquisition properly.

Figure 4-5 shows Forge Group's share price over its life as a listed company.

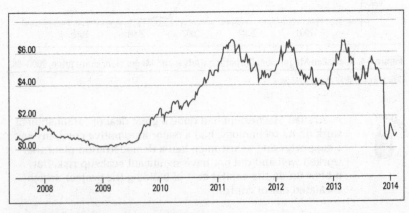

Figure 4-5: Forge Group share price, 2007–14.

Data source: © IRESS Market Technology

Valuation risk

Valuation risk is tied to the price of a share. A company may be well run, profitable, with a conservative balance sheet and part of a stable industry, but the shares are too expensive to buy. The shares are *overvalued*.

Valuation risk usually isn't a problem for investors with a long-term investment strategy because they can afford to wait for the quality of the stock to push the stock past its over-stated value, although a market slump such as the one that occurred between 2007 and 2009 can force them to extend their holding period beyond what they had expected.

However, short-term investors have to wait for the *price/earnings ratio* (P/E) to come back down to earth, which may not fit their investment strategy.

Political risk

Political risk refers to the uncertainty of return from a foreign investment because political or legislative changes in that country may be detrimental to investors' interests; or, in less stable countries, that coups and political violence can affect companies.

Australian companies, particularly mining and petroleum exploration companies, operate in some of the furthest-flung reaches of the planet, in some cases under regimes considered highly unsavoury and in countries considered unsafe for Westerners.

In early 2006, for example, an outbreak of fighting forced Australian company Range Resources to suspend its oil exploration operations in Somalia. In 2010 — and again in 2013 — outbreaks of ethnic and political unrest in the Kyrgyz Republic rocked the share prices of the group of Australian companies with activities there, including Manas Resources, Ram Resources and Nimrodel Resources.

Another case of political risk involved Australian mining company St Barbara, which operated the Gold Ridge gold mine in the Solomon Islands. Gold Ridge had already been abandoned by its Australian owners once before (in 2000) due to civil unrest, and St Barbara took it over in 2012.

The mine experienced incursions into the site, attacks on company vehicles, and vandalism and fire damage to mine infrastructure, only for the workers doing the repair work to then be attacked by locals. Then in 2014 deadly floods shut the mine and threatened its tailings dam, stretching St Barbara's relationship with the Solomon Islands' government to breaking point. In 2015, St Barbara sold the mining operation to local landowners for just $100, but not before the problems at Gold Ridge had slashed the company's value by 96 per cent.

In 2012, the Indonesian government shocked miners by introducing new laws that threatened to bring all foreign mining projects under government control. Although the foreign ownership restrictions eventually proved more lenient than expected, in 2014 Jakarta followed up that raft of new laws with a ban on exports of some raw materials, further confusing foreign miners working there.

Such outbreaks are an occupational risk of looking for ore and hydrocarbon deposits in the backblocks of the atlas: Then again, given the rest of the world's reaction to the RSPT/MRRT introduction (refer to the section 'Legislative risk' earlier in this chapter), Australia has lost a lot of its innocence when it comes to political risk.

A similar reversal of perception occurred during the uranium boom on the stock market in 2005, when Australian companies with projects in Africa received greater sharemarket support in many cases than companies with Australian ground. The reason for this was that for nearly 30 years, uranium mining in Australia had been restricted under a 'three mines' policy, which allowed mining only at the Ranger mine in the Northern Territory (owned by Energy Resources of Australia), the Olympic Dam mine in South Australia (formerly owned by WMC Resources, now owned by BHP Billiton) and the Beverley mine in South Australia (owned by Heathgate Resources, a subsidiary of General Atomic of the USA).

The Coalition government ditched the policy after taking office in 1996, but the Labor-controlled state governments effectively maintained it. In 2009, Australia's Labor Government approved the country's first new uranium mine in more than ten years, at Four Mile in South Australia (close to Beverley). The uranium industry has been in the doghouse since the Fukushima disaster of March 2011 shut down all but two of Japan's 50 nuclear reactors, but the local uranium industry is eyeing long-term demand from China and is on track for several more start-ups, including Cameco's Yeelirrie project and Toro Energy's Wiluna project, both in Western Australia. But for a long time, companies with uranium prospects in Africa were preferred to prospects in Australia — on the grounds of less political risk!

Currency risk

If a company operates in any currencies other than the Australian dollar, that company has *currency risk*. Currency risk is a bet that can have a number of outcomes. If the price of your foreign assets rises, you get a capital gain. The important question then concerns the value of those assets in their local currency. Here's what can happen:

- ✔ If the foreign currency strengthens against the Australian dollar (A$), your capital gain is magnified.

- ✔ If the foreign currency loses ground against the A$, your capital gain is reduced.

- ✔ Conversely, if your foreign assets fall in value, you don't want the foreign currency to weaken against the A$ because that increases your loss.

- ✔ With a falling asset price, you want the foreign currency to strengthen against the A$ to offset some of your capital loss.

Companies try to lessen or negate their currency risk by using the derivatives markets to lock in future receipts or amounts to be spent, at a predetermined rate. This practice of hedging is a form of insurance that can cost money. Hedging doesn't always work, as with the Sons of Gwalia example, which I discuss in the section 'Financial risk' earlier in this chapter.

Specific risk

Risk that is particular to a certain stock is called *specific risk*. A good example is Western Kingfish Limited, which was floated on the ASX in July 2007. Western Kingfish operated fish farms at Jurien Bay in Western Australia, where it produced yellow-tailed kingfish. In November 2008 a bacterial infection wiped out 75 per cent of the company's fish, plunging it into administration.

Fellow fish farmer Clean Seas Tuna had a similar issue in September 2010, with 'human error' wiping out 80 tonnes of kingfish while the fish were being bathed. The shares, which had already fallen by 58 per cent after the revelation of a $14 million half-year loss, promptly fell a further 15 per cent.

Clean Seas was also trying to breed southern bluefin tuna, but had to shelve that program because it couldn't get its fish large enough to survive the winter.

Clean Seas is on top of its kingfish problems and now sells its kingfish to Australian, European and Japanese consumers at the high end of the sashimi market. While a full-year net profit still eluded it as at mid-2015, the share price had at least recovered somewhat from its lows.

Stories such as these are a good reminder why, when building your portfolio, you shouldn't put all your eggs in one basket.

Sector risk

A risk not shared by the market as a whole, but affecting representatives of only one industry, is called *sector risk*. Mining companies' shares suffered from the proposed RSPT in 2010, despite the general health of their industry, because the proposed tax had a highly specific effect on their profits, and thus their attractiveness as investments. Doing your research and keeping up with market developments can help you to guard against sector risk.

Fraud risk

Any company with inadequate internal financial controls runs the risk of falling victim to *fraud* (an economic crime perpetrated against the company, whether by an insider or outsider).

In August 2009, electrical retailer Clive Peeters' senior accountant defrauded the company of $20 million: She was caught and jailed for five years.

Clive Peeters went into receivership in May 2010, after falling sales and crippling debt of $140 million forced the board to pull the plug. Harvey Norman bought the business in July 2010. The fraud wasn't responsible on its own for the demise of Clive Peeters, but it certainly contributed.

In 2014, the high-flying chief executive officer of biotech company Phosphagenics, Esra Ogru, was sentenced to six years in jail for creating an elaborate system of fake invoices and credit-card claims to defraud the company of $6 million, in a fraud that took place over nine years between 2004 and 2013. Since Phosphagenics alerted the ASX in July 2013 that 'invoicing and accounting irregularities' had occurred, the share price lost 82 per cent.

In 2015, former chief executive of generic drug maker Sigma Pharmaceuticals, Elmo de Alwis, and former chief financial officer, Mark Smith, pleaded guilty to falsifying the company's accounts in 2009 and 2010. The court heard that Sigma's accounts overstated the company's income and revenue by $15.5 million, inventories by $11.3 million, and net profit by $9.6 million.

Sigma's financial difficulties during 2009 and 2010 had already resulted in the company agreeing to pay shareholders almost $60 million in 2012, to settle a class action brought by disgruntled investors. The class action rested on the company predicting that it would record modest profit growth when it was conducting a $300 million capital raising in September 2009; six months later, Sigma shocked the market by revealing a $424 million write-down that led to a $389 million loss for the 2009–10 financial year (ending 31 January, 2010).

That unexpected loss — announced in March 2010 — saw the sharemarket halve Sigma's market value in a day. In April 2010, de Alwis stepped down, followed by Smith the next month. Sigma has doubled in price from the day after the 2010 loss announcement, but remains 16 per cent below the level from which it fell.

Fraud can even come from outside the company. In January 2013, coal miner Whitehaven Coal lost 9 per cent of its market value after an anti-coal activist issued a fake press release stating that ANZ Bank had withdrawn its $1.2 billion loan to help Whitehaven build a new coal mine because of environmental concerns. Whitehaven shares lost about $280 million in market value in a matter of minutes.

Agency risk

Agency risk refers to the risk that management and the board (the investors' 'agent') may act in the best interests of the agent rather than the investors. This comes to the fore when boards approve ridiculous salary packages for managers — for example,

James Hardie's chief executive, Louis Gries, was approved a salary of US$11.7 million ($15 million) for 2014–15 — or reject takeover offers in order to keep their jobs. Management may also engage in empire-building by making acquisitions that don't add value for shareholders.

An interesting example is Rio Tinto's US$38 billion 2007 acquisition of Alcan, which prompted more than US$30 billion of write-downs and cost former chief executive Tom Albanese his job. The Alcan buy was seen by many as a move to make Rio Tinto harder to take over (BHP's interest in Rio Tinto was known at that stage), but the move destroyed at least US$35 billion worth of value for Rio Tinto shareholders. Between 2007 and 2015, Rio Tinto wrote down the value of its asset base by 34 per cent, according to Citi Research, the worst downgrade by any major miner.

Similar criticism can also be levelled at BHP for merging with Billiton at a premium, and then demerging many of Billiton's assets years down the track. Citi reckons BHP marked down 12.5 per cent of its asset base over the period.

Non-financial risk

Non-financial risk can come from such areas as product liability, occupational health and safety, human resources and security issues. Political, environmental and market changes can also be termed non-financial risk. Although these elements don't have specific dollar values, they eventually have a direct impact on financial risk.

In the UK, Huntingdon Life Sciences was brought to its knees by animal rights activists protesting against the company's use of animals in scientific testing. The activists' campaign forced the stockbroking firms who made a market in Huntingdon shares (buying and selling to other brokers) to stop transacting the shares. The firms were afraid of being targeted by a similar campaign. As financial backers and customers of the company walked away under pressure from the animal rights campaigners, Huntingdon shares lost 80 per cent of their value in two years. Huntingdon moved its financial listing to New York, to take advantage of US securities laws that give greater anonymity to shareholders, but lost its market-maker (the broker that offers to buy and sell its shares). Again, you need to be up on the latest developments in the sectors affecting your portfolio shares.

Information risk

Information risk is when investors, who are buying shares, rely on such published information as a company's prospectus, announcements to the stock exchange, annual reports and brokers' research documents. All of these documents carry legal disclaimers that say, in a variety of ways, that they can't be relied upon, even if audited. As a wary investor, you need to get information from different sources to lessen the impact of information risk.

Avoiding the Turkeys

You can use a variety of techniques to assess whether any of the shares in your portfolio are at risk. The health checks you can apply to shares can be either fundamental or technical. *Fundamental analysis* looks at a company's financial performance — cash flow, balance sheet, revenue, earnings and dividends. *Technical analysis* involves charting share prices and trying to extrapolate from past trends.

Using technical analysis

Investors who follow charts like to identify support levels for stocks, that is, prices at which, in the past, the stock has turned upward. A stock falling through a support level on a chart is enough for most technically oriented traders to pull out of a company's shares. Even if you don't wholly trust technical analysis, you'll find that often, with the aid of that precious investment tool, hindsight, the charts tell a story of trouble before the news gets out to the market.

Watching cash flow

When you review a company's performance, always reconcile cash flow — the difference between revenue and outgoings as depicted in the cash flow statement — with reported profit. Those are the only earnings that matter. If you do this annually, you need to look beyond the company's reported result to the improvement in its balance sheet. Deterioration in cash flow (or worse, if cash inflow becomes cash outflow) is a signal that the risk has become higher.

Charting dividend changes

A lowered dividend, or a dividend that is only maintained at the previous year's level, is also a danger signal. Companies that pay a dividend go to almost any lengths, including borrowing, or dipping into their reserves, to maintain that dividend. A company cuts or suspends a dividend only under extreme financial duress. You need to follow the dividend returns of companies in your portfolio and know when your dividend is under threat, despite the spin-doctoring in company announcements.

Gauging institutional selling

Heavy institutional selling (when the super and managed funds sell their shares) is an indication that something isn't right with a company. The institutions follow a stock more closely than you do and know more than you do. If they're queuing up to sell shares, it isn't a good sign.

The exit of institutional investors from the share register of Sons of Gwalia after a profit warning in July 2004 was a sign that the market was concerned at the company's direction — concerns that were borne out. Your broker is able to provide this kind of information so you can protect your portfolio.

Investigating when directors sell

The directors of a company know its prospects better than anyone. These days, following all the announcements a company makes is relatively easy and directors must notify the sharemarket if they sell shares.

Normally, if directors sell small amounts of shares, you needn't worry. Like all Australians, the directors need cash occasionally. However, large sales by directors, such as 50 per cent or more of their holding, is a warning sign.

On the other hand, the public buying of HIH Insurance shares by its directors just two months before it collapsed in 2001 gave a signal to the market that was contradicted by what actually happened. An experienced investor weighs all the available information about a company's performance.

Chapter 5

Eggs and Baskets

● ●

In This Chapter

▶ Building a strategy for diversification

▶ Selecting a variety of shares

▶ Managing a balanced portfolio

▶ Relying on managed funds

▶ Investing overseas with managed funds

● ●

*D*iversification means using your investment money to buy different assets. Your goal in diversifying is to benefit from the performance of different assets that are usually not synchronised. If shares, for example, are performing poorly, property or bonds may be performing well. You want to include one or both of these in your portfolio in order to diversify across a range of investment options. You also want to diversify within an asset class. Say you already own mining shares — if you then buy a bank stock, it means a portion of your portfolio isn't dependent on commodity prices for growth. The aim of diversification is to ensure that, at any time, part if not all of your investment portfolio is performing well.

Few Australian investors cared about diversification prior to the deregulation of the Australian economy in the early 1980s. In the past, a savings bank account and a home mortgage were about the extent of a typical Australian investment portfolio. Since deregulation, a much wider range of options has become available. Today, an Australian investor's portfolio may contain any of the following:

✔ Australian shares, property and bonds

✔ Foreign shares, property and bonds

✔ Managed funds

✔ Hybrid securities

✔ Exchange-traded funds (ETFs)

Keep in mind that diversification is a good strategy for all types of investing. If you think of diversification in terms of the adage about eggs and baskets, then more baskets than ever before exist to accommodate your precious eggs. In this book, I talk mainly about diversification within a single asset class, shares, and in this chapter I cover risk versus return, growth and value stocks, investing overseas, using managed funds and active versus passive investing.

Spreading the Risk

Diversification is an essential strategy for protecting your investments over the long term. The second share you buy diversifies your portfolio, at least a little. Understanding how diversification works is a necessary step in acquiring a balanced portfolio. Three levels of diversification exist:

✔ You can own different asset classes, such as shares, government bonds and property.

✔ You can acquire different investments within one asset class, such as owning shares in BHP Billiton, Telstra and National Australia Bank.

✔ You can use geographical diversification, such as making an investment in overseas assets.

As an Australian investor, you can choose from about 2,200 stocks listed on the Australian Securities Exchange (ASX), which allows you to put together a highly diversified portfolio. You can put together a portfolio that includes higher-risk, higher-reward opportunities as well as conservative investments. You can place a small proportion of your total investment funds in higher-risk speculative shares, perhaps 5 to 10 per cent depending on your appetite for risk. (Refer to Chapter 4 if you need help in quantifying just what your risk level is.) However, high-risk investments need good research to ensure that those investments are more of a calculated risk rather than a wild stab in the dark.

Unfortunately, Australian investors have a poor record with diversification when buying shares. A total of 33 per cent of Australian adults — or 5.9 million people — own shares outright, according to the ASX Share Ownership Study for 2014.

Counting people who own shares indirectly through managed funds, 36 per cent of the adult population, or 6.5 million people, are share owners.

However, of the people who owned shares directly in 2010, 21 per cent of them owned just the one stock (the ASX no longer covers stock numbers for individual portfolios in its Share Ownership Study). Forty-five per cent of them had only three or fewer shares in their portfolio. (The average portfolio contained seven stocks, down from eight in 2006.) Of course, investors with two stocks are twice as diversified as those with only one, but neither is adequately diversified. They are share investors, but their meagre portfolio is at too great a risk for them to enjoy the benefits of ownership. The long-term outcome of their sharemarket investing isn't positive. A minority of shareholders in 2010 got close to qualifying as having a diversified number of stocks: 13 per cent owned seven to ten stocks, while 20 per cent had 11 or more stocks in their portfolios.

Over the past 30 years, the need for diversification has been clearly demonstrated as, one by one, all the asset classes crashed. First the sharemarket crashed in October 1987 (see Figure 5-1). Then, the property trusts were devalued in 1990.

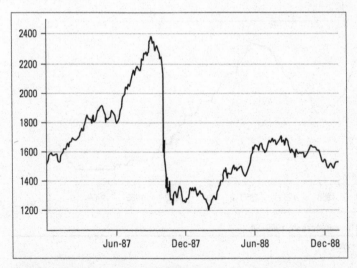

Figure 5-1: The sharemarket crash, 1987.

Source: Data from IRESS Market Technology

Figure 5-2 shows the total return (capital growth plus distribution income) of the Australian composite property (retail, industrial and commercial office) index. Cash rates fell by two-thirds from 1989 to 1994. Figure 5-3 shows the average interest rate for Australian cash management trusts.

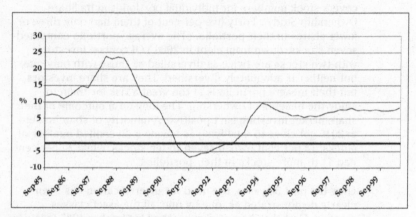

Figure 5-2: The property crash, 1990.

Source: PIR/data from the Property Council of Australia

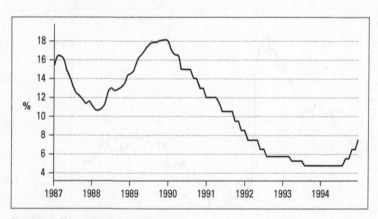

Figure 5-3: The cash crash, 1989–94.

Source: Data from RBA

The bond market slumped dramatically in 1994 (as shown in Figure 5-4) for the price of a ten-year bond (September 2004 Commonwealth Government bond).

Each of these slumps was preceded by large inflows of money to a different asset class. A market that's running hot tends to pull funds from other markets showing relatively low returns. This situation happens as well in the sharemarket when the *herd mentality* drives investor buying. Diversification of your portfolio is the best protection in this situation. Having a spread of investments reduces your risk and the volatility of returns.

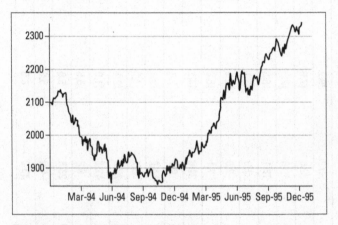

Figure 5-4: The bond market crash, 1994.

Source: Data from IRESS Market Technology

Table 5-1 shows the historical return from different asset classes available to an Australian investor. Each of these asset classes has enjoyed at least one year in which it was the best performer: A portfolio that was wholly invested in Australian shares has been the best performer, beating even international shares, on both a hedged and unhedged basis (note that over the three decades, the hedged and unhedged international shares investments come out almost evenly). But Australian shares are a more volatile investment than unhedged international shares. At the other end of the risk–return scale, cash isn't capable of consistently generating the return of a growth asset like shares. However, cash never returns a loss.

Table 5-1   Asset Class Returns

Financial Year (ending June 30)	Australian Shares	Australian Bonds	Cash	International Shares	International Bonds Hedged	International Shares Hedged	AREITs
1986	42.5	20.5	18.3	55.2	29.2	34.5	23.8
1987	54.0	12.1	17.3	32.6	17.6	33.2	41.3
1988	-8.6	19.4	12.5	-10.0	12.5	-5.3	-2.8
1989	3.5	3.0	15.7	18.1	16.3	18.1	-1.1
1990	4.1	17.8	18.5	1.9	13.1	5.3	15.2
1991	5.9	22.4	13.5	-2.0	15.3	-5.8	7.7
1992	13.3	22.0	9.0	7.1	15.8	-3.0	14.7
1993	9.9	13.9	5.9	31.8	14.7	17.3	17.1
1994	18.5	-1.1	4.9	0.0	2.1	6.7	9.8
1995	5.7	11.9	7.1	14.2	13.1	3.7	7.9
1996	15.8	9.5	7.8	6.7	11.2	27.7	3.6
1997	26.6	16.8	6.8	28.6	12.1	26.0	28.5
1998	1.6	10.9	5.1	42.2	11.0	22.1	10.0
1999	15.3	3.3	5.0	8.2	5.5	15.9	4.3
2000	13.7	6.2	5.6	23.8	5.0	12.6	12.1
2001	8.8	7.4	6.1	-6.0	9.0	-16.0	14.1
2002	-4.5	6.2	4.7	-23.5	8.0	-19.3	15.5

2003	-1.1	9.8	5.0	-18.5	12.2	-6.2	12.1
2004	22.4	2.3	5.3	19.4	3.5	20.2	17.2
2005	24.7	7.8	5.6	0.1	12.3	9.8	18.1
2006	24.2	3.4	5.8	19.9	1.2	15.0	18.0
2007	30.3	4.0	6.4	7.8	5.2	21.4	25.9
2008	-12.1	4.4	7.4	-21.3	8.6	-15.7	-36.3
2009	-22.1	10.8	5.5	16.3	11.5	-26.6	-42.3
2010	13.8	7.9	3.9	5.2	9.3	11.5	20.4
2011	12.2	5.5	5.0	2.7	5.7	22.3	5.8
2012	-7.0	12.4	4.7	-0.5	11.9	-2.1	11.0
2013	20.7	2.8	3.3	33.1	4.4	21.3	24.2
2014	17.6	6.1	2.7	20.4	7.2	21.9	11.1
2015	5.7	5.6	2.6	25.2	6.3	8.5	20.3
Average	11.8	9.5	7.6	10.2	10.4	9.2	10.9
Best	54.0 (4*)	22.4 (4)	18.5 (1)	55.2 (7)	29.2 (3)	34.5 (5)	41.3 (1)
Worst	-22.1 (2#)	-1.1 (4)	2.6 (6)	-23.5 (4)	1.2 (2)	-26.6 (3)	-42.3 (3)

*Denotes the number of times each asset class was best performer during a financial year between 1985 and 2015
#Denotes the number of times each asset class was worst performer during a financial year between 1985 and 2015

Source: © Andex Charts

Building a Portfolio

Before you start buying shares, decide your level of risk, what income you want from shares and your time frame for investing. With a well-diversified portfolio and a medium- to long-term horizon — at least five to ten years — you're giving your sharemarket investment the best chance to come out ahead of the other asset classes. Choosing your stocks well is the hard part. You need to follow a logical method in deciding on the stocks you buy.

Some investors use the *top-down approach*, which means that they take an overview of the state of the economy, determine which sectors are likely to do well and then examine the companies in those industries for the best candidates for investment. This strategy is sound because the economy drives the sharemarket. Other investors choose stocks by a *bottom-up approach*, which concentrates on the attributes of individual stocks rather than economic factors. This approach seeks to pick winners on their merits. Two popular approaches to choosing stocks involve buying growth shares or buying value shares.

Professional investors who are active managers of a share portfolio (those who try to add value to the portfolio by choosing stocks that can outperform the market) are usually either growth-oriented or value-oriented. Growth investors loved the tech boom of 1999 to 2000 because it briefly fulfilled their wildest dreams. Value investors hated it because the market paid no attention to their carefully chosen bargains. The market of the value investors' dreams was the one that came about after the market had halved, from March 2009 onward.

As a non-professional investor, if you can identify an undervalued bargain, by all means buy it, and if you're satisfied that you've identified a standout growth candidate, buy it too. Your portfolio can benefit from both approaches.

Buying growth stocks

Growth stocks are shares with earnings that increase faster than the growth rate of the economy. They have high earnings, a low dividend yield and a high ratio of price to net tangible asset (NTA) backing. The NTA backing represents the amount of tangible — that is, real — assets that stand behind each share. To work it out, subtract the value of any intangible assets, such as goodwill and brands, from shareholders' equity, and divide by the amount of shares on issue.

Investors expect growth stocks' earnings to increase rapidly. Usually these stocks are market leaders and innovators, with a unique and compelling investment history. They capture the admiration of the market, which is prepared to pay a large premium (measured by the price/earnings (P/E) ratio) to own them. The downside to this strategy is that any interruption to the expected growth pattern means an instant price reduction.

Travel agency chain Flight Centre is a good example. Floated in 1995 at 95 cents, Flight Centre revolutionised the travel industry in Australia by offering cut-price fares, and used its growing global distribution 'scale' to gain enormous buying power. The company has expanded its successful formula into overseas markets, including New Zealand, South Africa, Canada, the USA and the UK. Flight Centre's share price rose seven-fold between January 1999 and June 2002 — from $4 to $28.50 — because it was adopted by analysts as an international growth stock. At $28.50, Flight Centre was priced at 56 times historic earnings, versus an average P/E ratio of 16.6 times earnings for the S&P/ASX 200 industrials (excluding financial stocks).

But Flight Centre failed to anticipate that the airlines would slash the commissions paid to travel agents in a volatile travel market, and that online operators would make inroads into its market.

By 2004–05, earnings fell 17 per cent and by mid-2006, the stock was trading on 14 times its historic earnings. As an ex-growth stock, Flight Centre had become a value stock (see the next section for information on value stocks).

An investor buying Flight Centre in mid-2006, at $10 and 14 times historic earnings, saw it rise to $32 and 28 times historic earnings by December 2007, at which point its historic P/E had been running at 23.2 times earnings for five years. Flight Centre was back in town as a growth stock.

At this point, two things happened. First, in November 2007, Flight Centre bought Liberty Travel, one of North America's biggest travel agents. Second, the global financial crisis (GFC) arrived, bringing with it unprecedented discounting in the airline industry as carriers struggled to ride the GFC out. This discounting plunged the Liberty business into loss.

By March 2009, Flight Centre was down to close to $4, trading at less than three times historic earnings. (That was deep in 'value' territory: After a halving of the market, those kinds of once-in-a-lifetime P/Es were available for investors with the courage to buy them.) But with the market rebound, and helped along by a record profit in 2009–10, Flight Centre was back at $24.40 a share by October 2010, and a historic P/E of 16.8 times earnings. With a five-year average historic P/E at 23.2 times earnings through the worst of the GFC, Flight Centre had re-earned its stripes as a growth stock.

By mid-2015, Flight Centre had almost doubled in price, to $46.30, for a historic P/E (using 2013–14 financial year reported earnings per share) at 17.7 times earnings, and a projected (using analysts' consensus estimated 2014–15 financial year earnings per share) P/E of 17.8 times earnings — offering something for both 'value' and 'growth' investors.

Finding value stocks

Value investing is based on fundamental analysis. Value stocks are shares considered cheap because they're out of favour with the market, and are consequently priced low, relative to the company's earnings or assets. A value stock has a relatively low P/E ratio and a low price-to-NTA ratio, but a high dividend yield (because its price has fallen). Investors look for such value anomalies and buy the stock because they believe that the market will eventually recognise the stock's true value and the stock will be re-evaluated, or bid up in price.

The long-term average P/E on the Australian market is about 14 times historic earnings; the average dividend yield is about 4 per cent (although full franking, at the company tax rate of 30 per cent, adds about 1.4 per cent to that figure). Value investors usually look for stocks trading at P/Es well below the prevailing market P/E and well above the prevailing market dividend yield. But at all times they have to be aware of 'value traps', which are stocks that are trading where they are for good reason. The share price may have fallen for a very good reason. You can't just pick out the ten lowest P/E ratios or the ten highest dividend yields. The highest dividend yield, or the lowest P/E, may be a result of a sharp fall in the share price.

Knowing How Many Stocks to Buy

Professional investors believe they can minimise their risk with about 40 stocks in their portfolios. They believe that this number adequately diversifies away the risk. Unfortunately, for most investors, owning 40 stocks isn't an option. For an individual, no matter how much time you devote to monitoring your portfolio, you can't keep track of 40 stocks — unless you're very dedicated! As a single investor taking care of your own portfolio, you probably want no more than 15 shares, with a minimum of 10. Fifteen shares allows you to adequately monitor a portfolio and ensure that your investments are well diversified.

Picking your sectors

The Australian sharemarket hosts companies involved in a huge variety of activities. In March 2002, the ASX adopted the Global Industry Classification Standard (GICS), which was developed by Standard & Poor's (S&P) and Morgan Stanley Capital International (MSCI). The GICS structure consists of 10 sectors and 24 industry groups, from which investors can 'dig down' further to 67 industries and 147 sub-industries. A company is classified into the sector that most closely describes the business activities from which it generates most of its revenue.

The idea behind GICS criteria is that it's a worldwide standard by which companies can be uniformly classified according to their business activities. It doesn't matter where the companies operate or on which stock exchange they're listed: GICS ensures that companies, industries and sectors can be more accurately compared on a global scale. The GICS classification replaces the previous 24 ASX sectors.

When the ASX adopted the global standard, the new classification system had some drawbacks for Australian investors because the resources component of the market was split. The miners were placed in the materials index, which also contains stocks like James Hardie Industries (building materials) and Orica (chemicals and explosives), whereas the oil and gas companies were placed in the energy index. Investors couldn't readily see how the entire resources sector was performing, and what proportion of the index resources represented.

To redress this — and to support the metals and mining industry, which has been a major driver of economic growth in the 2000s — two new indices were launched in mid-2006, the S&P/ASX 300 Metals and Mining Index and the S&P/All Ordinaries Gold Index, to provide benchmarks for these important segments of the Australian sharemarket. In addition, for each tier of the market, separate indices are now calculated for resources (stocks in the energy sector and the metals and mining industry sub-sector) and for industrials (all others in the materials sector). Table 5-2 gives you the details.

Table 5-2   GICS Economic Sectors and Industry Groups

GICS Economic Sectors	GICS Industry Groups
Energy	Energy
Materials	Materials
Industrials	Capital goods; commercial services and supplies; transportation
Consumer discretionary	Automobiles and components; consumer durables and apparel; consumer services; retailing; media
Consumer staples	Food and staples retailing; food, beverage and tobacco; household and personal products
Healthcare	Healthcare equipment and services; pharmaceuticals, biotechnology and life sciences
Financials	Banks; diversified financial; insurance; real estate
Information technology	Software and services; technology, hardware and equipment; semiconductors and semiconductor equipment
Telecommunications services	Telecommunications services
Utilities	Utilities

Source: Standard & Poor's

Selecting shares from these sectors can give you a diversified and protected portfolio. However, if you try to cover the entire list of industry groups, your portfolio may become cumbersome and difficult to follow. On the other hand, if you choose the banking sector and buy shares in National Australia Bank, Commonwealth Bank and Westpac, you have a portfolio that's too dependent on banks.

Choosing core stocks

The Australian sharemarket is one of the most concentrated in the world. The S&P/ASX 50 Index — the market's largest 50 companies by value — accounts for about 63 per cent of the sharemarket's total value.

That leaves another 2,150 stocks making up the remaining 37 per cent. The 50 largest companies make up the *core stocks* to invest in, and are listed in Table 5-3.

Table 5-3   The Top 50 Companies on the ASX by Value as at June 2015

Stock	Market Value ($billion)
Commonwealth Bank	141.03
Westpac Bank	103.00
ANZ Banking Group	91.55
National Australia Bank	89.15
BHP Billiton	88.32
Telstra	75.80
Wesfarmers	44.36
CSL	40.88
Woolworths	34.69
Woodside Petroleum	28.69
Macquarie Group	27.51
Rio Tinto	22.94
Scentre Group	20.50
Westfield	19.30
QBE Insurance	18.89
Transurban	18.24
AMP	18.10
Suncorp Group	17.50
Brambles	16.50
Amcor	16.38
Insurance Australia Group	13.74
Origin Energy	12.98
Ramsay Health Care	12.51

(continued)

Table 5-3 *(continued)*

Stock	Market Value ($billion)
Federation Centres	11.68
Goodman Group	11.15
Sydney Airport	11.06
Oil Search	10.96
Aurizon	10.82
AGL Energy	10.67
ResMed	10.25
Newcrest Mining	9.94
Stockland Group	9.87
South32	9.71
APA Group	9.34
Crown Resorts	8.98
Caltex Australia	8.89
Lend Lease	8.85
Sonic Healthcare	8.62
Santos	8.07
Orica	8.06
James Hardie	7.93
ASX	7.76
GPT Group	7.64
CIMIC Group	7.31
TPG Telecom	7.26
Dexus Property Group	7.12
Coca-Cola Amatil	7.05
Qantas	6.85
Mirvac Group	6.82
AFIC	6.73

Source: Australian Securities Exchange Ltd

Most of the core stocks in your portfolio ideally have a record of rising profits and dividend payments. Check that these core stocks pay a fully franked dividend, which gives Australian resident shareholders a tax rebate on taxes already paid by the company on its profits. You can use the rebate, known as the *franking credit*, or *imputation credit*, to reduce your tax liability. In some cases, depending on the marginal tax rate, the franking credit can offset the entire tax liability. I discuss dividend imputation in greater detail in Chapter 10.

Investors love franking credits for the help they provide at tax-return time, but some of the major stocks on the Australian market have cut their franking rates due to the amount of their earnings overseas. Because they don't pay Australian tax on this profit, they can't generate franking credits. Although this isn't necessarily a bad thing — in fact, the profit that these companies generate overseas can act as a hedge against the possibility of their Australian earnings falling — the fact that they don't offer 100 per cent franking must be considered in the investment decision. Global share registry leader Computershare, for example, earns about 84 per cent of its profit overseas, so has not been able to generate enough Australian-taxed profit to pay a fully franked dividend. Other large-cap companies that have mostly been unable to pay a fully franked dividend because of overseas earnings are Orica, CSL, QBE Insurance, Amcor, Leighton Holdings (now known as CIMIC Group) and James Hardie.

The core stocks are the *blue chips*, considered the most reliable, least volatile issues on the market. However, blue chip status isn't forever. Remember that many big names such as Westpac, BHP, Westfield and AMP have at various times shocked the market with massive losses. And it's worth repeating that blue chip status did not save a company from a hefty fall in the 2007 to 2009 market meltdown.

Each sector has its Top 50 representatives. The market has given these blue chip shares a *capitalisation* (value) that reflects their reliable nature. The S&P/ASX 50 contains the *large-caps*, the largest 50 companies by market capitalisation, or value: This cuts out at about $5.4 billion. (Market value is not the only criterion for inclusion in the S&P/ASX 50; a liquidity, or turnover, is also required.) These are the elite group of stocks from which many of your core portfolio holdings come. Size, however, doesn't necessarily equate to blue chip status.

Evaluating second-liners

Outside the Top 50 come the *mid-caps*, usually considered to be the companies ranked 51 to 100 by value. This group is covered by the S&P/ASX Midcap 50, which ends at about $1 billion. Then come the *small-caps*, generally taken to mean those ranked between 100 and 300 by market capitalisation, as measured by the S&P/ASX Small Ordinaries Index. This means that, roughly, any stock between $20 million and $1 billion in size is a small-cap (although many institutional managers consider anything valued at less than $50 million as a *micro-cap*, with insufficient liquidity to warrant investment).

Institutional investors usually consider only the stocks comprising the S&P/ASX 200 Index — with a lower limit of about $260 million — to be *investment-grade* (suitable for investment). Companies whose stocks lie within the 200 to 300 range may make the grade, but haven't yet. But individual investors may have a different view than institutional funds of what constitutes investment grade. The institutions concentrate their analysis and efforts on the Top 100. Individual investors realise that they can use their research skills outside that range to find undervalued companies that the wider market has overlooked.

The small-caps are more volatile than the large-caps, and they tend to be hit harder when the market falls: The reverse is also true, that they run harder than the large-caps when the market is rising. But the reason why many investors find the small-caps attractive is that these stocks are far less researched stocks than those in the Top 100, meaning that investors who do their homework on an unknown or little-covered stock can 'get set' well ahead of the rest of the market, and make a return of many times what they put in.

This potential leverage is even greater in the 'micro-caps', which are the stocks that lie outside the S&P/ASX All Ordinaries Index (consisting of the 500 largest companies by market capitalisation). These companies are even less researched than the small-caps: Many go about their business virtually unnoticed. Not many institutional fund managers go anywhere near the micro-caps because these stocks have low liquidity, meaning that if the manager gets it wrong, the fund may not be able to sell the shares, and may make a 100 per cent capital loss. On the other hand, the fund may be one of the only — if not *the* only — institutions on the share register, and may be invited on to the board for that reason.

But the attraction for the retail investor is that you can find value you simply can't find in larger stocks. If you can get a micro-cap investment right, you're looking at a star investment. A compound annual growth rate of 30–50 per cent over ten years is possible. Twenty years ago, Harvey Norman was a micro-cap (its market cap is now $5.1 billion). Although the risk is far greater than investing in S&P/ASX 100 stocks, many investors like this sector of the market.

Outside the All Ordinaries Index, after you cull resources explorers and research and development stocks, you have almost 500 profitable industrial companies. That's a big universe in which to try to spot the next Harvey Norman.

But at some point, when delving around the approximately 1,700 stocks that don't make it into the All Ordinaries Index (the Top 500 by market value), you'll find yourself dealing with the specialised world of the specs, or speculative stocks.

Gambling on specs

In Australia, a *spec*, or speculative stock, once meant a mineral or petroleum explorer. Nowadays, spec refers to any stock that doesn't have a positive financial track record, but may have prospects. Usually these prospects are called *blue sky*, meaning the possibility exists of very large gains in the future. Mineral- and oil-exploring companies are still specs, but a host of biotechnology and telecommunications hopefuls have joined this category.

With specs, you pays your money and you takes your chances. Nobody really knows how specs are going to perform in the future because a reliable method of forecasting the potential of these stocks just doesn't exist. If the stock doesn't have a track record, buying a spec share is a gamble.

You can punt on a few speculative shares. If you set a limit on the amount you invest and you have a strategy for buying them, you can even come out ahead. Don't overlook the high risk involved when gambling on a good return. If you have a conservative portfolio, you may enjoy buying a few speculative shares. However, don't risk the children's school fees in a stock that promises a lot but is yet to earn a profit.

Diversifying through Managed Funds

When you analyse a diversified share portfolio, you have to keep in mind that it only contains shares. Full diversification requires another step. To protect your total investment, make sure your portfolio contains shares, property and interest-bearing investments, with a cash component kept in reserve. This kind of balanced portfolio is what a professionally managed diversified fund tries to put together.

A *managed fund*, or unit trust, is a good example of diversification in action. With a managed fund, small investors pool their money to buy assets that are larger in size and more numerous in spread than they could buy individually. A managed fund has greater buying power and can more easily diversify its assets than an individual investor can. Through managed funds, investors can share in the ownership of assets that they couldn't afford themselves, such as shopping centres, office blocks and airports. Managed funds also offer the most convenient means of investing overseas. Managed equity (share) funds have the built-in diversification of a large, professionally assembled portfolio. Buying into a managed fund saves you, the investor, the effort of building and researching your own portfolio.

Australian investors are big users of managed funds: Australia has the fourth-largest managed funds market in the world. According to research firm Rainmaker, in 2015, Australians had $2 trillion invested through fund managers and super funds (including managed funds, wrap platforms — which allow an investor to hold shares, managed funds and a cash account, all under one umbrella — and all kinds of superannuation); this is up 16 per cent since 2014, and has increased by 9 per cent each year over the past decade, which included the shock of the GFC. The nation's growing superannuation kitty also accounts for $2 trillion (about one-third of super is directly invested by funds, while about one-third of money invested by fund managers comes from non-super).

Managed funds have opened up virtually all of the major asset classes to individual investors. Approximately 1,770 funds are open for retail money. The $2 trillion managed funds pool is spread mostly across Australian shares ($446 billion), international shares ($415 billion), Australian bonds ($244 billion), property trusts ($52 billion), cash ($208 billion), direct property ($134 billion) and international fixed interest ($149 billion). Another $364 billion is invested in infrastructure, private equity, hedge funds and other 'alternative' assets.

Unlisted equity trusts are very popular. The largest of these are the Platinum International Fund, with $12.1 billion of investors' money; Vanguard's Australian Shares Index Fund, with $6.7 billion; the Fidelity Australian Equities Fund, with $4.5 billion; the Perpetual Industrial Share Fund, with $2.7 billion; the Schroder Australian Equity Fund, with $2.3 billion; and the Ausbil Australian Active Equity Fund, with $2.2 billion. Listed property trusts (LPTs) (see Chapter 8) are now a $121 billion component of the ASX, whereas property securities funds — these funds offer investors access to a portfolio of LPTs, managed by professional fund managers — are a $10.8 billion sector (having held $27 billion at their 2007 peak).

The other basic kinds of managed funds are

- Bond (or fixed-interest) funds, which own portfolios of government, semi-government and corporate bonds

- Cash management trusts (CMTs), which invest in term deposits, cash bank bills or short-term money market securities (instruments that can be quickly converted to actual cash)

- Mortgage funds, which hold a portfolio of mortgages over various kinds of property

Deciding to be an active or passive player

When buying into a managed fund, you not only buy a diversified portfolio, you also buy the expertise of the managers, which is important if the fund is active in trying to beat the index. This means that the fund manager's goal is to perform better than a particular index, such as the S&P/ASX 200. The fund manager may achieve this by buying undervalued stocks and selling overvalued stocks. Overall, this managed fund is betting that the skills of its stock pickers can earn it a better return than the market as measured by the S&P/ASX 200 Index. Active fund managers may have difficulty in picking the consistent winners and outperforming the market. However, when they succeed, these fund managers can beat the index handsomely. But there is a cost (in fees) of investing in managed funds.

Investors who don't want to invest in aggressive funds that try to beat the index can instead buy into passive or

(continued)

(continued)

index funds. An index fund replicates a particular index, reducing the worry about analysing the market.

Depending on the fund, this index could be the S&P/ASX 200 Index (for an Australian share fund) or the Morgan Stanley Capital International (MSCI) World Index (for an international share fund).

The manager of an index fund or exchange-traded fund (ETF) constructs a portfolio that closely tracks a specific market index by holding all or, in the case of very broad indices, a representative sample of the securities in the index. The index funds buy the poor performers as well as the standout risers, but their investors know that the fund won't underperform the index because their portfolio is the index.

Index funds have lower brokerage costs than active funds because these funds only buy and sell shares when the composition of the index they track changes. If you're paying fees to have your investment actively managed and the manager fails to beat the index, you're losing money.

After several relatively lean years early in the 2000s, and then the GFC-triggered market slump of 2007 to 2009, investors have become mutinously conscious that many funds are more concerned with how their performance fares against the relevant benchmark index, instead of how the fund actually performs. In simple terms, fund managers don't mind the fund performing poorly — what

fund managers do mind is the fund performing poorly on its own.

Investors in an older-style, typically growth-oriented equity fund were asked to pay an entry fee of as high as 5 per cent (the adviser, or a discount broker, may rebate this back to the investor in full). These days, most modern fund products (and wholesale funds) don't have entry fees, unless the investor goes directly to the fund manager. There may also be a platform fee, if that is how the investor invested in the product. A retail investor will face ongoing charges, which can be summed up in the management expense ratio (MER) and are typically about 1.4 per cent a year.

Another problem that investors may find with managed funds is that through 'process homogenisation' — once known as the herd mentality — the larger managers have focused on relative return (that is, relative compared to their peers), crowding together with a tracking error of 2–3 per cent, and not wanting to deviate too far from the index. By definition, this makes outperformance difficult to achieve.

Investors who have adopted an index (or passive) strategy — who want a fund that replicates a particular index — don't mind this approach. But those who want active management — they're paying for the skill of the fund manager's stock pickers to beat the performance of the index — do mind paying for what they're not getting, leading to a crisis of confidence in many of the big-brand managers.

In the past decade, the growing sophistication of the Australian investment marketplace has seen new kinds of managed funds emerge:

- 'Absolute return' funds, which invest for maximum return, without reference to any benchmark index (and carry higher risk as a result)

- Debt securities funds, which invest in sovereign (government) and corporate debt (or bonds)

- 'Hedge' funds, which claim the ability to make money regardless of what the share and bond markets are doing

- Income funds, designed to generate a reliable income for investors

The latest innovations are:

- **Private equity funds:** These funds invest in private companies, which are not listed on the stock market. In 1994, $71.1 million was invested in private equity: Australian investors now have $25 billion invested there.

- **Global property securities and infrastructure securities funds:** In the same way that global equity funds invest in overseas shares, global property securities and infrastructure securities funds invest in the much larger markets in those assets overseas. Global property securities is a $2 trillion market: Global infrastructure securities is estimated to be even bigger, at $3.3 trillion.

- **Socially Responsible Investing (SRI) funds:** These funds' investments are screened from an ethical or social perspective. They're either directed away from unacceptable investments — for example, arms makers, gambling companies and alcohol/tobacco companies — or actively channelled to acceptable investments, such as companies showing good environmental or social behaviour, or whose products demonstrably serve a good purpose. SRI is a small but growing market in Australia. According to Rainmaker Information, ethical/SRI investment held $10 billion at March 2015, up from $6.2 billion at June 2010.

Investing outside Australia

One strategy for managing your portfolio is to have some of your investments outside Australia. True diversification involves investment not only across a range of asset categories but foreign investment as well. The Australian sharemarket accounts for less than 2 per cent of the total capitalisation (or value) of the world's sharemarkets. Your share portfolio (or asset portfolio in general) isn't truly diversified unless it contains shares outside Australia.

Over the long term, international shares generate returns reasonably close to Australian shares. For example, according to research house Andex Charts, over the 20 years to June 2015, Australian shares (MSCI Gross Total Return Index) returned 9.1 per cent a year, compared to 7.7 per cent a year for international shares (MSCI World ex-Australia Gross Total Return Index). But the true value of having international shares in your portfolio is not just the return aspect. The true value is the added diversification these international shares give you, in the 98.2 per cent of the 'investable' stock market universe that is not in Australia.

The problem is not just that the Australian market is small. The Aussie market is also highly concentrated, dominated by a small number of companies (and sectors) that account for the lion's share of market capitalisation. For example, about 60 per cent of the Australian market is made up of interest-rate-sensitive stocks: Banks and financial companies; real estate investment trusts (REITs); infrastructure stocks; building materials stocks; developers; and Telstra. The result is that most Australian share investors are not well diversified.

Also, the composition of the Australian market in recent years means that local investors don't have access to some of the more advanced exposures. For example, the Australian exchange doesn't have any major telecommunications suppliers or aerospace companies. Nor can Australians invest on a large scale in the technology industry, or in the large-cap drug companies, or even in a basic defensive exposure like food. Investors who want to be well diversified have to look outside this market more than ever before.

For the vast majority of Australian investors, *international equities* means shares from one of the major sharemarkets, most of which are in countries that are members of the Organisation

for Economic Co-operation and Development (OECD). Table 5-4
charts Australia's peer group of First World sharemarkets (these
are the countries used in the MSCI World Index).

Table 5-4	Developed Sharemarkets	
Australia	Hong Kong	Portugal
Austria	Ireland	Singapore
Belgium	Israel	Spain
Canada	Italy	Sweden
Denmark	Japan	Switzerland
Finland	Netherlands	United Kingdom
France	New Zealand	United States of America
Germany	Norway	

Source: MSCI

Outside the first tier are the emerging markets, as shown in
Table 5-5. Shares from the emerging markets are a separate and
more risky asset class than the shares from the major world
markets.

Table 5-5	Emerging Sharemarkets	
Brazil	India	Russia
Chile	Indonesia	South Africa
China	Malaysia	South Korea
Colombia	Mexico	Taiwan
Czech Republic	Peru	Thailand
Egypt	Philippines	Turkey
Greece	Poland	United Arab Emirates
Hungary	Qatar	

Source: MSCI

Both portfolio theory and funds management practice accept that the addition of foreign shares to a domestic share portfolio lowers the portfolio's level of risk without jeopardising the return or, conversely, increases the return for the same level of risk. The addition of shares from emerging markets can also, surprisingly, lower overall risk. The key to success in diversification is having a wide enough net to protect your overall investment.

Trailing the emerging markets are the 'frontier' markets — the stock exchanges in places like Argentina, Bulgaria, Croatia, Jordan, Nigeria, Tunisia and Vietnam.

For Australian investors, the question is not whether to invest overseas, but how much of the portfolio to invest. Managed funds already take advantage of international markets. Professional management of a fund portfolio includes management of the currency risk, which can be a problem for overseas assets if not handled properly.

Investing overseas requires some expert knowledge and constant monitoring, but it can be done.

Knowing your way around the Australian sharemarket's 2,200 stocks and making decisions about which stocks you want to buy isn't easy. If you decide that you want to invest in US shares, your decision-making process can become even more complicated. That's why many people — even those who are self-reliant investors in the Australian marketplace — look to managed funds for their international exposure. These people prefer to buy the diversification strategy and investment expertise offered by a managed fund. If you want to look after your overseas investments personally, you can, but monitoring these investments adequately is difficult, even in the internet age. You're probably better off investing in emerging markets through a managed fund, unless you're a keen and intrepid traveller.

The large number of investment opportunities available means you can readily assemble a well-diversified portfolio with some of your assets working for you outside the Australian economy. The downside to this increased sophistication is that intelligent investment is more complicated than ever before. However, by practising some basic diversification strategies, you can increase both your opportunities and your successes.

Part III
Buying, Buying, Sold

Five Ways to Spend Less Time Worrying About the Stock Market

- **Be honest about your limitations.** You can use an online broker without any assistance at all if you know what you're doing. Most online brokers give you a huge amount of information, company research and education on stock market investing, both fundamental and technical.

- **Use all the information you can find.** You can find a cornucopia of information available about companies on the internet. Never buy a stock just on a tip: make sure to do your own research.

- **Get familiar with the exchange-traded fund (ETF) world.** ETFs are a great tool for asset allocation and portfolio construction: Make sure you get to know them. ETFs have opened up asset classes, international markets, commodities, currencies, trading strategies and investment styles that were previously hard to gain access to, all in one listed stock.

- **Don't set and forget.** Stay on top of your share portfolio, and always be ready to make a tough decision on even a favourite stock.

- **Make tax work for you.** Make sure you understand how you can extract the most benefit from the tax-effectiveness of franked dividends.

In this part...

- Discover how to buy and sell shares.
- Find out when to buy and sell shares.
- Choose your share portfolio.
- Decide what kind of broker suits you best.
- Understand the effects of tax on your shares.

Chapter 6

Buying and Selling Shares

. . . .

. . . .

*B*uying and selling shares can be easy. All you need is an account with a stockbroker, because a broking firm licensed by the Australian Securities Exchange (ASX) must perform all transactions on the securities exchange.

You can buy and sell virtually any quantity of any listed share through your broker, whether you make the transaction over the phone or on the internet. The broker makes the transaction on your behalf and charges you a fee, called *brokerage*.

You can also buy shares before they list on the sharemarket, when a company makes an *initial public offering* (IPO), known as a *float*. Buying shares through an IPO is free of brokerage, but the catch is that you must first obtain a prospectus for the float. In the 1990s the general public could easily buy shares in large floats, such as the Commonwealth Bank and Telstra. However, most floats are a lot smaller and harder to get into than those mammoth floats.

In this chapter, I cover how the ASX's trading system works, how the ASX Trade platform tracks trade histories and prices, and how to place an order with your stockbroker. I also take you step by step through a trading day on the ASX.

Finding the Market

The actual sharemarket exists on a computer screen that's
linked to the ASX's electronic trading system, called ASX Trade,
which provides individual share information from the Australian
share market, and access to the trading venues, even those
not operated by ASX. Launched in 2010, ASX Trade provides,
for every one of the approximately 2,200 stocks listed on the
market, among other data, such vital statistics as the last sale
price, the buy quote (*bid*) and the sell quote (*offer*, or *ask*).
These statistics tell you the price at which the shares last
traded, the price that buyers are presently prepared to pay for
the shares and the price that sellers are prepared to accept.

ASX Trade hosts two trading services:

- **TradeMatch** is the main market, and handles retail orders.
  It handles about 70 per cent of all trading. TradeMatch is
  a 'lit' market, meaning the bids, offers and volumes are
  displayed, and the market sees each transaction as it is
  struck.

- **Centre Point** is a 'dark' market, meaning that buyers and
  sellers are matched anonymously. Institutional investors
  strike 'block' trades (trades involving large numbers of
  shares) in Centre Point, to lessen the impact of such large
  orders hitting the market. Centre Point pricing exists
  between two price steps in the ASX market. High-frequency
  traders, who use complex algorithms to analyse trading
  patterns and execute orders based on market conditions,
  also use Centre Point. But depending on the broker you
  use, so can retail investors.

ASX Trade also gives access to the second Australian stock
exchange, Chi-X, which trades company shares already quoted
on the ASX, but doesn't list or supervise the companies (refer to
Chapter 2 for more).

Brokers access ASX Trade through a range of interfaces.
The ASX's own trading terminal software is ASX Best, which
was introduced in 2011. It is an order router that connects
into ASX through the exchange's electronic 'pipe,' called
ASX Net. Some brokers use alternative interfaces to the
market, such as IRESS Trader (provided by ASX-listed financial
software company, IRESS Limited), and some have their own
proprietary interfaces.

Through ASX Best — or another interface — every stockbroker
now has direct access to the sharemarket from his or her
desktop. Investors don't see or interact with ASX Trade — only
brokers do. Clients of online brokers see a re-presented version
of ASX Trade, based on a feed direct from the ASX, when they
log in to their broking account.

Computerisation did away with the physical trading floor, which
had disadvantaged investors and stockbrokers who lived away
from the capital cities. Their orders usually cost more and took
longer to fill because each transaction had to be routed through
a big-city agent firm. Since the introduction of an electronic
trading system in 1987, if a bid is the one that matches the offer,
the bid gets transacted immediately. Every user can see the
prices of all transactions and the number of shares involved.

Setting the pace — how the ASX trades

Only stockbroking firms have direct access to ASX Trade. You
place an order with your stockbroker, by instructing your broker
personally, or by trading online (which still goes to ASX Trade
via a broker) and the order is placed into ASX Trade through
ASX Best (or another interface.)

ASX Trade provides details on the exact number of buyers
and sellers for each stock. Brokers can trade shares at the
push of a button. (See Chapter 9 for a full explanation of how
brokers work.) As you place your buy and sell orders, the
firm's Designated Trading Representative feeds the information
into ASX Trade. Bids and offers are lined up, with bids
tabulated from the highest down and offers shown with the
lowest at the top.

The trading program matches buyers and sellers automatically,
giving priority to the highest bid and lowest offer price in the
queue. This is called _Price Time priority_. If prices are equal, the
orders that were entered in the system first are filled first, which
means that large orders have no priority over small orders.
When a bid and an offer match, a transaction occurs.

Price quotes are in cents and fractions of a cent, as in Table 6-1.
All of this information is updated continuously as the market
changes.

Table 6-1	Price Steps for Equities, Rights Issues and Warrants	
Price Range (cents)	**Minimum Bid (cents)**	
Up to 9.9	0.1	
10–199.5	0.5	
200 and above	1.0	

The ASX Trade platform is a state-of-the-art system that allows fast, informative communication at a glance.

A *ticker* moves across the top of the screen, from right to left, and shows trades as they occur, in groups of stock code, price and number of shares.

A *Price Information window* is used to view current market prices in a selected stock or a number of stocks. This window displays specific information relating to the performance of a stock, such as the stock identity (ID); a description of the stock (Short Description); the total quantity available at the best bid (BQty); best buy price (Bid); best sell price (Ask); and the total quantity available at the best ask price (AQty).

ASX Trade also shows the difference between the buy price and the sell price — this is the *spread*, which shows you how the shares are priced in current buy and sell situations:

- ✔ **Open:** The price of the first trade for the current trading day
- ✔ **High:** The highest traded price for the current trading day
- ✔ **Low:** The lowest traded price for the current trading day
- ✔ **Last:** The price of the most recent trade
- ✔ **LQty:** The quantity of the most recent trade
- ✔ **Close:** The price of the last trade at the close of trading on the previous trading day

Users also see:

- ✔ **Volume:** The volume traded during the current trading day
- ✔ **Value:** The value traded during the current trading day in dollars

Getting order depth

Order depth shows the full *market depth* for a particular stock, displayed order by order. The *Order Depth window* is a list of bids (the prices that buyers are prepared to pay) and asks (the prices that sellers are prepared to accept). In the Order Depth window, the buyers are on the left, with the highest bid at the top; the sellers are on the right, with the lowest offer at the top. Market participants can see all the orders at individual prices. The Order Depth window can also be viewed with all orders at the same price aggregated.

The Order Depth window allows brokers to view all of their own orders currently in the market. No other broker can see this information.

Brokers enter, amend or cancel their orders via the Order Depth window, which is also where they make any inquiries.

Getting trade history

The *trade history* is used to view information about individual trades. For each buy and sell trade, the Trade History window shows the following information:

- ✔ **ID:** The stock identity.

- ✔ **Qty:** Quantity of shares bought or sold. The shorthand for a thousand is 'T'; for a hundred thousand, it's 'HT'; and for a million, it's 'M'. (For example, 10,000 shares is 10T; 700,000 shares is 7HT; and 2 million shares is 2M.)

- ✔ **Prc:** Traded price.

- ✔ **Time:** The time of the trade.

- ✔ **As of:** The *as of* date of the trade. If the trade was entered with a date different from the current trading day, it will be displayed in this column.

- ✔ **TType:** The trade type. If the trade is cancelled, the trade is displayed again as a trade reversal; that is, it's displayed as Rev.

Broker numbers are not displayed for trades executed on stocks.

Paying your way

Most stockbroking firms require you to put up a certain amount of money before they accept your first order to buy shares. Not to put too fine a point on it, the stockbroker wants to know that you can pay for the shares, and that the firm won't be left holding the baby.

After you establish an account, you can then place buy and sell orders over the telephone, by email, or through your broker's website. As you sell shares, the broker pays the proceeds into the account. The account comes in handy later when you settle your trades.

Making a Trade

In order to buy or sell shares, you have to give your stockbroker an *order*, which the broker enters into ASX Trade. If your buy order matches the best sell order, the transaction takes place in full view of everybody connected to ASX Trade anywhere in Australia. You can give your broker an order by telephone, over the internet, in person, or by email, fax or letter. If you use the internet and have an account with an online stockbroker, you can buy and sell shares with the click of a mouse.

However, you always need a broker to fulfil your order. If the market is moving quickly, success may mean being able to place the right kind of order. Getting, or getting rid of, the shares you want at the price you want may depend on what kind of order you lodge.

Placing an order

The main types of order on the ASX are limit orders, market-to-limit orders and best-limit orders.

If you want the shares as quickly as possible and won't haggle over the price, you use a *limit order*, which is entered at a defined price: This order can execute at any price that is equal to or better than its limit price, but the order won't execute at a worse price. A limit order ensures that you won't pay more than you specify for the shares you're buying, and, if you're selling, that you won't accept less than you specify.

With a limit order, you set the price at which you want to buy or sell the shares. It doesn't matter what the current market price is — you only trade at a price that's acceptable to you. For a buy order, you set the price below the current market price to try and get the shares at a cheaper price; for a sell order, you enter a price higher than the current market price to try and get a better sale price.

A *market-to-limit order* starts out as what used to be called an *at-market order*, which gets filled at the best price available in the market at the time of the order. But if the order isn't completely filled and the price moves away, it converts to a limit order, with the price defined at the price you paid for the filled portion of your order.

For example, suppose you entered an order for 1,000 Telstra shares as a market-to-limit order. The market price is $6.24, but you only get 600 shares 'filled' at this price before the price changes to $6.26. An order is then created for the remainder of the shares you want (in this case 400 of them) and it is entered as a limit order at $6.24, which is the price you paid for your first 'fill'.

In this case, you can leave the order as it is, or go into your pending orders and amend it. If you are keen to buy and the market price has risen, you may either amend your order back to a market-to-limit order, or change the price on your limit order to a higher price, near or a bit above the current market price. Similarly, if you want to sell and the market price has dropped, you may want to lower the price of your limit order.

If you don't like using market-to-limit orders but still want the current market price, you can use a limit order at a higher price than the current price (if buying) or a slightly lower price (if selling). Your order will still execute at the best price, but it gives you more chance of having your whole order filled straight away.

A *best-limit* order is an unpriced limit order that is priority-queued at the current best bid price (if selling) or best ask price (if buying). It appears in the market as a limit order with a specified price.

Brokers use numbers of shares rather than dollars when discussing trading. If you ask for '10,000 Commonwealth Bank' when you actually mean $10,000 worth of Commonwealth Bank shares, you may wind up being billed for close to $820,000!

Utilising market depth information

Market depth information is now available from online brokers and information services. *Market depth information* allows you to see the various buy and sell orders entered into the trading system at a limit, but yet to happen. Being able to see how many shares are on offer and at what price can help you buy and sell more effectively.

If your order is queued up behind a much larger order at the same price, you can tweak your bid (higher for a buy, lower for a sell), effectively starting a new queue, which means your order can get through quicker.

Finetuning your order

Traders take a different view of the order process to investors. Investors usually choose their stocks to hold long term and really aren't interested in quibbling over a few cents here and there on the purchase price. However, for traders, executing the trade as close to perfect as possible — that is, getting the price absolutely right — can make all the difference. Several methods are available to both investors and traders.

These methods are:

- ✔ **Good for date:** The order expires at the end of the specified trading day.

- ✔ **Good for day:** You can lodge a *limit* order for the day only. If the limit order isn't filled, ASX Trade *purges*, or cancels, the order at the end of the current trading day.

- ✔ **Fill or kill:** *Fill or kill* orders fill the order entirely when possible, or not at all.

- ✔ **Fill and kill:** *Fill and kill* means fill as much of the order as you can, immediately, and cancel the rest.

- ✔ **Stop-loss:** If you're a trader looking to get in and out of shares quickly at a profit, you'd be wise to consider the downside, or the possibility of loss. In many cases, traders set a *stop-loss* order with their broker, which tells the broker to sell the shares if they fall to a certain price. A stop-loss order means if the price falls — that is, if the trade goes wrong — traders can retrieve their capital quickly, take a small loss and live to fight another day.

If you're a long-term investor who has carefully chosen the stocks for your portfolio, you're not going to be too worried by the immediate downside (unless the stock starts to look terminal, in which case you chose badly!).

✔ **Straight-through processing:** Internet share trading allows investors to place their order directly into the market place, as though they had their own access directly to ASX Trade. A broking firm takes the order placed by the investor via the broker's website and places the order into ASX Trade. *Day traders* — traders who want to buy and sell a stock before the end of the trading day — in particular like straight-through processing.

If you're making trades without a broker's advice, only one person is to blame if things go wrong — you. Most broking firms still believe that their advisers can help you make the most of your investments (but there's an obvious conflict of interest there!). However, they may help you avoid a badly planned order.

Closing an order

After you place a buy or sell order, you want the order filled quickly. If you're a buyer who's prepared to pay the lowest price sellers are asking for the amount of shares they have on the market, your purchase can go through while you're still on the telephone.

How long the order hangs around depends on the kind of order. Most orders operate on a *good until cancelled* basis. ASX Trade will purge any orders overnight that meet the following criteria:

✔ **Expired:** Orders can be entered with an expiry date. ASX Trade checks the expiry dates of all orders at the close of each trading day. The system removes expired orders daily.

✔ **Price:** The order price is too far away from the current market, defined as the best buy (or sell) price for the close. How far is too far depends on the market price.

✔ **Purged:** The basis of quotation changes, for example, ex-dividend (XD).

✔ **Session State:** Orders for a stock that has been suspended (prohibited from trading) during that trading day.

Working the Trading Day

Equity Automatic Trading takes place on ASX Trade between 10.00 am and 4.12 pm on weekdays (except public holidays that occur in Victoria and New South Wales on the same day). Not all shares are open for trading at 10.00 am. The start of the trading day is staggered to allow orders recently placed into the system to be processed smoothly.

These orders may have been entered the previous day, after the close of trading. Between 4.12 pm and 6.50 pm, the equity market enters an *adjust* phase, where orders cannot be entered. Brokers are able to trade during this period; however, the ASX imposes strict rules in relation to trading after hours. Brokers can conduct *housekeeping* on their trading books, cancelling or amending orders.

Orders may also be entered in the morning, during *pre-open*, which begins at 7.00 am. During pre-open, Designated Trading Representatives can enter orders, amend or cancel the previous night's orders and generally prepare for the trading day, but are unable to trade. Figure 6-1 shows these phases on ASX Trade.

Transferring off-market

You don't have to use the sharemarket to trade shares. Off-market transfers of shares between parties without using a stockbroking firm as the intermediary are executed through the use of an *Australian Standard Transfer Form*.

You can also conduct off-market transfers of securities electronically through *CHESS* (Clearing House Electronic Sub-register System), which is an ASX computer system that manages the settlement process (see the section 'Playing CHESS Isn't a Game', later in this chapter). You can transfer shares held in CHESS. You don't need an Australian Standard Transfer Form for transfers through CHESS; for this type of transfer, you need to go through your stockbroker.

Off-market transfers are usually private arrangements between family members or transfers from deceased estates. To obtain an Australian Standard Transfer Form, contact the share registry of the company whose shares you wish to transfer.

Trading Sessions

Actual Market Times

Time	*Equity 1–5+ / Interest Rates*	*Warrants (excludes Index, Commodity and Currency Warrants)*	*Index, Commodity and Currency Warrants*
5.30 am			
6.00 am*			
7.00 am	Pre-open	Pre-open	Pre-open
9.40 am			
9.50 am*			Open
10.00 am*	Open	Open	
4.00 pm	Pre Closing Single Price Auction (CSPA)	Pre CSPA	Pre CSPA
4.10:30 pm**	CSPA	CSPA	CSPA
4.12 pm	Adjust	Adjust	Adjust
4.20 pm			
4.30 pm			
4.42 pm	Adjust on	Adjust on	Adjust on
5.30 pm*			
6.50 pm	Purge orders	Purge orders	Purge orders
6.59 pm	System maintenance	System maintenance	System maintenance
7.00 pm	Close	Close	Close
8.00 pm			
8.10 pm			

+ *Equity Market A–B: 10:00; Equity Market 2 C–F: 10:02:15; Equity Market 3 G–M: 10:04:30; Equity Market 4 N–R: 10:06:45; Equity Market 5 S–Z: 10:09*

* *Random +/– 15 secs*

** *Random +/– 30 secs*

Figure 6-1: A day in the life of ASX Trade.

Source: © Australian Securities Exchange Limited

Estimating the costs for trading

When you buy or sell shares, you're charged a fee called *brokerage*, which covers the broker's costs and a profit margin. Stockbrokers earn their income from brokerage on transactions, although some brokerage firms are changing to annual fees for managing a client's portfolio. However, brokerage is still the main game, which means your broker is happiest when you're transacting. Buying or selling really doesn't matter to your broker.

Most brokers apply a tiered scale for charging brokerage, in which the commission rate decreases as the dollar value of the transaction increases. Many charge a flat fee for smaller trades, with brokerage moving to a percentage of the total trade for transactions over a certain amount.

Brokerage fees differ significantly between stockbroking firms. The level of service offered usually determines the fee. If you want research, portfolio management and other services, you can expect to pay more in fees. The charges may be a percentage of the transaction, with discounts on higher-value transactions. Some firms may charge a flat fee for transactions up to a certain size, and most firms charge a minimum fee for all transactions.

A broker can provide a range of value-added services, including advice on which shares to buy or sell, recommendations, research, portfolio management, financial planning and access to new floats that the firm is handling. Investors can choose between so-called *full-service* brokers — offering stockbroking with all the trimmings — and *execution-only* (or *discount*) brokers. Chapter 9 gives a detailed explanation of how brokers work.

You may be able to negotiate a special scale of fees with your stockbroker, based on your volume of business with the firm. Full-service brokers charge a minimum amount of as low as $80–$100 (plus GST) for small purchases, rising to $200. Alternatively, they may charge you 1.2 per cent of the trade, or 0.9 to 1 per cent of the value of the trade for larger purchases (above $30,000). Above the minimum, brokerage rates are usually negotiable and depend on the dollar value of the transactions and the frequency of trades.

Stockbroking is a customer- and service-oriented profession. Stockbroking is also very competitive, so if you feel you're paying too much brokerage, let your broker know that you're prepared to take your business elsewhere.

Some full-service brokers may be prepared to charge 0.5 to 0.7 per cent brokerage on trades above, say, $60,000, but if you try to screw the broker down to 0.5 per cent, you may then find that you get less attention.

A lot of full-service brokers take on accounts as 'managed accounts', which can be discretionary — where the broker buys and sells the stocks — or consultative between the broker and the client, and all shades in between. Many self-managed superannuation funds (SMSFs) like the managed account arrangement. In this structure, the client may pay a management fee of 1 per cent of the value of the portfolio up to, say, $500,000: above $500,000, the fee may then drop to 0.75 per cent a year. Such clients may also be paying brokerage of 0.4 per cent, but these arrangements can be highly negotiable.

Discount brokers (these days, the term usually means online or internet brokers) provide a competitive environment for the broking industry. Some investors aren't interested in receiving advice, or a newsletter, or having any relationship with their broker other than taking and executing orders. They want to trade as impersonally as possible and so online brokers suit their needs.

When discount stockbroking was unleashed on the market in the 1990s, many Australian investors were sceptical. Commonwealth Securities' first minimum brokerage price of $75 a trade was competitive, but hardly screamingly cheap.

Now you can trade online for less than $10 — heavily qualified — up to a trade value of $10,000, or as low as 0.03 per cent of the value of a $100,000 trade. Some brokers stipulate that clients also open a cash management or deposit account to ensure that funds are available for some transactions. You pay GST on brokerage, but that GST is tax deductible after you've sold the shares.

You can find the lowest — and average — brokerage rates for online brokers as at March 2015 in Table 6-2.

Table 6-2	Best Online Brokerage Rates, as at March 2015	
Trade Value	Lowest Brokerage (per trade)	Average Brokerage (per trade)
$1,000	$9.90	$19.15
$5,000	$9.90	$19.15
$10,000	$9.90	$20.08
$25,000	$18.75	$27.54
$50,000	$25.00	$50.71
$100,000	$30.00	$96.48

Source: CANSTAR* (based on the number of platforms considered for Online Share Trading star ratings in March 2015)
* Consider only the Online Brokerage Fee

Making the final settlement

After your broker completes your trade, you receive a contract note setting out the particulars of the transaction. *Settlement —* paying for the shares you bought or handing over the shares you sold — must take place within three business days after the transaction (a system called T+3).

After you place an order and the order is filled, you're required to fulfil your side of the transaction, even if you haven't yet received the contract note. Many brokers can offer you a cash management account to make settlement easier. If your broker has sold shares for you, the broker then deposits the proceeds (minus costs) into your account. If your broker has bought shares for you, the broker debits your account. You don't have to use this arrangement, but many investors find it's convenient.

Playing CHESS Isn't a Game

The Australian Securities Exchange has a paperless settlement system, the Clearing House Electronic Sub-register System — or CHESS. Prior to CHESS, shareholders used to receive share certificates for each parcel of shares that were purchased (which usually only clogged up your desk drawers until you sold the shares, and most times you couldn't find the certificates anyway).

CHESS was introduced in 1993 as an electronic transfer and settlement system that improved the bureaucracy of the Australian sharemarket. CHESS operates as a central hub that exchanges money and shares at the same time. The ASX registers all shareholdings electronically on CHESS, and they're known as *uncertificated holdings*. The cost of using CHESS is included in your brokerage fee. The CHESS Securities Clearing House (SCH), on behalf of companies, issues holding statements to shareholders who are sponsored by brokers or institutions that participate in CHESS. You get a separate statement for each security you have in CHESS. You also get a statement whenever your security holding changes because of a transaction during the month.

To register your ownership of shares on CHESS, you need a *Holder Identification Number* (HIN). To get this, you need to be sponsored by a broker who is connected to the CHESS computer system. Your CHESS sponsor registers you on CHESS by opening a CHESS account in your name. The stock exchange then sends you a notice confirming your CHESS registration and gives you your HIN. You can register shareholdings in any number of companies under your HIN. Of course, appointing a broker as your CHESS sponsor restricts your selling to that broker. If you want to sell through any broker, use Issuer-Sponsored Registration.

Alternatively, a company whose shares you buy can sponsor you. Here, you register on an Issuer Sponsored Sub-register and receive a Shareholder Registration Number (SRN), which records your shareholding in that company. When you buy shares in a company, you automatically get an SRN. If you want to transfer the registration of these shares to CHESS, you can ask your CHESS sponsor.

If you hold shares in more than one company and choose to be *issuer-sponsored*, you have a different SRN for each shareholding. As your portfolio grows, you have to deal with multiple SRNs. Transferring the registration of these shares to CHESS, under one HIN, is much easier on the memory.

Shareholders don't have to manage the paper mountain of printed share certificates. CHESS holding statements accumulate over a financial year (1 July to 30 June). During the financial year, you get a new statement page that reflects transactions from 1 July. The statement tracks share transactions in the same way that bank account statements track cash transactions. The end result is less paper and more accurate records.

Chapter 7

Knowing When to Buy and Sell Shares

The basic rule for investing in shares is to buy low and sell high. You buy shares when they're cheap and sell them when they're expensive. The trouble is, how do you know what's cheap or expensive? Only hindsight tells you that for sure. You may buy a share and then see its price fall. Conversely, you may sell a share and then watch its price rise. If you sold the share at a profit, remember that you made a profit; and if you bought believing the shares were cheap, don't worry that they're now even cheaper.

In this chapter, I discuss the whys and wherefores of when to buy and when to sell, how to analyse the market, the differences between being a trader and an investor, and ways to keep your tax to a minimum.

Getting Ready for the Action

No accurate method exists by which you can determine the best time to buy or sell shares. Whether you're a long-term investor or a trader focused on short-term opportunities, you have to work this out for yourself. Many people collect and interpret data in order to know when to buy and sell shares, but even the professionals don't always get it right.

An experienced investor knows that no perfect method for determining when to buy or sell a share exists, although you can always find a salesman or a software system that claims to have the key. If only the process were that simple! Whether they use fundamental analysis, technical analysis or even astrology, these systems are far from infallible. Don't be fooled by software programs that promise to make you rich. If the system were foolproof, you can be sure it would be a very tightly held secret.

Before you buy or sell shares, you have to satisfy yourself that the shares are likely to rise or fall. If you're using a software system to give you trading tips, you have to be able to validate the information it's giving you. Whether you do this through your own research or through consulting a reputable broker or adviser, seeking a second opinion is always wise.

When you invest in the sharemarket, the only way to have the odds in your favour is to do your homework. You have to study the companies, research their operations, review their history and estimate their potential for profit. This may require reading the company prospectus or annual report, sifting through broker research, trying the company's products or services yourself and even talking to the directors or managers. You may decide to follow the price and the volume of trades and try to understand the many things that they imply. Read, study and ask plenty of questions — and then go back and study some more.

Loving your shares

Emotions play a part in sharemarket investing. Although buying shares means acquiring a financial asset, the main purpose of the investment is to earn money for you. If a share doesn't perform to expectations, sell it and find one that will make you money. That's the objective. However, when you buy a share, you're also starting a relationship. You researched the company or read about it and you're enthusiastic. As with your everyday relationships, the possibilities seem endless, the expectations are all for the best and you're truly optimistic. Perhaps, if this relationship goes well and your stock makes you money, you may come to believe you could never bring yourself to sell. If that happens, you've lost sight of the purpose of investing in shares.

Sometimes investors are paralysed by the fear that after they sell a share the price goes higher and they could have got more for it if they'd hung on. If this happens, remember that by locking in your capital gain, you protect yourself from the possibility of loss; taking a loss on a share feels a whole lot worse than not making as much profit on a share as you could have.

A profit is only a profit and a loss is only a loss when it is *crystallised* — when you actually sell the shares. Price fluctuations in the sharemarket continually alter your paper profit or loss, but good or bad, the change in the value of your holdings isn't real until you act on it.

Sometimes you may fulfil your expectations and justify your emotional attachment to the shares. When you're ready to sell, you face two possibilities — either you've made money on the shares, or you haven't. You can bank the money and pay the tax, or learn your lesson, claim the loss and get on with your life in the sharemarket.

If a share purchase goes bad, convincing yourself that the shares can return to your buying price if you just hang in there long enough is easy. However, that's a dangerous assumption to make. Taking the loss and moving on to better investments may be more suitable.

Buying smart

To buy smart, you buy a share when it's undervalued by the market and likely to rise in price and generate a capital gain.

You can't know what's going to happen to the share price in the future. However, you can make a well-informed guess, based on knowledge, research and help. You're making an educated guess but that's all it can ever be. Sharemarket investors and traders make these assessments every day.

Every sharemarket participant is trying to buy stocks cheaper and sell stocks at a profit. But for every buyer, a seller exists — someone whose view of the stock is the exact opposite of yours. To ensure your side of the transaction is the correct one, do your homework and trust your opinion. That way you can be confident that you're a better-informed investor than the person on the other side. But you won't get every decision right.

Selling smart

Usually, you sell a share when you decide it's more likely to fall than rise. If you bought shares for less than you sold them, that's good, and all you have to worry about is the capital gains tax. If you need cash, selling a profitable shareholding is a quick way to generate free money to spend on things like children's education or overseas travel. I've cashed in shares to spend on travel, and it's an enjoyable feeling, as though the money came out of thin air.

TIP

Averaging down or up

Averaging down means buying more of a share if the price falls. Investors do this to lower the average cost per share of the holding. For example, say you bought 1,000 shares of a company at $5. The price drops to $3, so you buy 1,000 more shares. The average cost of your shareholding is now $4. Instead of the stock having to rise above $5 before you're ahead, your break-even point is now $4. If the share price falls further, you can lower your average buying cost even more. But the risk you're taking is that the stock never recovers, in which case all you've done is throw good money after bad.

The debt-laden 2000s and the global financial crisis (GFC) reckoning that followed — with the spectacular share price falls that ensued — was a trap for investors who thought they were averaging down. Say you bought shares in childcare centre operator ABC Learning Centres in December 2006 at $8.60, when the company announced its US expansion. The stock had risen all the way from its $2 issue price in March 2001, it was recommended by many brokers, and plenty of investors simply assumed that it would replicate its Australian success in the US and thus consolidate a fragmented market. But ABC Learning Centres had bitten off more than it could chew. Its share price began to slide, but as the price got lower, you averaged down by buying more shares. You bought at $6 in October 2007, at $5 in January 2008, at $4 in March 2008, at $1 in July 2008; all the way to a final close of 14 cents in 2009 before the company went into receivership and liquidation. Lowering your average cost turned out to be a one-way ticket to oblivion — unless you eventually claimed the capital loss (see Chapter 10). Averaging down only works if a stock recovers and moves higher than your average buying cost. When you average down, you're taking a big risk, but you can make it work in your favour if you confine it to stocks that you research thoroughly. Then, when the market overreacts to a piece of news and dumps the stock temporarily, averaging down can pay off.

Say you bought 100 Woolworths shares at $34 in November 2007. Like all stocks, Woolworths was hit by the GFC. By February 2008, with the shares down to $27, you decided that the worst must be over for the stock, and you bought a further 250 shares. You now own 350 Woolworths shares and, all up, they cost you $10,150. Your average cost is now $29 — Woolworths needs to move higher than this figure for you to be in the black.

In June 2008, with Woolworths still on the slide and down to $24, you add another 200 shares, costing you $4,800. Your average cost is now $27.18.

By October 2010, Woolworths has rebounded to $30, and you're 10 per cent up on your Woolworths holding. Add in almost $1,800 of dividends and you're up by 22 per cent. If you had stayed with just your original purchase at $34, you'd still be down 12 per cent.

By May 2014, Woolworths is at $37, taking your average gain to 36 per cent. Averaging down has worked because the stock has risen strongly.

However, Woolworths gets a bit complacent, and its arch-rival Coles (owned by Wesfarmers) starts to beat it regularly in sales growth. Also, its Masters Home Improvement joint venture has a troubled start. Institutional investors aren't impressed, and they sell the stock down. By mid-2015, Woolworths is back down at $27, which is below your average cost. Fortunately, you've now received more than $5,000 worth of dividends, so you're up by 33 per cent. With Woolworths having fallen in price by 27 per cent from its 2014 peak, you may want to average down again. If you buy another 250 shares at this point, at $27, your average price becomes $27.12. Any rise from here — if the company regains

competitiveness, and the market starts to like the company's story again — and you're back in the black on capital gain, as well as dividends.

If Woolworths had kept rising from May 2014, and you had bought the most recent parcel of shares (say, at $40), your average price would now be $31.18. 'Buying the dips' decreases your average cost and increases your capital gain — assuming that the 'dips' turn out to be temporary.

'Value' equity fund managers are quite prepared to average down, on the grounds that if they like a stock at $10, they like it even more at $5. Of course, that approach assumes that they have researched the stock thoroughly, and believe that the market is missing something that they know.

On the face of it, a better strategy is to *average up;* that is, as a company's share price increases, you should buy more of its shares. The theory here is that while you increase your average buying cost, the company is also prospering, the good news is flowing and the stock is steadily rising. In averaging up, you're putting more money into your winners. That's true, but your investments are following the law of diminishing returns. Averaging down — if it works — adds a lot more value.

Another method of averaging is *dollar-cost averaging*, which involves making regular investments of the same amount of money in a stock or managed fund. You're not trying to predict the best time to buy, but dollar-cost averaging makes market fluctuations work for you because you buy more shares when prices are low and fewer shares when prices are high.

However, share purchases can go wrong, and you may have to sell shares for less than you paid. In such a case, if you're a disciplined share trader, you may have a concrete rule on how much you're prepared to let the share price fall before you sell. If you're a long-term investor, you may be prepared to ignore the price fall to salvage something from a disaster. The good news is that the Australian Tax Office allows you to use your capital losses to offset against the capital gains that you've (hopefully) made on other shares, in that or future years.

In the absolute worst-case scenario, if you buy the wrong share, you can lose all your investment. This can happen even if you do your homework and satisfy yourself that the shares are a good buy. That's part of the risk.

Going into Analysis

Two tribes seem to dominate the sharemarket according to the pundits — the fundamentalists (fundies) and the technically oriented (techies). Fervent followers of each school exist. Professionals say that fundamental analysis tells you which shares to buy or sell and technical analysis tells you when to buy or sell. I don't believe these are exact tools, but they're useful and investors can profit from knowing how to apply them.

Fundamental and technical analysis are not for everybody. Remember, peaks and troughs on a share price chart can be seen only with hindsight. However, these tools can be helpful.

Using fundamental analysis

Investors make their decisions based on fundamental analysis. *Fundamental analysis* concentrates on the financial health of the company, as shown in its regularly published accounts. Among the most important indicators are

- ✔ Profitability
- ✔ Dividend yield
- ✔ Cash flow
- ✔ Assets
- ✔ Owners' equity
- ✔ Liabilities

Fundamental analysis involves relating the company's reported numbers to its price to work out whether the market price is cheap or expensive. It's used to measure risk and to find out whether the company's financial situation is improving or deteriorating. One of the drawbacks of fundamental analysis is that company accounts are furnished only every six months or, in the case of new companies that have listed on the stock exchange without a track record of profitability, every three months. These companies are required to post a statement of cash flows every quarter. Using fundamental analysis, you may spot a trend and try to confirm that trend in the next issue of company statements.

Fundamental analysis is a tool best suited for medium- to long-term investment. Fundamental analysis doesn't suit a trading strategy because it relies on out-of-date data. Four important calculations in fundamental analysis are the price/earnings ratio, the dividend yield, and interest and dividend cover. Other areas that are worth close investigation are gearing, asset backing and cash flow.

Determining the price/earnings ratio

The *price/earnings ratio* (P/E ratio) is a basic tool of fundamental analysis. The P/E ratio is the share price divided by the earnings. The P/E ratio compares the share price to the earnings and determines the value of the earnings bought at that price. Analysts use the P/E ratio to compare companies against their own track record, their industry peers and against the overall market.

To calculate the P/E ratio, you can either use the reported earnings of a company from its most recent financial year annual report or the prospective earnings forecast by broking firms. Investors who use an historic P/E ratio feel it shows actual figures based on real earnings whereas those who use a forecast figure are trying to look into the future. Then again, buying shares means forecasting future growth.

It used to be said that investors should look for a company with a low P/E ratio. The general rule was that a value of 10 or lower is cheap and that 20 or above is expensive. However, analysis can be a bit more complicated. For example, a stock may have a P/E ratio of 20 because its growth prospects are better and the market is prepared to pay a premium for it, or a stock may have a P/E ratio of 8 because the market feels the stock won't grow. These days, investors understand that the market goes through phases in which these parameters change.

A P/E ratio on its own doesn't tell you much. You have to use this calculation as a comparison. For example, you can compare a company's P/E ratio to the following:

- ✓ The average P/E ratio of its sector group, for example, banks, transport or telecommunications
- ✓ The average P/E ratio of the market as a whole
- ✓ The history of the company's P/E

By using these comparisons, you can see whether the share is rated at a premium (relatively overvalued) or at a discount (relatively undervalued). Comparing P/E ratios can show you whether the share price of the company is too high or too low.

The American fund manager John Neff built his career on low P/E ratio investing, looking for P/E ratios 40 to 60 per cent below the market average. He says:

> *Low P/E stocks can capture the wonders of P/E expansion with less risk than skittish growth stocks. An increase in the P/E, coupled with improved earnings, turbocharges the appreciation potential ... Unlike high-flying growth stocks poised for a fall at the slightest sign of disappointment, low P/E stocks have little anticipation, no expectation built into them. Indifferent financial performance by low P/E companies seldom exacts a penalty.*

A low P/E ratio can be that way because the market doesn't rate it very highly. Successful investing is about finding opportunities in shares that are undervalued, but not all of them go on to be winners. Sometimes a dog is a dog.

Calculating the dividend yield

To calculate the *dividend yield* — the percentage return of dividend income from a share investment — divide the dividend by the share price and multiply by 100 to convert to a percentage.

You can't compare the dividend yield to the yields on other investments because the dividend is only part of the earnings stream of the company. Some of the earnings are retained or reinvested in the business, and the dividend yield doesn't account for any capital gains (or losses) on the shares.

However, you can compare the dividend yield of the company to the same areas as you did with the P/E ratio; that is, other companies in its sector, the market as a whole and company price history. These comparisons can reveal whether the share is relatively overvalued or undervalued. You want to buy shares with a high yield and sell shares with a low yield. The dividend yield falls as the price rises.

You need to be careful because a high yield can be a sign of distress (remember risk versus return). The moral here is that you can't use dividend yield or any single determinant on its own as a guide to buy or sell.

Finding interest and dividend cover

Interest cover denotes the number of times that earnings cover (can pay for) interest payments. An interest cover of four is adequate, while three or below is cause for worry. An interest cover of five or above means that the company has sound management.

Dividend cover is the ratio of earnings to the dividend. A ratio above 1 shows that the company has earnings left over after paying the dividend. A company with a dividend cover above 2 is considered highly reliable: The dividend comprises less than half of the company's earnings for the year. Dividend cover below 1 means that the company needs something more than earnings to pay its dividend. Companies can borrow from their reserves of retained earnings from prior years to pay a dividend. As a one-off situation this is fine, but it's not sustainable in the long run, and is usually considered a warning sign.

Mature companies have a lower dividend cover because they don't need to retain cash to finance their growth. For these companies, a dividend cover of 1.5 is fairly standard.

Using gearing

Gearing describes the ratio of borrowings to shareholders' equity (or shareholders' funds). A company finances assets from shareholders' equity or through liabilities to external creditors.

The gearing ratio shows the relative proportions between these two sources of funding. Pre-GFC, investors didn't like to see a gearing level above 100 per cent. Now they prefer to see much more conservative gearing, at 50 per cent or lower.

Understanding asset backing

Theoretically, each share represents a share of the company's assets, not counting debt. The *net tangible asset* (NTA) backing is a figure based on the assumption that if the company were dissolved and all its debts paid, these assets would be left to be sold. Intangible assets are not counted in this figure.

The market price of a share should be higher than its NTA backing. Ideally, a price premium would exist because the business is flourishing, selling its goods or services, and being well managed. A company that's trading below its NTA backing is cheap, but this may be an indication that it won't survive. Price-to-NTA is a good indicator of relative value, but don't use it on its own.

Watching the cash flow

A company's gross *operating cash flow* comes from selling its product or service. From this, you deduct the cost of these sales, such as paying staff, advertising and marketing costs, research and development expenses, leased assets, and other working capital outlays. Other deductions include any dividends or interest paid and income tax paid. What is left over is net operating cash flow. If net operating cash flow is positive, the company is generating cash. When it's not positive, the company is consuming cash.

A company with negative cash flow can turn this around and bring in cash through its investing activities or by selling businesses, shares, intellectual property or any other assets. The company can receive cash from dividends on its investments, make further issues of equity or options, or borrow from banks or other sources. However, funds garnered from investing or financing are only an adjunct to a company's main activity, which is selling products or services. If a company can't generate positive operating cash flow, investors become wary of purchasing shares.

Working with technical analysis

Technical analysis is the study of the changes in the price and volume of a share that have occurred over a period of time. Using technical analysis, you can chart the share's history and begin to make extrapolations and projections about the share. Ideally, this kind of analysis allows you to make predictions about where the share price will be at a given point in the future. You can also use technical analysis to study an index or a currency, or any commodity that is traded and sold.

 On any share price chart, you can draw a trendline using technical analysis. When an upward trendline is breached, the signal says sell. When a downward trendline is breached, the signal says buy.

Charting resistance and support levels

A *resistance level* is a point on a chart that the share price has historically not been able to break through, and from which the share price has fallen away. If the stock is approaching a resistance level, its track record may indicate a sell. But if the stock manages to move through resistance, it's generally headed higher.

A *support level* is a point on a chart at which the share price has historically rebounded. If the stock is approaching a support level, its track record may indicate a buy. But, if a stock falls through a support level, traders sell the stock as soon as they can because it's heading for a lower support level.

Following a moving average

The *moving average* (MA) can appear on a chart in the form of a curving trendline. If you take a specified period of consecutive price data and divide it by that number of time periods, you get the MA. For example, you can take the last 20 days of closing prices, add them together and then divide by 20 to produce a single price. You can plot this price on the chart alongside the market price.

 A moving average identifies a trend after it has already started and is known as a lagging indicator. When the price closes above the MA, it's a buy signal, and when the price moves below the MA, it's a sell signal.

Understanding breakout trading

A *breakout trade* is a form of share buying based on trend theory. When a stock is on an uptrend, it forms a series of waves with higher highs and higher lows. When the share breaches a wave high or a long-term resistance level it means that the share's uptrend is confirmed. Buying at this point is termed a breakout trade.

Breakout trading sounds strange to novice investors who think that success comes from finding a stock that's languishing near its lows and watching it return to its highs. Breakout trading seems contrary to logic. How can a share be a bargain when it's at its highest price? The answer is that if the uptrend continues, that current price is ultimately a bargain.

Investing or Trading

Investors and traders have different goals when they buy and sell shares. An *investor* wants to identify stocks that provide maximum capital growth over a long period of time. A *trader* buys and sells shares to make a profit without a preconceived idea of how long to hold the shares. This is how they differ:

- ✔ Investors look for a promising share prospect with low risk and the possibility of increased capital gain. They research the company, understand risk versus return and know that earnings affect share prices. Investors want the right stocks at the right price, and they believe that sooner or later, the share price is going to rise. They're patient and prepared to wait for the true value of their shares to be reflected in the share price.

- ✔ Traders move funds in and out of the sharemarket; whether they're buying or selling doesn't matter. A trader expects to take an amount of money and use it to buy blocks of stocks, which the trader can sell for a profit. Not all the trades are going to be successful, but an experienced trader with a disciplined approach expects to make more profits than losses.

Buying as an investor

Investors look for particular elements when buying shares. They want a stock that's predictable and shows growing earnings. They want a share in a successful company to show a profitable trend within five years. Investors may allow a year of flat or even declining earnings, but in the remaining four years, they want earnings growth of at least 10 to 15 per cent a year. The company's business and the sector of the economy in which the company operates must show the potential to create this earnings growth.

Other factors investors are interested in when buying shares include:

- ✔ **Capable management:** Investors want to see a settled board of directors and a management team that can demonstrate a track record of success; they also want to know that these people own shares in the company.

- ✔ **Reasonable price:** A share with a rising trend in earnings, which trades on a low P/E ratio relative to its peers and the market, is just what an investor looks for.

- ✔ **Low gearing:** The lower the borrowings, the better, because the less interest a company pays, the higher the proportion of earnings that's ploughed back into the company, and the greater the dividends for shareholders.

- ✔ **High cash flow:** A company with a strong cash flow from its business is effectively self-financing and less prone to external shocks, such as interest rate rises.

Efficient market theory is a point of view that says the market knows all there is to know about every stock at any time and values each of them accordingly. However, investors know that at any time plenty of undervalued gems (and overvalued stocks) are in the market and, with a bit of diligence, you can find them.

Keeping the dividend

Prior to the GFC, investors believed that there was one major status symbol that a listed company would fight tooth and nail to keep. It wasn't S&P/ASX 200 Index status, it wasn't a sumptuous glass-and-granite Sydney or Melbourne CBD address and it wasn't an investment-grade credit rating. What investors really thought was sacrosanct was the dividend.

The expectation was that solid companies — certainly companies that thought of themselves as blue chips — would always lift their dividend. But the straitened financial circumstances that companies found themselves in during the GFC forced a reappraisal of this belief.

Where the cash to pay the kind of dividend largesse that shareholders had come to expect did not exist, company management bit the bullet and cut their dividend payouts during the downturn. Among them were Wesfarmers, BlueScope Steel, Rio Tinto, Westfield and Lend Lease. Some stocks, including Sigma Pharmaceutical, James Hardie Industries, Australian Agricultural

(continued)

(continued)

Company, Elders and Transpacific, ceased payments altogether.

Even the big four banks, long the darlings of income seekers, suffered in 2009 as bad debt provisions affected the ability to pay dividends. Commonwealth Bank cut its payout by 14 per cent, Westpac reduced its dividend by 18 per cent, and shareholders in ANZ and National Australia Bank suffered 25 per cent dividend cuts. Macquarie Group shareholders had to stomach a 46 per cent dividend fall, while Suncorp slashed its dividend by 63 per cent as it also struggled with bad debts.

In contrast, companies such as Woolworths, QBE Insurance, Origin Energy, BHP Billiton, Newcrest Mining and CSL managed to increase dividends during the downturn, while Telstra held its payout steady.

The market still usually views cutting a dividend as a signal to sell the shares; however, there's a lot more understanding about the fact that in difficult times, cutting a dividend may be a necessary step. But the companies that do so had better resume dividend growth as quickly as possible!

Companies can protect their dividends by retaining some of their earnings in a reserve account. Telstra revealed in 2005 that it had dipped into reserves and borrowed to help pay its special dividends. With adequate reserves, a company can still pay a dividend in a year when profits are low or even non-existent, but most companies do this only in limited circumstances.

Dividends aren't a bonus for owning shares; over long periods, the dividend return typically delivers half of your total return from owning shares.

Selling as an investor

Investors sell a share when it delivers the return they expect or if the share's story changes and the risk of holding it increases. Investors also sell because of financial need. You may have to finance an emergency or settle a long-planned-for payment. You enter the sharemarket to see your capital grow and build wealth. You can cash in part of this wealth at any time — for the children's school fees, a new car or an overseas holiday. Shares are a financial asset that store buying power today for future use.

Investors who adhere to the buy-and-hold strategy don't want to sell. They're trying to replicate the miracle of Westfield Holdings. If you had invested the equivalent of $1,000 in the float of Westfield in September 1960, and reinvested every dividend and bonus that Westfield had paid to you, by October 2011 your investment would have been worth about $242 million. (Westfield Group no longer makes this calculation.)

You can't take the money with you, but shares can play a major part in building inheritable wealth for your family. Even if you're a buy-and-hold investor, you're wise to continually monitor your share portfolio. Ask yourself if you'd buy the stock today. If the answer's no, you should think about selling it and reinvesting the proceeds in a stock you'd like to buy.

The doyen of the buy-and-hold strategy is Warren Buffett of the US investment company Berkshire Hathaway. Buffett is a phenomenally successful money manager, and his company has what it calls 'permanent holdings'. But Buffett does sell when a stock is overvalued or even undervalued. According to Philip Fisher, you hold on to a share until it has done the job or its circumstances change and you don't think it ever will do its job.

Buying as a trader

If you buy a stock expecting to sell it in a matter of days, even hours, then you're not an investor, you're a trader. Trading in the sharemarket is okay if you know what you're doing and accept the risks. If you try to compress the wealth-creating power of the sharemarket into a short time frame, the sharemarket gods can get very angry.

Traders don't worry too much about the fundamentals of a company, particularly if they're *day traders*. As the name suggests, *day trading* is the buying and selling of shares within the same trading day. Day traders are also not too concerned with the P/E ratio of the stock. The P/E ratio is only a consideration for those who are committing money to the stock for a period of years. Traders are concerned with price movement and volume; that is, the technical indicators and the price momentum of the stock.

Day trading is a particularly difficult and stressful form of share investing that's decidedly not for the novice or the long-term average investor. Although knowing how day traders operate may be interesting, I must caution you that this kind of investing is only for professionals.

Selling as a trader

A trader sells when their shareholding drops to a specified point. When a trader buys, they put a *stop-loss* in place that stipulates the amount of loss they're prepared to take before selling the shares. Stops are set in terms of a dollar (or percentage) amount, or they're set by using some form of technical parameter, such as when a moving average is crossed. Although the trading mantra says to let profits run, a trader may also decide, after reaching a certain amount of gain, to get out of the trade and look for the next profitable share. Instead of a stop-loss, you can call this a *stop-profit* because that's exactly what it does. To the trader, though, the operative word is 'profit'.

Relying on Your Broker

You can't rely completely on your stockbroker. Although some of their buy recommendations may be good investments, selling is another matter. Stockbrokers talk about underweighting a stock, lightening it, reducing it or even trimming it, but they rarely bring themselves to say 'sell'. Some subscription-based investment websites (and newsletters), however, are wholly independent and answer only to their subscribers, and are quite willing to make 'sell' calls.

Sell calls can cause problems for a broking firm. Companies don't like having their shares rated 'sell'. A disgruntled company can blacklist a broking firm from analysts' briefings, conference calls and site visits. If the broking firm has an underwriting arm, a sell recommendation can be even more problematic. The broking firm can forget about any underwriting work from companies it describes as sells. Supporting issues in the after-market (the days after a stock is floated) is an important part of getting underwriting and if the broker has been unfriendly, the work won't be there.

Brokers make their money when people buy or sell shares. In fairness, brokers spend more time and effort on buy recommendations because they're directed at an unlimited number of people; that is, anyone who sees the recommendation is a possible buyer. However, only those people who own the shares can sell them — unless they're short-sellers (see the sidebar 'Selling short' for more).

A common complaint of the small investor is that 'my broker never tells me when to sell'. Even if a broker was convinced that a share was about to fall and had the time to call every client on his list, he probably couldn't get to every client before the share price fell. The broker naturally wants to take care of his best clients first because they pay his wages.

Selling short

'He who sells what isn't his'n, Must make it good or go to prison.' This mantra of legendary 19th century Wall Street trader Daniel Drew is no longer true in terms of prison, but anyone who sells shares short and gets it wrong still pays a hefty price.

Short-selling is a reverse of what you're meant to do on the share-market. Short-selling is selling a stock first, and buying back the stock later. You don't have the stock when you sell it; you have to borrow it from someone and then sell it. Then you buy it back. Short-selling is rife in the US markets but not so popular in Australia.

Short-sellers profit if the price falls. Then their selling price is more than their buying price. They pay their fees and borrowing costs and pocket the difference.

If the price rises, the short-sellers are in trouble. To cover their short position — because they have to deliver the shares they've sold — they have to buy the shares back on the market. If the price has risen, they've paid more than their selling price. For this reason, short-selling is definitely not for the inexperienced sharemarket participant.

Because you don't own the shares when you sell them short, you must borrow them from someone. Stockbrokers and institutional investors can lend the shares to you, but they charge a borrowing fee and also require collateral for the loan. If your broker permits short-selling, the Australian Securities Exchange (ASX) requires the broker to obtain margin cover of 20 per cent of the value of the trade before placing your short-sold order. If the price of the shares you've short-sold rises by more than 10 per cent, you must provide additional margin cover of 100 per cent to your broker.

Because of the ASX's T+3 settlement period, a short-sold position must be settled within three days; if not, a hefty fail fee will apply. Therefore, to make a profit, the price of the shares must fall within three days. You buy the shares, deliver them, pay your broker's fees and borrowing costs and pocket the difference.

The ASX maintains a list of the approved securities that may be short-sold; no more than 10 per cent of the shares on issue may be short-sold.

(continued)

(continued)

In early 2016, 365 stocks were on the list, which is updated daily. Short-selling is not allowed when:

✔ The stock is under a takeover offer

✔ The order price is lower than the last sale price

Short-selling is a common strategy employed by managers of hedge funds and absolute return funds, many of whom run long-short funds, which simply aim to capture returns from both rising and falling share prices, within the same fund. In this way, the funds can, in theory, generate a positive return no matter how the sharemarket (or other financial markets) are performing.

Such funds have been termed alternative investments and rose in popularity among retail investors annoyed at the losses posted by their Australian and international equity funds in the early 2000s. But not all of these funds were able to perform well in the GFC, losing too much on the 'long' side.

Short-selling was blamed for some of the excessive volatility at the peak of the GFC market turmoil in late 2008, and for some of the large price falls in stocks targeted by the short-sellers, particularly financial stocks. Some short-selling by hedge funds was deliberately targeted at stocks in which key executives had margin loans to buy their shares; the short-selling triggered margin calls, which pushed the share price even lower and had a disastrous impact on market sentiment.

In response, in September 2008, the Australian Securities and Investments Commission (ASIC) and the ASX temporarily banned short-selling. The ban was lifted in May 2009 for 'covered' short-selling, where the sellers had borrowed the stock before selling it; but 'naked' short-selling (where the sellers never even borrowed the stock) remained banned. Following the ban, ASIC and the ASX introduced stricter disclosure rules for covered short-selling.

Looking and Listening

Knowing when to buy and sell shares means that you need to be attuned to what is happening in the business community. You need to do your research, and you also need to be aware of events such as takeovers, profit warnings, index changes and more.

Analysing takeovers

A hostile takeover bid is an emotion-packed event for the sharemarket. If more than one company is involved and a bidding war ensues, the rest of the sharemarket eagerly watches the protagonists slug it out. The shareholders of the sought-after company have the most to gain, mainly because a takeover usually boosts the share price.

When a company's share price is beaten down, or one of its competitors sells its business for a large amount of money, speculators look for possible takeovers. Market rumours swirl around potential takeovers, and some traders buy on rumour, hoping to sell on fact.

Any company listed on the sharemarket is up for sale, from the biggest blue chip to the smallest minerals explorer. Anybody can come along, any day, and lay money on the table. If the price is right, the board has a duty to recommend that shareholders accept it.

Taking note of profit warnings

When a company announces a downturn in profits, it means its investment story has changed for the worse. The opposite is true for an upgraded profit forecast. Traders often act quickly when they hear a profit warning. However, as an investor, if you don't believe that the long-term outlook for the company has altered and yet the stock is suddenly substantially cheaper, you may want to buy more shares. When a profit warning does alter the long-term prospects of a company, you can then think seriously about selling the shares.

Watching index changes

Thanks to the growth of index funds, changes to the composition of the major indices bring both guaranteed buying of the stocks added and guaranteed selling of the stocks discarded, as institutions alter their portfolios to reflect the new make-up of the index. Trading on index changes is short-lived, but generally this trading produces relatively reliable price gains.

Capitalising on turnaround situations

The sharemarket is hard on a poorly performing stock, which usually means the company is in difficult straits. Later, when the company has a new management team, has cleaned up its balance sheet and is back with a plan for business growth, the sharemarket may still be ignoring it. This situation is one in which an astute buyer can make a lucrative investment if they know what they're doing. Investors who follow market fundamentals can benefit from these turnarounds.

Being a contrarian investor

Contrarian investing is buying when buying seems absolutely the wrong thing to do and selling when exuberance reigns. Psychologically, a contrarian investor is going against the herd instinct, which requires considerable self-belief. However, as we now know, selling all your technology shares in March 2000, or buying back into the battered blue chips in March 2009, was a very wise thing to do. It just took a lot of guts at the time!

Contrarian investors can make huge gains if they're brave and patient. Contrarians have great faith in their process of share assessment. However, as the fund manager John Neff says: 'Don't bask in the warmth of just being different. There is a thin line between being a contrarian and being just plain stubborn. At times, the crowd is right. Eventually, you have to be right on fundamentals to be rewarded.'

Watching for insider activity

When individual board members buy or sell shares in their company, investors watch carefully. Naturally, shareholders are happier when board members buy rather than sell shares. In fairness, directors should be allowed to raise cash by selling shares without setting off the market. If directors change their shareholdings, this news has to be announced on the stock exchange but not on the actual day of the transaction; these changes are listed as notices of record. Investors watch the transactions of insiders in the hope of detecting a trend; investors want to know whether a transaction is a one-off or whether a flurry of buying or selling is about to occur.

Taxing Considerations

Letting tax considerations drive investment decisions is always a bad move. Whether you're buying or selling shares, your main objective is to buy future growth. If you concentrate only on gaining a tax advantage, you may lose out in the long term. By all means consult an accountant about your tax liabilities in buying and selling shares, but don't make your decisions based on tax advice solely.

Minimising capital gains tax

Some people decide not to sell profitable shares because they don't want to trigger a capital gains tax (CGT) liability. You can't avoid this tax unless the shares you sell were bought before the law was introduced (19 September 1985). Nothing can protect capital gains from a sudden change in market sentiment, which can turn a gain into a capital loss very quickly.

Selling to take a tax loss

May and June are known as the tax-related selling season. At this time, investors may bite the bullet on shares they're holding at a loss. If they choose, they can take the loss and offset it against capital gains earned in that tax year, or carry the loss forward for future use. Then, if they want to stay with the shares, they can buy them again at the current price.

Offsetting your annual tax with a capital loss is a perfectly legal deduction. However, CGT can be a problem if it overwhelms your investment strategy. Financial advisers always warn against such decisions. (See Chapter 10 for a guide to tax and shares.)

Chapter 8

Buying What You Know

. . . .

In This Chapter

▶ Appreciating ordinary shares

▶ Choosing specialised stocks

▶ Taking a punt

. . . .

*I*f you want to buy shares, you're not starved for choice. About 2,200 shares are available on the Australian sharemarket and more are being added every month (of course, companies occasionally get delisted, too). These companies cover virtually every activity that can legitimately be conducted for profit. The ASX presents a dazzling array of opportunities. You can't help but be impressed by the ingenuity and potential on display.

However, you can't own everything, so don't try to stretch a portfolio too far. If you own 20 stocks, you own too many. Diversification is great, but has its limits. A share portfolio becomes difficult to monitor properly when it grows beyond 15 stocks. That means if you're taking charge of your own sharemarket investments, you have to narrow your sights compared to an institutional investor who may hold 50 or more stocks. In this chapter, I tell you all about the different types of sharemarket sectors and stocks, and show you how to choose what goes in your portfolio.

Acquiring Ordinary Shares

Ordinary shares, those tiny building blocks of a company's equity, can be anything but ordinary in their performance. Most activity on the sharemarket centres on ordinary shares or what the Americans call *common stock*.

Each ordinary share entitles the owner to:

- ✔ A proportional share of the company's profit after expenses.

- ✔ A proportional share of the company's assets after the liabilities have been met in the event of liquidation of the company.

- ✔ A vote for the board of directors in the company.

The ordinary share is one of the great inventions of the financial world. It may be ordinary, it may be common, but an ordinary share is a fabulous opening to the wealth created in the economy.

Buying blue chips

Named after the highest-value chip in poker, *blue chips* are the sharemarket's elite stocks. Blue chips have an established track record over many years of consistently rising profits and fully franked dividends.

The blue chips have large market capitalisations, which guarantees plenty of liquidity in the market. They boast well-established businesses, high-quality assets and — usually — good management. Blue chips typically have high dividend yields, in the range of 4–7 per cent (except biotech CSL, which is more of a capital-growth stock than a yield generator). Over time, blue chips prove to be reliable wealth generators.

But blue chips sometimes fall from grace. At various times, companies such as Westpac, BHP Billiton and AMP have all turned in billion-dollar losses and lost their blue chip status. And when the market is being routed across the board as it was in 2008, even the bluest of chips are not immune.

Investors must always understand that the sharemarket is the most volatile of the asset markets — and the blue chips, as the highest-profile stocks, can be most affected by this volatility. Indeed, because the expectations are higher on blue chips, they can be savagely treated in the short term if they disappoint the market. If you expect a blue chip share only to rise and never to fall in value, you've got another thought coming. For example, if in mid-2007 your portfolio had contained Commonwealth Bank, Westpac, ANZ Bank, Telstra, Woolworths, BHP Billiton and Rio Tinto, it would have been considered an excellent blue chip portfolio. But each of those stocks was pounded by the global financial crisis (GFC), during which the Australian market slumped by 54 per cent. If your portfolio held an equal amount of these blue chips, by February 2009 you would have been staring at a portfolio that was down by 52 per cent.

At least the companies in your portfolio had the cover-all excuse of a once-in-a-generation market slump to explain their slumps. But even in isolation, blue chips can lose their status temporarily. For example, even before the GFC, building products maker Boral turned in five consecutive years of falling profit in the 2000s, and had its credit rating lowered. Problems in AMP's UK life insurance businesses in 2003 caused a $5.5 billion loss: The share price fell from $45 to a low of almost $3.50, blowing up $18 billion of shareholder wealth.

In 2001, National Australia Bank (NAB) made $4 billion in write-downs on its disastrous purchase of US mortgage business HomeSide. NAB had just regained the market's trust from that effort when it announced in early 2004 that unauthorised foreign exchange trading by some of its treasury staff would cost a further $360 million in write-downs.

The latter debacle cost NAB boss Frank Cicutto his job. It wasn't so much that the foreign exchange scandal was a financial disaster — in effect, NAB had to put aside only an amount equivalent to three-and-a-half weeks of pre-tax profit. Instead, what sent the NAB share price falling and ended Cicutto's reign was the fact that the company had given shareholders two nasty shocks in three years. NAB needed drastic action to begin the process of regaining the trust of institutional shareholders. The bank had only just done so when the GFC hit.

At the turn of the century, property giant Lend Lease was a successful and stable blue chip company. That was until it sold its funds management arm, MLC, to NAB, and expanded into the US. Without the earnings from MLC, Lend Lease was wholly exposed to the vagaries of the property and construction sectors. The volatility increased when Lend Lease lost the management rights to Australia's largest diversified property trust, GPT, in 2005 after launching a takeover bid. Subsequently the GFC erupted, during which Lend Lease's exposure to the troubled US and UK property markets saw the stock punished severely. However, Lend Lease has mounted an impressive recovery since 2009 and is once again making its case for blue chip status.

Newspaper giant Fairfax Media — publisher of *The Age*, the *Sydney Morning Herald* and *The Australian Financial Review* — was once considered a blue chip because of the reliable earnings from the 'rivers of gold', its newspapers' classified advertising revenue. But its shares now trade for 30 per cent less than they did when the company was refloated out of receivership in 1992. What's worse for long-suffering Fairfax shareholders is that the three internet-based businesses that stole the lion's share of the rivers of gold — jobs website seek.com.au (ASX code: SEK), real estate sales website realestate.com.au (REA), and auto sales website carsales.com (CRZ) — are each now valued by the sharemarket at more than Fairfax; collectively, they're now valued at over six times more than Fairfax.

Telco giant Telstra is considered a blue chip yield generator for an income portfolio, consistently generating a dividend yield in the range of 5–7 per cent. But the stock's fall in price from the T2 float price of $7.40 — let alone the $9.20 at the peak of the tech boom — to a low of $2.58 in October 2010 means the stock can't be considered a blue chip in terms of capital growth. When Telstra was floated the market viewed it as a high-tech growth prospect, but in the 2000s a bungled move to expand into Asia, regulatory interference and the realisation that heavy competition in the company's domestic market made earnings growth difficult altered the way that the market viewed the stock. However, since the lows of 2011, Telstra stock has gained 140 per cent on the back of its deal with the government on the National Broadband Network (NBN).

In the run-up to the 2007 federal election, the opposition Labor Party announced that if it won office it would build the 'super-fast' NBN. Subsequently, the new Labor Government went ahead as intended and committed to build the network. Initially, it was thought that the NBN would bypass Telstra's existing copper network — harming Telstra's revenues, margins and profits. However, in June 2011 Telstra signed a $16 billion (pre-tax) deal with the NBN in return for the gradual decommissioning of Telstra's copper network and cable broadband service, the progressive migration of its customers to the NBN and the leasing of important Telstra infrastructure to the NBN. Simply put, Telstra is a very different company to the one that Telstra subscribers to all three tranches of its float bought shares in — although it has continued to deliver on the yield front.

According to company reports, Telstra is the most widely held Australian stock, with 1.4 million shareholders; followed by AMP, with 855,000; Commonwealth Bank, with 780,000; Westpac, with 596,000; BHP Billiton, with 555,000; NAB, with 533,000; Wesfarmers, with 514,000; ANZ Bank, with 500,000; and Woolworths, with 442,000.

Blue chip stocks are exposed to the same systemic risk as any other stock on the market. Blue chip status means nothing if the market is falling across the board. The blue chips usually lead the market higher, but when the market suffers a correction, the blue chip stocks plunge too. You can do poorly in blue chips if you buy and sell them at the wrong time, so you need to watch these stocks as closely as your other stocks.

Looking at industrial and Resources companies

Traditionally, the main kinds of companies listed on the stock exchange have been divided into industrials and resources. *Resources* companies are easy to identify; they include mining and petroleum companies that drill, find, extract, process and sell Australia's mineral commodities. Any company engaged in these activities is a resource company; one that isn't engaged in these activities is an *industrial* company.

Choosing industrials

The industrial part of the sharemarket is the largest by value and by number of companies. These companies are involved in a vast array of activities, not only manufacturing products but developing drugs, banking, making wine, growing cotton, setting up telecommunication networks, operating tugboats, collecting financial receivables and building solar-power systems. The more you investigate the Australian stock market — especially the world beneath the Top 200 — the more the variety of what listed companies do will amaze you. You want a feel of the different types of companies that make up the stock market? It's time to examine the Global Industry Classification Standard (GICS) sectors of the S&P/ASX 200 Index.

Financials: Banks and financial services

At the top, the dominant GICS sector is *Financials*, which accounts for about 41 per cent of the S&P/ASX 200 Index.

Naturally, the Financial sector heavyweights are the big four banks: Commonwealth Bank, Westpac, ANZ and NAB, in order of size, as well as global insurer QBE and Australia's home-grown investment bank Macquarie Group (an *investment bank* doesn't take deposits and make loans; instead, an investment bank trades on its own account, delivers corporate advice and financial services packages, and manages investment opportunities).

The sector also contains the smaller banks — Bendigo & Adelaide Bank and Bank of Queensland — as well as insurance and financial services heavyweights Suncorp Group, AMP, Insurance Australia Group, Perpetual, IOOF and Platinum Asset Management. The big listed investment companies (LICs), Australian Foundation Investment Company and Argo Investments are large financial stocks, and the stock exchange itself is a constituent of this sector — the company that operates it being ASX (Australian Securities Exchange) Limited.

A variety of smaller financial services businesses round out this part of the sector.

Banks receive and pay the prevailing price of money in the form of interest. A rise in interest rates means added revenue on the asset side of the bank balance sheet and extra cost on the liability side. Banks can lend more than they borrow because they can create credit. Bankers generally don't like high interest rates because it raises the cost of borrowing and lending money. However, depending on the liability costs, a bank can do well in a rising interest rate environment. For example, if a bank has a high proportion of its liabilities in savings and cheque accounts paying a low interest rate, an interest rate rise will increase the bank's profits.

Banks also have *non-interest income* — revenue generated not from borrowing and lending but from their fees and charges. Non-interest income accounts for about 31 per cent of the banks' revenue, down from 41 per cent in 2006.

The insurance influence on the sharemarket grew in the 1990s with the demutualisation of several large mutually owned life insurance offices. These companies changed their status from mutually owned societies to companies limited by shares; shares were then offered free to their policyholders *pro rata* according to the policies held. In this way, AMP, AXA Asia–Pacific (formerly National Mutual) and Insurance Australia Group (formerly NRMA Insurance) migrated to the sharemarket, bringing millions of first-time investors with them. (*Note:* In March 2011, AXA Asia–Pacific merged its Australian businesses with AMP and sold its Asian businesses to its French parent company, AXA.)

Financials: REITs

The Financials sector also includes the *real estate investment trusts* (REITs), formerly known as *listed property trusts* (LPTs). REITs are unit trusts that own property and are traded on the sharemarket. REITs give individual investors the chance to share ownership in property assets, such as city office blocks, shopping centres, industrial parks and tourism properties, which they couldn't afford to invest in as individuals. REITs own about two-thirds of the institutional-grade property in Australia.

Big REITs such as Westfield Corporation (refer to Chapter 3 for more on the incredible success of Westfield), Stockland Group, Scentre Group (which owns and operates Westfield's Australian and New Zealand shopping centre portfolio), General Property Trust (GPT), Mirvac Group, Goodman Group and Dexus Property Group are near the top of this part of the Financials ladder, as is builder and property developer Lend Lease.

The REITs offer property investment, but with all the advantages of a stock exchange listing. All or part of the property holding can be sold instantly rather than having to sell the actual properties.

Until the GFC hit in 2007, REITs were considered a reliable source of high yields because they're required to distribute all of their taxable profit to unit-holders: Most REITs usually pay out about 80–90 per cent of their profit as distribution, compared to about 60 per cent of the major listed industrial companies' profit going out as dividends. Over the past 20 years, the average gross yield from an investment in LPTs/REITs has run at about 8.8 per cent, or twice the average yield on the sharemarket.

REITs do not boast the tax advantages of a fully franked share dividend so this outperformance is not as good as it looks. Their distribution has a *tax-advantaged component*, which comes from the trust's building depreciation allowance — income-tax free — and a *tax-deferred component*, which reflects other taxation deductions available to the trust during the period. However, these components are not as effective in reducing an investor's tax liability as fully franked dividends from shares.

The REIT sector changed markedly over the 2000s. Whereas until the late 1990s the LPTs were simple landlords passing on rental income to their unit-holders, with profit coming from rental income minus expenses, the sector became much more entrepreneurial. The stapled-security structure, where a share in a property company trades indissolubly with a unit in a property trust, became more common. The stapled securities were able to add earnings streams other than mere rent collection; for example, property development, syndication, management and property services. However, while these activities increased the REITs' non-rental earnings, they also increased their exposure to equity market risk. Added to this was the fact that through the 2000s the sector had binged on debt, with average gearing across the REITs rising from about 10 per cent in 1995 to 30 per cent in 2001 and then to 46 per cent in 2007.

The reckoning when the debt bubble exploded in 2007–08 was painful. As global credit supply dried up, property markets in the US and Europe collapsed, along with investors' returns. The average return of A-REITs (Australian REITs) fell from 20 per cent between 2004 and 2007 to 50 per cent in 2008–09. The sector's value slumped by more than 70 per cent. Those with a large percentage of offshore assets fared the worst. Some weaker REITs did not survive.

Since 2009, however, the A-REITs have raised more than $26 billion in equity to repair balance sheets and drive down gearing. The average gearing ratio is down to 31 per cent. More importantly, 85 per cent of the REITs' income is now from rent, slightly up from 84 per cent in 2007; also, the 'quality' of remaining non-rental income has improved, with a larger percentage of this coming from stable sources such as wholesale funds management. The sector now distributes only 80–90 per cent of its incomes, retaining the rest for capital spending and tenant incentives (for example, to attract tenants, the trust may offer a six-month rent-free period, or to pay for the tenant's fit-out requirements.) The volatility of the sector has been greatly reduced and it is once again considered defensive.

At the time of writing, you can find 51 REITs listed on the ASX, with a combined value of $115 billion — an amount that is down about 16 per cent from the pre-GFC peak in 2007.

The REITs are categorised by the kind of property they own, for example:

- ✔ **Retail:** Scentre Group, Charter Hall Retail REIT, BWP (Bunnings Warehouse Property) Trust, Vicinity Centres, SCP Australasia Property Group.

- ✔ **Office:** Dexus Property Group, Investa Office Fund, Cromwell Property Group, 360 Capital Office Fund.

✓ **Industrial:** Goodman Group, 360 Capital Industrial Fund, Industria REIT.

✓ **Diversified:** General Property Trust, Stockland Group, Mirvac Group, Charter Hall Group, Abacus Property Group.

One of the recent developments in the sector is the advent of *specialty REITs* — REITs outside the normal categories of office, retail and industrial property. As the term suggests, specialty REITs offer specific exposure to a niche sector of the property market, for example, healthcare properties, retirement and aged care properties, childcare properties, tourism properties, hotels, agribusiness properties (farms, feed-lots, orchards, vineyards), and even data centres (facilities purpose-built to house computer systems and associated equipment: these often need specialised environmental and security protection, and large, reliable power sources).

Examples of specialty REITs include National Storage REIT, which invests in self-storage centres; Generation Healthcare, which is the only currently listed REIT that invests solely in healthcare assets; Ingenia Communities Group, which owns a portfolio of 'seniors living' properties; and APDC Group, which owns three data centres, which it leases to listed data centre operator NEXT DC Limited.

Telecommunications services

Prior to the float of the first portion of Telstra shares in November 1997, the *Telecommunications* sector didn't exist. An index was created to hold Telstra, which was subsequently joined by Cable & Wireless Optus (now owned by Singapore Telecom) and Telecom New Zealand.

At 6 per cent of the S&P/ASX 200 Index, the sector holds Telstra, Spark New Zealand (formerly Telecom New Zealand), telecommunications services providers TPG Telecom, M2 Group, Macquarie Telecom, Kiwi fixed-line communications company Chorus, and a host of smaller telecommunications and services providers.

Utilities

A *utility* is a business that provides an essential service, such as electric power, telephone, natural gas, water and sewerage. *Infrastructure* is defined by the huge fixed assets that provide these services. Infrastructure can be economic infrastructure, such as the physical systems used to provide electric power, gas, water and sewerage; roads, railways, ports and airports; and telecommunications installations. The sector can be extended to social infrastructure, including hospitals, schools, parks and sporting facilities.

Traditionally, governments provided the infrastructure and ran the utilities, which were monopolies. However, a wave of privatisation and deregulation in the 1980s and 1990s allowed for competition among utilities and opened them to private ownership.

The utilities sector on the ASX is usually considered an economically defensive sector — in theory, a sector that does not fluctuate with economic and market cycles — and which pays a reliable dividend stream, but full franking (see Chapter 10) is not uniform. However, the low-interest-rate environment of the 2010s has seen share investors come to view the utilities as a relatively safe source of strong yields.

The utilities sector encompasses companies considered to be electric, gas or water utilities, or companies that operate as independent producers and/or distributors of power. The major stocks include AGL Energy (formerly the Australian Gas Light Company, which was listed in 1871), electricity and gas transmission and distribution group AusNet Services, gas pipeline operator APA Group, energy utility asset owner DUET Group, electricity distributor Spark Infrastructure, plus three New Zealand stocks: Electricity producers Mighty River Power and Meridian Energy, and electricity and natural gas retailer Genesis Energy.

Infrastructure assets can be long-term cash flow generators — almost an Australian equivalent to the US 30-year bond, which Australia doesn't have. Professional investors like infrastructure assets, which are known as *patronage* assets because everyone uses them. These assets generate a long-term cash flow with a high yield and little volatility, and prior to the GFC were considered one of the best defensive sectors for investors in the event of a bear market.

Infrastructure and utilities stocks are certainly not a set-and-forget investment, with potential regulatory issues often affecting stock value.

Industrials

The *GICS Industrials* sector is a grab-bag that accounts for 7.1 per cent of the S&P/ASX 200 Index. That's to be expected from a sector designed to include companies involved in the manufacture and distribution of capital goods, including aerospace and defence, construction, engineering and building products, electrical equipment and industrial machinery; the provision of commercial services and supplies, including printing, data processing, employment, and environmental and office services; and the provision of transportation services, including airlines, couriers, marine, and road and rail transportation infrastructure.

Leading the sector are construction and engineering giant CIMIC Group (formerly known as Leighton), global pallet and information management company Brambles, employment website Seek, and the big transport stocks: Toll road operator Transurban, airlines Qantas, Virgin Australia and Air New Zealand, airport operators Sydney Airport and Auckland International Airport, transport infrastructure group Asciano, and the big engineering services providers such as Downer and Monadelphous.

Rounding out the sector are manufacturing survivors such as shipbuilder Austal and household and commercial premises fittings maker GWA Group, which still makes household names such as Dorf tapwear, Caroma baths and showers, Clark kitchen sinks and laundry tubs, Gainsborough doors and handles, and Gliderol garage doors.

Consumer Staples

The *Consumer Staples* sector is the fifth-largest in the S&P/ASX 200 Index, representing 6.6 per cent of index capitalisation. It holds the stocks that make and sell items that are considered essential household spending — although some people may argue the toss on some of these. For example, if you're not fond of a tipple, you may wonder why brewing and wine group Foster's is a 'staple' of the consumer diet, although for many Australians, it is!

Supermarket giants Woolworths (Safeway) and Wesfarmers (owner of Coles Group) are part of the sector for their food-retailing reach, but these companies also have discount stores (Woolies has Big W; Coles has Target and Kmart). Coles Group's other store brands include hardware chain Bunnings, Liquorland and Officeworks, while Woolies' stores also include Dan Murphy's and BWS, among others.

Grocery wholesaler Metcash is part of the Consumer Staples sector, as are beverage group Coca-Cola Amatil, the world's second-largest bottler of Coca-Cola trademark products (and the largest in terms of geographical spread), vitamins and nutritional supplements maker Blackmores and personal care and hygiene products company Asaleo Care. New Zealand-based dairy products group Fonterra is also part of the sector, as are Australian food producers Bega Cheese (dairy), Warrnambool Cheese & Butter (dairy), Australian Agricultural Company (beef), Tassal (fish) and Select Harvests (almonds), as well as global wine group Treasury Wine Estates.

Consumer Discretionary

Amounting to 4 per cent of the S&P/ASX 200, the *Consumer Discretionary* sector comprises stocks whose business depends on non-essential consumer spending, whether directly through buying their products, or indirectly, for example advertising. The Consumer Discretionary sector contains the stocks that make and sell products to consumers, operating as a *cyclical* sector, which is highly dependent on the health of the economy (consumer spending makes up two-thirds of the Australian economy).

The big media groups are here: News Corporation, Fairfax Media, Seven West Media, Nine Entertainment, Ten Network and Sky Network Television, plus radio network Southern Cross Media. Media stocks are considered especially cyclical because of their heavy reliance on the strength of advertising revenue, which in turn depends on the level of economic activity.

Gaming and leisure heavyweights Crown Resorts (casinos), The Star Entertainment Group (casinos), Tabcorp (TABs, gaming and racing media), Tatts Group (lotteries and wagering), SkyCity Entertainment Group (owner of casinos in Australia and New Zealand) and global poker machine business Aristocrat Leisure are there, as are the big internet-based sales businesses, jobs website seek.com.au, REA Group (operator of real estate sales website realestate.com.au), auto sales website carsales.com and travel and accommodation booking site webjet.com.au.

The Consumer Discretionary sector contains household-name retailers, such as department store icon Myer Holdings; electronic goods, homewares and furniture retailer Harvey Norman; electronic goods and music retailer JB Hi-Fi; travel agency chain Flight Centre; clothing retailers Oroton, Noni B and Kathmandu; Premier Investments, which owns Smiggles, Peter Alexander, Just Jeans, Jay Jays, Portmans, Jacqui E and Dotti; and global surfwear and youth lifestyle clothing group Billabong International. Also included are lighting retailer Beacon Lighting;

car-part seller Super Cheap Auto; four-wheel-drive accessories maker ARB; and the Pacific Brands portfolio of Australian clothing, bedware and footwear brands, which includes Bonds, Berlei, Jockey, Sheridan and Tontine.

Consumer Discretionary also hosts such diverse stocks as funeral director InvoCare, appliance maker Breville, pizza chain Domino's, furniture retailer Nick Scali and ferry operator Sealink Travel.

Healthcare

Making up 6 per cent of the S&P/ASX 200 Index, the *Healthcare* sector includes Australia's major global medical device makers, the hearing-implant specialist Cochlear and sleep-disordered breathing-device manufacturer ResMed. It also includes global plasma products and vaccine group CSL (the former Commonwealth Serum Laboratories, one of Australia's first privatisations, listed in 1994). Drugmakers, wholesalers and retail pharmacy operators Sigma and Australian Pharmaceutical Industries are part of the sector, as are medical diagnostics company Sonic Healthcare, hospital operator Ramsay Health Care, hospital and pathology business Healthscope, medical and pathology centre operator Primary Health Care, and healthcare and protective products maker Ansell, as well as a host of drug and diagnostics developers.

Information Technology

The *Information Technology* sector is headlined by global share registry and trading systems operator Computershare; sharemarket information and trading systems developer IRESS Market Technology; IT services business SMS Management & Technology; financial management software groups Reckon, MYOB and Technology One; data centre operator NEXT DC; technology consultant DWS Advanced; and 'big data' specialist UXC. It also holds stocks as varied as financial technology company Praemium, aerial imaging company Nearmap, and internet domain name registrar and managed services business Melbourne IT.

Materials

The *Materials* sector is the second-largest in the S&P/ASX 200 Index, accounting for 15 per cent of index capitalisation. It straddles the industrial and resources worlds, containing packaging giants Amcor and Orora, chemicals groups Orica, Incitec Pivot and Nufarm, and the well-established companies that provide materials for the Australian building and construction industries — the likes of Boral, CSR, James Hardie, Adelaide Brighton, DuluxGroup and Brickworks (which also holds a substantial share portfolio).

At the top of the materials sectors are Australia's big miners, led by global diversified mining giants BHP Billiton and Rio Tinto, the largest and third-largest mining companies in the world (split by Brazil's Vale). Australia's largest gold producer, Newcrest Mining, is there, as is iron ore producer Fortescue Metals, copper and gold miner OZ Minerals, aluminium producer Alumina and copper miner Sandfire Resources. Then come troubled steel-makers BlueScope Steel and Arrium, and Sims Metal Management, the world's largest metal recycler. Australia's big mineral sands producer Iluka is there, as is Zimplats, which mines platinum in Africa. Also included are nickel producers Western Areas, Panoramic Resources and Mirabela Nickel.

Energy

Weighing in at 5 per cent of the S&P/ASX 200 Index, the *Energy* sector holds Australia's big petroleum producers, Woodside Petroleum, Origin Energy (which also generates electricity), Santos, Oil Search, AWE, Drillsearch Energy and Beach Energy, as well as petrol marketer Caltex Australia. Gas players Karoon Gas and Liquefied Natural Gas (LNG), and coal producers New Hope, Whitehaven Coal and Yancoal Australia are sector stocks, as well as African uranium miner Paladin Energy and local producer ERA. Rounding out the Energy sector heavyweights is engineering group WorleyParsons, which provides professional services to the energy and resources industries.

Biotech

Approximately 130 true *Biotech* stocks are on the Australian Securities Exchange (ASX) — companies involved in drug discovery and development, diagnostics or medical devices. However, only a handful of these are profitable industrials (those in the GICS Healthcare sector); the rest are at various stages on the long path to commercialisation of drugs, diagnostics and medical devices.

Success in Biotech investment requires patience.
A pharmaceutical company is required to conduct extensive pre-clinical laboratory testing before testing a compound in humans can begin. Pre-clinical trials involve thorough testing of the compound in animals (for example, mice) to prove the compound appears to be safe, and possibly effective in mammals.

Pre-clinical testing usually takes three to four years, and has a success rate of about 1 per cent. If successful, the company provides the relevant information to the US Food and Drug Administration (FDA), requesting approval to commence testing the drug in humans — known as an Investigational New Drug (IND) application. If the FDA approves the IND (the review takes 30 days), the company is cleared to test the compound in human volunteers in Phase I clinical trials. These trials aim to determine how the drug acts in the human body, and to investigate any side effects that may occur as dosage levels are increased. Phase I usually lasts from several months to one year.

Once a drug has been shown to be safe in Phase I, Phase II trials aim to evaluate the efficacy — the clinical effect — of the new treatment, in a testing period that may last from several months to two years. Phase II trials determine the dosage and treatment schedules. Phase II is where most experimental drugs fail — approximately only 30 per cent of drug candidates successfully complete both Phase I and Phase II testing.

Phase III trials then seek to confirm the clinical benefits of the drug in large numbers of patients; this large-scale testing aims to provide a more thorough understanding of the drug's effectiveness, benefits, and the range and severity of possible adverse side effects. Phase III trials usually take one to four years to complete.

Upon successful completion of Phase III, the pharmaceutical company submits the results of all the studies to the FDA so as to obtain a New Drug Application (NDA), which means that the drug can be sold to the public. The FDA has initiated a fast-track approval process for new drugs seen to potentially satisfy a significant unmet therapeutic need. For example, NDA approval for the AIDS drug treatment, indinavir, took just 42 days.

The irony is that despite working with such long lead times, the Biotech sector is dominated on the stock market by retail investors, who think in the short term. Like resources exploration, Biotech attracts an announcement-driven trading mentality. Companies trade very strongly on the expectation of a clinical trial result, and if the result is not what the market wants to hear, the stock gets punished.

Australian drug developers generally lack the money to take a discovery from the lab bench to the market, and need to bring in partners along the way. It costs about $25 million US dollars for a drug candidate to complete Phase I and II trials. Many Australian

Biotechs have a solid candidate, but they don't have that sort of money — meaning that they'll need a partner with deep pockets. Smart investors understand that the further companies move along the pathway, the probability of success, the value and the ability to do a deal with a partner all increase.

Cleantech

The latest technological wave to grab the attention of investors is *Cleantech*. This term is used to describe companies involved in renewable energy, carbon dioxide emissions control, biofuels, energy efficiency, water purification technology, salinity, carbon sequestration projects, alternative engine technology, electrical switching devices, clean coal technologies and new materials.

The Australian market has many stocks that qualify as Cleantech candidates. The grouping is similar to Biotech in that many of the stocks involved are yet to commercialise their technologies. But profitable companies such as waste handling and recycling companies Cleanaway (formerly Transpacific Industries) and Tox Free Solutions are showing that Cleantech operations are no barrier to strong financial performance.

Exploring Resources

The GICS sectors of Energy and Materials contain the Australian stock market's *Resources* stocks. Because of Australia's mineral wealth, the sharemarket is renowned overseas as a Resources market. Some international investors still appear to regard Australia as little more than a gigantic mine to be invested in only when commodity prices are rising. These overseas investors hope to get a double benefit if share prices and the Australian dollar are rising.

In the mid-1980s, the Resources sector represented about two-thirds of the Australian sharemarket's capitalisation; now it accounts for about 19 per cent (Table 8-1 illustrates how the mineral exports market has changed since the mid-1990s) and 38 per cent of listed companies by number. Although Resources activity has grown tremendously, the difference is better explained by the fact that far more of the depth and breadth of the Australian economy has moved on to the sharemarket, and the industrial side of the market has swelled.

Table 8-1   Value of Australian Mineral and Petroleum Exports

Commodity	1994–95 Export Value ($m)	2014–15 Export Value ($m)	Change (%)
Energy			
Crude oil	2,581	8,658	235
LNG	1,796	16,924	842
LPG	230	811	253
Bunker fuel	764	1540	101
Other petroleum	1,075	551	−49
Coal	10,276	37,909	269
Uranium	281	532	89
Total Energy	17,003	66,907	293
Metals and Minerals			
Aluminium (all forms)	6,772	11,119	64
Copper (all forms)	1,192	8,514	614
Gold	7,012	13,052	86
Iron ore	4,148	54,411	1212
Iron and steel	2,056	692	−66
Lead (all forms)	638	1,853	190
Manganese	302	1,272	321
Mineral sands (titanium)	972	1,081	11
Nickel	1,465	3,584	145
Silver	70	231	230
Tin	75	150	100
Zinc (all forms)	1,160	3,095	167
Zircon	232	263	13
Diamonds	718	313	−56
Other minerals	2,360	5,416	129
Total Metals and Minerals	29,172	105,047	260
Total	46,175	171,954	272
% of GDP	6	12	100
GDP	747,264	1,580,000	111

Source: Australian Bureau of Statistics, September 2015, International Trade catalogue no. 5465.0

Mining and petroleum drilling companies extract, process and sell Australia's minerals, oil and gas. Australia possesses virtually the full set of mineral commodities, making for one colossal industry.

The main reason why investors invest in resources is to capture the upside of the global economic cycle, and to have commodity price exposure in the portfolio for diversification purposes. Australia's resource companies have enjoyed several years in the sun, powered by the rise in commodity prices, driven by the massive industrial expansion in China.

Between 2000 and 2010, commodity prices racked up huge rises: Alumina by 60 per cent, copper by 340 per cent, lead by 350 per cent, nickel by 170 per cent, zinc by 70 per cent, tin by 300 per cent and oil by 200 per cent. Even the bulk commodities, iron ore, thermal (power) coal and coking (steel-making) coal, were up by 530 per cent, 260 per cent and 420 per cent respectively, driven by established markets like Japan's and China's — and to a lesser extent, India's — increased need for steel and power.

As the massive Chinese industrial expansion hoovered up Australian commodities as fast as they could be mined or pumped, the commodity price strength helped push many Australian miners' share prices to record levels. In 2010, the Reserve Bank of Australia (RBA) said that the resources boom in Australia fuelled by Asian demand for minerals could last 20 years.

The Chinese annual GDP growth rate was the driving force for this expansion, averaging nearly 10 per cent between 1979 and 2014. While this breakneck pace was a massive factor in lifting hundreds of millions of Chinese people out of poverty, it was fuelled by massive investment in infrastructure, relying on low wages and polluting industries. A new Chinese leadership took over in 2013, and this government is trying to change the focus of the Chinese economy to domestic consumption, as is the case with other developed economies.

Consistent with this shift, China's economic growth rate has been declining, coming in at 6.9 per cent in the second half of 2015 — and economists anticipate that China's annual economic growth will fall further in the near future, as the country's economy takes on more characteristics of a developed-world market.

A growth beginning with a '6' is still huge for an already large economy — China's economy is a US$10.4 trillion beast — and the managed slowdown has been well-foreshadowed. However, this slowdown has had a major impact on commodity prices, along with the inevitable rising supply — as projects begun in the 2000-to-2010 boom-time come on stream — and shaky confidence in North America and Europe.

The upshot is that from the 2000s commodity-price peaks to mid-2015, alumina has fallen by 29 per cent, copper by 49 per cent, lead by 57 per cent, nickel by 79 per cent, zinc by 58 per cent, tin by 54 per cent and oil by 67 per cent. In the bulk commodities — Australia's major exports — iron ore is down 73 per cent, thermal coal down 77 per cent and coking coal has slumped by 72 per cent.

The major beneficiaries of the boom-time rise were the giants of the Australian resources market, BHP Billiton and Rio Tinto. These two offer a diversified exposure to a range of commodities. In BHP Billiton, for example, investors capture not just mineral diversification (coal, iron ore, copper, uranium and potash) but they also have petroleum working for them; BHP Billiton is a Top 50 global oil company in its own right. Rio Tinto offers diversified exposure in coal, iron ore, uranium, alumina, precious and base metals, diamonds and industrial minerals. The benefit of buying into BHP Billiton or Rio Tinto is the broad commodity diversification that you get within those stocks.

The slump in the iron ore price on the back of the Chinese slowdown hurt BHP Billiton and Rio Tinto, because iron ore is such a big contributor to their earnings: BHP is down 40 per cent from its peak price, while Rio Tinto is down 55 per cent. But the reckoning has been much tougher on the single-commodity, 'pure-play' iron ore producers (as in, they are purely influenced by the iron ore price), which do not have any diversification benefit: Fortescue Metals, for example, is down 84 per cent, while smaller iron ore miners Atlas Iron and Mount Gibson Iron are down 99 per cent and 95 per cent respectively. Ouch.

Other diversified miners operate in the base metals area, such as Independence Group (nickel, copper, gold, zinc and silver) and Metals X (tin and gold).

Some investors like to target their investment more specifically by buying pure-play companies like Newcrest Mining, Iluka, Sandfire Resources, Alumina and Western Areas, thereby taking a view on the specific commodities (gold, mineral sands, copper, aluminium and nickel respectively). In this way, the investor receives greater earnings leverage if their view on the commodity is right.

Other single-commodity exposures include Oz Minerals, Aeris Resources and Hillgrove Resources (copper); Panoramic Resources, Mincor Resources and Poseidon Nickel (nickel); and Energia Minerals (zinc). In mineral sands, Mineral Deposits has brought the Grande Côte project on-stream in Senegal, MZI Resources is developing the Keysbrook project in Western Australia, and Astron Corporation is developing both the Donald project in Victoria and the Niafarang project in Senegal.

In gold, Newcrest Mining dominates local production; other domestic producers include Northern Star Resources, Regis Resources, Beadell Resources, Evolution Mining, St Barbara, Doray Minerals, Resolute Mining, Alkane Resources and Silver Lake Resources. A number of ASX-listed stocks produce gold in other countries, including OceanaGold (New Zealand), Kingsgate Consolidated (Thailand) and AngloGold Ashanti (South Africa, Brazil, Argentina, Mali and Australia).

Emerging local gold producers include Bulletin Resources, Blackham Resources and Gold Road Resources, while ASX-listed companies poised to enter production overseas include Anova Metals (USA), West African Resources (Burkina Faso), Sumatra Copper & Gold (Indonesia) and Orinoco Gold (Brazil).

In oil and gas, the market hosts heavyweight producers Woodside Petroleum and Santos, as well as smaller producers such as Oil Search, Beach Energy, AWE, Senex Energy, New Zealand Oil & Gas, Cooper Energy, Bounty Oil & Gas, Strike Energy and Central Petroleum.

There is also a small group of Australian-listed players that operate in the US oil and gas industry, including Liquefied Natural Gas Limited, Sundance Energy, Samson Oil & Gas, and Maverick Drilling & Exploration and Incremental Oil & Gas.

The main issue for the investor contemplating the Resources sector is whether to take the lower-risk route — the large-cap diversified miners, such as BHP Billiton and Rio Tinto — or to invest in the pure-play companies, such as Iluka, Hillgrove Resources and Alumina, where you're taking a view on their specific commodities (mineral sands, copper and aluminium, respectively). The risk is higher with those companies, but you receive greater earnings leverage.

Even riskier are the highly speculative junior explorers, where the investor is looking for a strong capital gain related to specific projects that the company has.

Entering the mineral market

The prices of resource shares generally anticipate movements in commodity prices. Resource shares are attractive to buyers when the Australian currency is weak because the supply contracts of the miners are written mostly in US$, while they report their profits in A$. The Resources sector is even more attractive in times of economic expansion: World economic growth translates to growth in global industrial production, and Australian mineral commodity producers supply a great deal of the global industrial production.

Mining shares usually don't offer generous dividend payments. Mining companies have a stable cost of production and can usually predict their operating costs. These companies measure profits by sales income minus operating costs, so fluctuations in the prices of the commodities they mine — and in the A$/US$ exchange rate — are the key to their profitability.

The nation's two largest export commodities are coal and iron ore. Up until 2009, iron ore was mostly priced through annual discussions between Asian steel-makers and their (largely Australian) suppliers; but these days, the biggest influence on the price is the daily 'spot' price (for immediate delivery), although some purchasing contracts are still struck on forward (futures) pricing for particular indices of iron ore grades.

Up until recently, coking (steel-making) and thermal (electricity) coal prices were mostly determined by annual (or quarterly) negotiations between suppliers and users, but more recently (as prices have fallen) buyers have been keener to look at 'floating' prices based on benchmark indices for coal from different markets.

The prices of Australia's precious and base metals exports, however, are far more volatile, being set daily on the frenzied commodity exchanges of New York, Chicago and London.

Mineral exploration is an uncertain occupation. Companies look for deposits of resources, whether minerals or hydrocarbons (oil and gas), with varying degrees of success. Their experts must be able to interpret complex geological and other data and then find the deposits. They also have to find enough to mine economically. For example, in the exploration for oil and gas, about one in ten wells is successful. Australian investors are patient and have invested in minerals explorers such as Oil Search, which began looking for oil and gas in Papua New Guinea in 1931. The first revenues from this venture came in 1991, and the first dividend to shareholders followed a year later.

Exploring for resources

Since the beginnings of the stock exchange in Australia (refer to Chapter 2) the Resources sector has given the market a lot of its romance, in the tradition of the exploration company hitting paydirt with a drilling hole, resulting in a share price surge. In particular, the names of nickel explorers Poseidon and Tasminex live on as synonyms for instant riches — and the inevitable bust. On one day in January 1970, Tasminex shares surged from $3 to $96 on the basis of a false report that the company had struck nickel at Mount Venn in Western Australia. Fellow nickel explorer Poseidon made that jump look paltry, rocketing from 50 cents to $280 in a few months, on news that it had struck nickel nearby at Windarra.

It's legend that Poseidon — which actually did mine nickel at Windarra — eventually went into receivership in 1976 (although an unconnected company, Poseidon Nickel, is developing the multi-mine Windarra project), and that Tasminex never mined nickel at Mount Venn (now known as Tasmania Mines, the company mines magnetite — an iron ore used in the coal industry — in Tasmania. Mount Venn is now owned by a company called Global Metals Exploration, but it is a very long way from being mined). But if the great 1969–70 nickel rush has faded from memory, there are more recent reminders for stock market punters of share prices taking off for the stars.

In November 2001, explorer Minotaur Resources released drilling results from its Mount Woods joint venture in outback South Australia, showing a massive copper intersection at the Prominent Hill prospect, and triggering an 870 per cent rise in the Minotaur share price — from 17 cents to $1.65 — the day after the exploration results were announced. The stock peaked three weeks later at $2.55. Now owned by OZ Minerals, Prominent Hill produced its first copper–gold concentrate in February 2009.

Or, punters could look back to the uranium boom of 2005, in which internet security firm turned minerals explorer Fast Scout (now known as Strike Resources, which these days focuses on iron ore projects in Peru) out-Poseidoned Poseidon, rocketing 1,800 per cent in two days, after agreeing to buy a stake in some uranium exploration tenements. (It didn't even have to drill a hole, let alone find any of the stuff!)

In July 2006, explorer CuDeco's shares exploded from 30 cents to a peak of $10 in just a few days, on the release of spectacular drilling results from its Rocklands copper project in Queensland. But the ASX was not impressed, suspending the company for a week and requesting that it restate its estimates resource figure (as well as stopping the directors exercising share options, which were suddenly well in-the-money). The company filed a new resource estimate, more than halved in size. Reinstated to trading, the stock slumped 75 per cent in two days. CuDeco hopes to produce its first copper (plus gold and cobalt) from Rocklands in 2016.

More recently, in July 2012, nickel explorer Sirius Resources was trading at 5 cents until news of two huge nickel discoveries, first Nova, then Bollinger, in Western Australia's Fraser Range area sent the stock soaring to $5 by March 2013 — a 100-bagger. Sirius was taken over by Independence Group in 2015.

The excesses of the 1969–70 nickel boom prompted the first serious look at corporate governance in Australia. These days, the veracity of stock exchange announcements — and the qualifications of the geologists who sign them — are strictly enforced. A rigid system is in place: The Joint Ore Reserve Committee (JORC) Code for Reporting Mineral Resources and Reserves, which defines the criteria for publicly reporting resources and reserves.

Under the JORC code, a company proceeds from resource to reserve: An *ore reserve* is considered to be the economically mineable part of a measured or indicated mineral resource. Ore reserves are subdivided into *probable reserves* and *proved reserves*. Announcements must be signed off by a 'competent person', which means a member of either the Australian Institute of Mining and Metallurgy or the Australian Institute of Geoscientists.

Despite the tighter regulation of announcements and the claims made in them, some tricks of the trade remain. Prime among these are *nearology* and *flexibility*. An outbreak of nearology occurs when one spectacular drilling result sparks a flurry of announcements from any company with ground that shares the same postcode. In the past decade, nearology has been seen in the Gawler Craton (SA), the Musgrave Ranges (SA/NT border), the East Kimberley region (WA) and the Bryah Basin (WA).

After Sandfire Resources' breakthrough copper–gold discovery at De Grussa in the Bryah Basin in May 2009, the share prices of more than 20 junior companies with exploration projects in the region pricked up. Flexibility occurs when a particular commodity is running hot, and deposits can be re-packaged to take advantage. For example, if nickel is running, gold projects can be re-presented as nickel projects. Or the projects could be copper projects under the right circumstances, or the drilling data can be re-interpreted as highly prospective for diamonds.

Certainly, the potential for excitement in the explorers never goes away. Investors have to beware of the way that announcements are presented because the Australian stock market hosts explorers looking for virtually everything that can be mined.

The explorers — whether looking for minerals or hydrocarbons — are highly speculative. In fact, you're not investing when you play in this market, you're punting. The risk is higher because no financial fundamentals exist at all. Rather, you're looking for a strong capital gain related to the company's specific drilling programs or projects. This mode of sharemarket participation is very announcement driven and fits the day-trader mentality of trading momentum to a tee.

In the 2000s, nickel explorers were the ones running when the nickel price went to $17,000 a tonne. Then copper stocks were hot, then coal, then iron ore, then uranium was on the go. At these times, the cafés and bars in West Perth — the home of the nation's minerals explorers — are abuzz with activity. But investors have to be wary of the odd company that decides that minerals exploration is hot, dry and remote work, and that it is easier by far to mine the sharemarket.

Eureka! It's uranium

Between 2002 and 2007 the sharemarket saw a boom in uranium, and it began to benefit from changing views regarding nuclear energy as an energy source that doesn't contribute to carbon dioxide emissions, the growing need for non-fossil fuel power sources and China's economic growth story. Australia is a major player in the uranium industry; it's the equal-largest supplier of the commodity with Kazakhstan and Canada, with about 20 per cent of the market each. All of Australia's production is exported; in 2014–15, Australia exported 5,515 tonnes of uranium oxide (or 'yellowcake') worth about $532 million.

But Australia has the largest known recoverable resources of any country. It has just under one-quarter of known recoverable resources, 1.4 times the quantity of recoverable resources of Kazakhstan and 2.6 times those of Canada. Australia has the world's largest deposit of uranium oxide, at Olympic Dam in South Australia. Australia's uranium resources are also considered cheaper to extract than other countries' deposits. Of Australia's recoverable resources, 37 per cent are expected to cost less than US$40 a pound to extract and 27 per cent less than US$80 a pound.

For nearly 30 years, uranium mining in Australia was restricted under a 'three mines' policy, which allowed mining only at the Ranger mine in the Northern Territory (owned by Energy Resources of Australia (ERA), which is 68 per cent owned by Rio Tinto), the Olympic Dam mine in South Australia (formerly owned by WMC Resources, now owned by BHP Billiton) and the Beverley mine in South Australia (owned by Heathgate Resources, a subsidiary of General Atomic of the USA). Beverley closed in 2014.

Although the 'three mines' policy was ditched in 1996, there are still only three operating mines: Ranger, Olympic Dam and the Four Mile deposit in South Australia, just a few kilometres from Beverley, which was approved in July 2009. Discovered in 2005, the Four Mile deposit was the biggest uranium discovery in Australia for 25 years. Heathgate Resources runs the project.

Other mines have been foreshadowed in South Australia and Western Australia, with Toro Energy's Wiluna project in the latter expected to enter production in 2016. The proposed Kintyre mine in the Pilbara region of Western Australia, owned by Canadian company Cameco (the world's biggest uranium miner), was conditionally approved by the Australian government in April 2015.

Yellowcake entered the GFC trading at a record spot price of US$136 a pound in mid-2007 — up from US$7 a pound in 2000 — but the slump took prices down to about US$40 in 2010. By March 2011, uranium had recovered to above US$70, but the disaster at Fukushima in Japan — after which Japan's entire nuclear reactor fleet was taken offline — saw it plunge to US$28 in just a few months. In mid-2015, the Japanese had still not re-started their nuclear power supply, but uranium had edged back up to US$36.25 a pound.

Notwithstanding the Fukushima disaster, in late 2011 BHP Billiton committed to a US$30 billion expansion of the Olympic Dam copper/gold/uranium mine, to make it potentially the world's largest uranium mine and the second-largest copper mine. Falling commodity prices in the wake of the China slowdown (check out the earlier section, 'Exploring resources' for more on this) influenced BHP to shelve the plan, but by mid-2015 the mining giant was keen to get going on this project again.

ERA is the Australian sharemarket's only pure-play local uranium producer, and Paladin Energy is the only other miner. Paladin mines uranium at its Langer Heinrich project in Namibia and its Kayelekera project in Malawi. Paladin (which is also listed in Canada) also owns the Valhalla and Skal uranium deposits in Queensland and the Manyingee and Oobagooma projects in Western Australia. Paladin is living testament to the uranium boom — and bust. As the uranium price rose from US$10 a pound at the end of 2002 to $140 in mid-2007, Paladin surged from 1.6 cents to $10.80 (the peak coincided with the first production from Langer Heinrich). But as the uranium price plunged post-Fukushima, Paladin sank back to the 20–40 cent range, where it remains.

ERA was also planning an expansion of Ranger, but put that plan on ice in June 2015 due to weak uranium prices. (Ranger is on a lease and is surrounded by Kakadu National Park, and the expansion plans had attracted controversy.) From a 2009 peak above $16.50, ERA's share price had slid to 35 cents by mid-2015.

Other Australian uranium hopefuls include Vimy Resources, Cauldron Energy, Alligator Energy, Summit Resources and Energy Metals. Uranium mining has a problem because, not only does the normal exploration risk of defining a resource and economic reserve and taking the project through to mining exist, you also require government permission to mine uranium. Then, a company has to be allowed to export it.

Producing platinum

Australian explorers are trying to crack the geological secrets of the land for missing commodities. For example, the platinum group metals — platinum, palladium, rhodium, ruthenium, iridium and osmium — are not yet mined. A viable deposit of platinum group metals (PGMs) is the Holy Grail of Australian mining. Companies such as Rimfire Pacific Mining (which is exploring around Australia's only historic platinum mine, at Fifield in New South Wales), Platina Resources and Impact Minerals are attempting to hit the jackpot. Two platinum producers are listed on the ASX — Aquarius Platinum and Zimplats — but their mines are in Africa. The ASX-listed Nkwe Platinum hopes to join them soon, with its Garatau project in South Africa.

Rare earths

Another gap in the mineral portfolio was filled by Lynas Corporation, whose rare earths deposit at Mount Weld in Western Australia is a world-class resource of these 17 chemically similar rare metallic elements. The market for these metals is growing rapidly in China, Japan, Europe and North America because the materials are used in the electronics, automobile, glass and telecommunications industries. Mount Weld is considered to be richest deposit of rare earths in the world, and the first non-Chinese supplier of rare earths to the global market. Based on the resource size, Mount Weld could supply 10 per cent of world demand for rare earths — a market worth $1.25 billion a year — for 20 years.

Lynas' strategy is to create a reliable, fully integrated source of rare earths from mine through to customers. Lynas built a concentration plant in Western Australia and a processing plant in Malaysia, and began production in 2011, with a deal struck in November 2010 for Japanese buyers to take 30 per cent of annual production. But Lynas has been slammed by a combination of the downturn in rare earths prices, continued operational difficulties and community opposition to its processing plant in Malaysia, and the company is operating at break-even.

Lynas Corporation provides another example of how fraught with difficulty investing in mining can be. When the company bought the Mount Weld deposit from Rio Tinto back in 2001 for $12 million, the shares were trading at around 13 cents and the company was worth about $9 million. The offtake agreement with the Japanese customers in November 2010, which effectively gave the green light for production to start, lifted the company's share price to $1.61 and its market value to $2.7 billion. Beginning production in 2011 saw Lynas shares surge to $2.38, for a valuation of $3.5 billion. But the litany of pitfalls the company has since faced saw the share price slide to 3.7 cents in mid-2015, for a valuation of $129 million.

Gold producer Alkane Resources is developing its Dubbo zirconia project in New South Wales, built around one of the world's largest in-ground resources of rare metals and rare earths. At Dubbo, Alkane plans to produce zirconium, niobium, yttrium and rare earth elements — mainly lanthanum and cerium — as well as neodymium, praseodymium, dysprosium and terbium. Explorer Arafura Resources also hopes to produce ten rare earth elements — primarily neodymium, praseodymium, dysprosium, europium and yttrium — from its Nolans Bore rare earths deposit in the Northern Territory.

Buying gold: A special case

Gold has the same structural issues as other resources. However, gold is a special case. The problem is that the gold market is artificial. The physical market — the annual trade in gold mined — is dwarfed by the market in gold derivatives: Exchange-traded commodities (ETCs) backed by gold, gold futures and options contracts. US gold analyst Paul van Eeden has calculated that daily trade in gold derivatives roughly equals the amount of actual physical gold produced each year. Van Eeden estimates that the actual uses of gold — jewellery, industrial and dental — account for about seven days' worth of trading on the gold markets a year. Miners and consumers of gold are bit players on the gold-mining stage; the derivatives market controls the gold price. Gold is not a supply/demand-driven market. The exchange rate of gold is market driven because the price is determined by the value of the US dollar.

The trick to investing in gold stocks is to identify companies that have a mine life long enough to be around when the next big gold rally arrives, whenever that happens — not a recommended investment strategy for an average investor!

Investors interested in gold can find an alternative to gold stocks. The ASX has two vehicles that enable retail investors to buy gold in its own right. The first of these products, Gold Bullion Securities (ASX code: GOLD) was launched in March 2003. Each GOLD security gives the investor ownership of one-tenth of an ounce of gold bullion, held in the London vaults of custodian bank HSBC Bank USA. GOLD securities may be sold at any time on the ASX, or (subject to certain conditions and fees applying) holders may redeem them at any time for cash or in exchange for gold bars. The price of a GOLD security is one-tenth of the A$ gold price.

Later in 2003, GOLDs were joined on the ASX by the Perth Mint Gold Quoted Product, or PMG (ASX code: PMGOLD), which is a *security* (technically a warrant) that gives you the right to own one-hundredth of an ounce of gold. That right may be bought and sold on the stock exchange. The gold is held in Perth as bar or coin, and guaranteed by the Western Australian Government.

Both products enable investors to trade in gold as if the investors owned physical bullion. This type of investing is a very clean and efficient way of 'playing' the gold price; instead of buying the corporate risk attached to a gold miner, an investor buying either GOLDs or PMGs is only 'buying' the gold price. There are no company-specific factors like mine life, resource security or hedging activity to complicate matters. The stocks simply track the A$ gold price very closely, and may be sold at any time on the ASX. There is brokerage on the purchase or sale, and the management expense ratio (MER) of the investment is 0.40 per cent a year.

Gold is also tradeable on the ASX through a range of exchange-traded products (ETPs), which offer exposure, through a listed stock, to the price changes of physical gold. ETPs also offer an investment in physical silver, platinum, palladium, and a basket of the three, plus gold.

Finding Specialised Stocks

Some of the stocks in your portfolio fulfil specialised roles. For example, those in listed investment companies widen your investment in the market dramatically. If you feel you don't know enough about the market and lack confidence, unit trusts may be the way to go. Other types of investment also exist that can offer you specific tax advantages.

Listed investment companies (LICs)

Unit trusts are professionally managed and follow a diversification and asset allocation strategy that's available only to the most sophisticated sharemarket investors. Two types of trusts exist — trusts that are listed on the sharemarket and trusts that are not. *Listed investment companies* (LICs) own a portfolio of other listed shares; in effect, these companies operate as a share that invests in other shares. Like their unlisted cousins, listed investment companies offer built-in diversification and professional management at a cheaper rate for investors.

Non-listed equity trusts are very popular, but the industry often comes under fire for the high fees it charges investors. LICs are more competitive because the brokerage fee on the purchase of a LIC is usually about half the entry fee of an equity trust. The annual management fee for a listed trust is even smaller.

The share price of a LIC tends to fluctuate around (but mostly under) its asset backing or the value of its *net tangible assets* (NTA). The NTA is the market value of that company's share portfolio divided by the number of shares on issue. Sometimes the share price of a LIC can fall below NTA, and investors may buy an interest in the portfolio for less than the cost of establishing that portfolio. For example, over the ten years to June 2015, LIC Argo Investments traded at a discount to NTA of up to 9.3 per cent and a premium to its worth of as much as 17.3 per cent.

An equity trust is *open-ended* and the value of the underlying units in an equity trust is determined by the NTA. An investor in an equity trust buys the units by paying the NTA plus fees. LICs are *closed-end* investment vehicles because, after the initial capital raising, the shares trade at a price set by the market. (No new money comes into the fund unless new shares are issued or through a dividend reinvestment plan.) As with any other stock, supply and demand as well as the health of the sharemarket affects the share price.

Historically, during stronger market phases, the investment companies are at a premium to NTA. Buying at a premium to NTA works against the investor because the trading opportunity lies in riding the move from discount to premium. Longer-term investors can have an investment that tracks the market. Long-term investors who buy investment companies at deep discounts to asset backing are rewarded because their original investment keeps working for them over the years. At June 2015, about 77 per cent of Australian LICs were trading at a discount: The average discount was 12.4 per cent.

LICs are the tortoises of the sharemarket. They never pick up speed but, over time, generally achieve returns in line with the market average. Selecting a LIC on the basis of discount to NTA may not be the best strategy: The better-performing LICs trade at a premium, and the poor performers often trade at a discount. The most important criterion in evaluating a LIC is its track record.

LICs are permitted to report NTA figures before and after provision for unrealised capital gains. Some of the investment companies aim to make a profit and pay a dividend purely from the dividend flow in their portfolio. Others aim to add to profit by trading the portfolio. Most LICs distribute income in the form of fully franked dividends. For LICs with a dividend reinvestment plan, investors can choose to increase their investment exposure rather than receiving cash.

The better-performing LICs have outperformed the equity market accumulation indices (which count dividends as reinvested) over quite long periods. For example, according to Zenith Investment Partners, since its inception in 1946 — Argo was started by a group of South Australian stockbrokers that included cricket legend Sir Donald Bradman — Argo has earned a total return (capital gain plus dividends) of 9.9 per cent a year, versus 7.2 per cent for the S&P/ASX 300 Accumulation Index (and its predecessors.) Australian United Investments and Choiseul are the best-performing LICs, in terms of long-term growth in NTA.

The LIC market

The LIC market in Australia is relatively small — about $27 billion, compared to $446 billion in unlisted Australian equity trusts — and is dominated by longstanding companies like Australian Foundation Investment Company (AFIC) at $6.9 billion and Argo Investments at $5.4 billion in size. AFIC was founded in 1928 and closely aligned with the JBWere group, while Argo Investments was founded in 1946 in Adelaide by a group of stockbrokers that included the world's greatest cricketer, Sir Donald Bradman.

There are 65 LICs listed on the ASX, most of which invest in Australian shares. Those with a large-capitalisation Australian stocks focus include AFIC, Argo, Australian United Investments (AUI), Milton Corporation, Carlton Investments and Djerriwarrh Investments (which specialises in the buy-and-write options strategy). Those with a small-capitalisation Australian stocks focus include Mirrabooka Investments, WAM Capital, OzGrowth and WestOz Investment Co.

Globally focused LICs include Templeton Global Growth, Platinum Capital, Hunter Hall Global Value, Magellan Flagship Fund, PM Capital Global Opportunities and AMP Capital China Growth, which is entirely focused on China 'A' shares (stocks traded on the Shanghai and Shenzhen stock exchanges).

Other LICs with a specific focus include Contango Microcap and Acorn Capital Investment Fund, which mainly target Australian 'microcap' stocks; Australian Leaders Fund, Cadence Capital and NAOS Emerging Opportunities Company, which are 'long–short' funds, meaning they can short-sell stocks (sell them without owning them by borrowing the stock, hoping to profit from a price fall).

Exchange-traded funds (ETFs)

Exchange-traded funds (ETFs) are one of the fastest-growing investment products in the world. An ETF is effectively a stock that represents a portfolio. For example, the StreetTracks S&P/ASX 200 Fund (issued by State Street Global Advisors; ASX code: STW) is designed to closely track the performance of the S&P/ASX 200 Index, because it comprises all of the companies in the index.

Like shares, ETFs are traded on ASX Trade, the ASX's electronic trading system, and settled through the CHESS clearing system. Like equity funds, ETFs offer an individual investor a simple means of gaining exposure to a portfolio of shares (or other assets). But ETFs are much cheaper.

For a start, no entry fees (often up to 5 per cent in older-style retail-managed funds) or exit fees exist for retail investors, who pay brokerage only when buying or selling the ETF units, and no minimum transaction size exists either. And the ongoing *management expense ratio* (MER) — the cost of investing in a managed fund — is much lower than that in the typical managed fund. The MER of a standard retail equity trust is typically 1.4 per cent. An index ETF could be managed for as low as 0.09 per cent a year.

There are 123 ETFs listed on the ASX, each giving single-stock exposure to an index, asset class, portfolio, strategy, commodity or currency. The sector is worth $18.48 billion. ETFs are a fast-growing sector of the investment market: They're much cheaper than managed funds, with no entry and exit fees, and an annual fee that can be as low as five basis points (0.05 per cent) a year, or up to 0.7–0.8 per cent a year for more specialised ETFs. Also, investors only pay normal ASX brokerage when buying and selling ETFs.

One way to use ETFs is as the core holding in a 'core/satellite' strategy, which combines low-MER passive funds with the outperformance potential of alternative investments. The investor gets the performance of the sharemarket as cheaply as possible, and seeks outperformance through an aggressive allocation to, for example, absolute-return fund managers.

ETFs are the cheapest way that an individual investor can 'buy' the overall market. ETFs provide simple, easy diversification with the great advantage of the liquidity of a stock exchange listing.

Through ETFs, Australian investors can invest in a wide range of Australian and global share indices, fixed interest, cash, currencies, commodities, tailored portfolios, investment strategies and 'styles' (for example, some investment managers look mainly for 'value' stocks, others are 'growth' stock specialists: Refer to Chapter 5 for an explanation of these terms). Most global ETF exposures are denominated in US$ and *unhedged* (meaning that investors are exposed to currency fluctuations), but some are hedged back into A$.

ETFs share three main characteristics:

- Open-end rather than closed-end funds. This means that the number of units on issue and available to be traded on the stock exchange will fluctuate, according to demand.

- Involved in a simultaneous primary market (for ongoing unit creation and redemption) and secondary market, which is traded on the exchange.

- Designed to ensure that the unit price on the secondary market does not diverge too far from the net asset value (NAV) of the units.

How index ETFs work is that institutional investors operate in the primary market by creating and redeeming units *in specie* (in kind). Every day, the ETF manager announces a basket of shares (or bonds, or property trusts) that an institution must hand over to own a certain minimum parcel of units in the ETF. Retail investors buy and sell the units on the market, for the market price. An actively managed ETF differs in that investors can subscribe for and redeem units in cash: The prospectus stays open all the time.

Deciding What to Buy

With the market divided into specific sectors, you can get a feel for the sectors with which you're most comfortable. Some sectors need a bit more research and effort in order to make successful investments; resources and some of the telecommunications companies operate in a complex environment. As with all share investment, the more you know about the companies that you invest in, the sounder your investment.

Buying what you know

If you use a company's goods or services, you know that company well, and you understand what makes them attractive to consumers. You can see where the revenue is coming from to pay you, as a shareholder, your earnings stream and dividend wage.

One of the annoying (because it's true) clichés of the sharemarket is that if you can't explain to someone sitting next to you at a dinner party what one of your stocks actually does, you shouldn't own that stock.

Brand power

An extension of the 'buying what you know' policy is *brand power*. The type of companies that have become trusted blue chips of long standing are companies with a trusted brand name that have been around for a long time. Brands don't get to be household names without earning the trust of investors as well as consumers. However, beware a brand that has had huge expenditure put into it and looks established, while the company behind it has not yet made a profit, or has profits that are unreliable. Watching Qantas' share price slide from $5.86 in 2007 to $1.05 in 2013, as the company struggled with high fuel and operating costs, competition from deep-pocketed Middle Eastern carriers in its international business and a price war in its domestic market — on the way to a $2.8 billion loss in 2013–14 — is a salutary lesson for investors in the danger of confusing a strong brand with financial strength (although Qantas shares have since mounted a strong recovery).

Companies that dominate

Competition benefits consumers but not investors. If the competition is hot, margins remain down and also earnings — and that's not good. The sharemarket may be the seat of capitalism, but it likes a monopoly best. What the sharemarket wants most is reliable and predictable earnings. A company that dominates its market delivers stability.

The big four Australian banks enjoy enormous size and scale, plus they're considered to have implicit government protection — which is enshrined in the 'four pillars policy' that prevents them from merging, their 'too big to fail' status and the fact that they're allowed by the Australian Prudential Regulation Authority (APRA) to apply lower risk weightings to their home loan assets than the regional banks, because they're 'systemically' more important, and thus considered to be under more intense regulatory supervision. Commonwealth Bank, Westpac, ANZ and NAB thus collectively enjoy competitive advantage.

Ramsay Health Care holds a very strong competitive advantage due to its scale, being the largest operator of private hospitals in Australia: Its 70-plus hospitals and day surgeries are in the pick of locations in Queensland, Victoria, New South Wales, South Australia and Western Australia (the company has also expanded into the United Kingdom, France, Malaysia and Indonesia, and has a joint venture in China). Hearing-aid maker Cochlear has very strong global reach and patented technology. CSL has been recognised by investors globally for its size and manufacturing scale, giving it a cost advantage over competitors in a market where demand for blood plasma continues to grow. Challenger holds an 80 per cent share of Australia's annuity market, and regulatory barriers are in place to discourage other players from entering the market.

Gaming companies Tatts and Tabcorp have lost varying extents of monopoly to regulatory reform. Echo Entertainment's Star City is also poised to lose its monopoly in Sydney when Crown Resorts opens a casino at the Barangaroo development from 2019 — although in 2015, Echo turned the tables on Crown by winning the tender to redevelop Brisbane's Queen's Wharf and move its Treasury Casino, which will remain Brisbane's only casino, into it.

Top management

Effective management is absolutely vital to the financial health of a company and to your investment. Good management positions your company at the forefront of its market. If the managers fail, so does your investment.

You can follow the track record of the management teams that run the companies in which you're investing. If you don't have confidence in their abilities, don't wait until the board shares your opinion. Fire them first by selling the shares.

Assessing management is difficult, and made more so by the publicity that some chief executive officers (CEOs) attract. The financial media can fall in love with high-profile CEOs, especially if they're good with a quote, while stock market analysts can be bedazzled by a seeming Midas touch. In the late 1990s, it was Peter Smedley (former CEO of Colonial, then Mayne) who was a market favourite. Then in the early 2000s it was AMP's extrovert American chief executive George Trumbull, who was larger than life while taking AMP on an acquisition binge that later went awry.

Former Telstra CEO Ziggy Switkowski was another whose love affair with the media and market ended acrimoniously, when he agreed in 2004 to step down two years early. His departure followed a series of disastrous expansions — including a failed move into Asia that lost the company $3 billion — that cut the market value of Telstra in half. Switkowski was followed by American Sol Trujillo, whose high-profile time in the top seat at Telstra was marked by an adversarial relationship with the Federal Government, the Australian Competition and Consumer Commission (ACCC), employees and customers — not to mention a 25 per cent slide in the share price.

Then came the boom of the mid-2000s, in which the luminaries of the debt boom such as Eddy Groves of ABC Learning Centres, Phil Green of Babcock & Brown, David Coe of Allco Finance Group, John Kinghorn of RAMS Home Loans and Michael King of MFS were all over the media, not only in the finance pages, but in the lifestyle pages too. Their high profiles could not prevent the credit crunch and GFC exposing their companies as unsound once the debt taps were turned off.

In contrast, not many investors would have heard of the likes of Greg Roebuck, founder and CEO of Carsales.com, Andrew Bassat, chief executive of Seek, Paul Perreault, chief executive of CSL, Hamish Douglass, chief executive of Magellan Financial Group, Chris Rex, chief executive of Ramsay Health Care and Graham Turner, managing director of Flight Centre. Relatively unknown they may be to the wider public, but they all lead management teams doing an excellent job of creating value for shareholders.

Retreating behind defensive stocks

Defensive stocks, considered safe in troubled times, are the most liquid shares in the Top 50. A true bear market such as prevailed over late 2007 to early 2009 depresses share prices across the board, and designing a portfolio that performs well in such a market is difficult. In this situation, professional investors sell many of their shares to increase their cash holding.

In the extreme case of a recession, bank shares, high-yielding property trusts and patronage assets (refer to the earlier section

'Choosing industrials') are the best defensive havens because interest and rental income are fairly constant. In the worst cases, you can also move the rest of your portfolio to cash. Defensive stocks are non-cyclical because they experience solid profits regardless of the motions of the broader economy. Even if their prices fall in a bear market, they should not fall by as much as other stocks.

The food retailers are also being viewed as safe havens: The supermarket stocks, Woolworths and Wesfarmers (which owns Coles), are usually considered premier defensive stocks, but Woolworths' 28 per cent price fall over 2014 and 2015 — as it under-performed against Coles — tarnished this reputation somewhat (and cost chief executive Grant O'Brien his job). Telstra is viewed as a defensive stock for its strong yield, as are CSL and Ramsay Health Care, the former with its strong global cash flows and the latter backed by the growing demand for healthcare as the population ages.

Utilities are sound defensive performers, because people still need electricity and gas: Energy stock AGL and gas pipeline operator APA Group are both good examples of defensive utilities. Sadly — for the human frailty it speaks of — gambling is also a robust defensive exposure, in the form of stocks such as Tatts Group and Tabcorp.

Other defensive stocks are those with dominant market positions. A good example of that in the Australian market is Computershare, the world's largest share registry business. Australian banks also proved to be sound defensive holdings during the GFC. Although their profits suffered as their bad debt provisions mounted, and they were susceptible to movements in credit markets, the fact that they had very little exposure to US housing or to the European debt problem held them in good stead.

The nature of a defensive stock ultimately boils down to the price you pay. For instance, the banks may have been better defensive options when they were at their lowest value, around May 2012, but that may not be the case if you buy them at relatively high share prices.

Cycling your way to recovery

Cyclical stocks are shares whose sales and earnings are affected most by the economic or industry cycle. When the local economy seems to have bottomed or come out of recession, the usual strategy is to sell your defensive stocks, such as the banks, and buy cyclical stocks, such as building materials, media and resources, to ride the recovery.

The big mining and energy stocks — BHP Billiton, Rio Tinto, Fortescue Metals, Woodside, Oil Search and Santos — are typically *high-beta* (that is, they tend to move with the market index) because they are most leveraged to the world growth cycle. Other cyclical stocks — which tend to move with business and economic cycles — include Nine Entertainment, Ten Network, AMP, IAG, Suncorp, Qantas, Virgin Australia and Brambles, and discretionary retailers such as Myer, JB Hi-Fi and Harvey Norman. Financial stocks such as ASX, Perpetual and IOOF are also considered cyclicals, as are jobs website seek.com.au, car sales website carsales.com and real estate website realestate.com.au, operated by REA Group.

Stocks with links to the housing market are also considered cyclical, such as building materials suppliers CSR, Boral, DuluxGroup and Adelaide Brighton.

Scooping the small-caps

Small-cap stocks are those with a small capitalisation or market value. However, if you're a large fund manager, small capitalisation may be any share valued at less than $1 billion on the stock exchange, or it could be those outside the Top 50 by market capitalisation, or the Top 100.

Picking successful smaller companies is harder than picking good big companies because, generally, you have to do your own research. Find out as much as possible about the company; start by reading its announcements to the ASX and you can get a lot of information on the company's performance, as well as order its most recent annual report from its website.

Small-cap stocks are difficult to research. However, because most investors are concentrating on the larger stocks, you may be able to find an overlooked company that is already making a profit. When the rest of the market finds your stock, you can sell at a profit. That's the theory, anyway! Many small companies don't ever get picked up. If you have an eye for a good product with growing earnings and dividend streams and a sound balance sheet, buying small can be rewarding.

Punting on speculative stocks

Speculative stocks are those with the most risk but which offer potentially the highest returns. They have no track record and offer only the excitement of a good blue-sky story — the prospect of riches.

Because the Australian sharemarket relied on the Resources sector for such a long time, investors have a history of backing speculative companies. Mineral exploration companies are often in the middle of a boom-and-bust speculative investment. The Poseidon incident in 1969 is one of the most famous speculative debacles. Poseidon was a nickel explorer whose shares rose from 50 cents to $280 in four months. There was never any viable nickel. In 1999 through 2000, investors bought speculative stocks (in this case technology stocks) that were doubling, tripling and quadrupling in a matter of days. The fundamentals of investment such as profit, dividend and interest cover were irrelevant. When the companies didn't produce earnings, technology shares tumbled. In the 2000s, the speculators favoured any stock drilling for copper or uranium, or working in drug development.

The Australian sharemarket is full of speculative situations: There are still the resources explorers, which can soar on good drilling results, and they have been joined by many technology and biotechnology stocks that have a similar leverage to good news. Good drug trial results and announcements of tie-ups with big global pharmaceutical companies usually have the same effect on a biotech company's share price that spectacular drilling results have on a resources explorer's.

While it is risky, investing in speculative shares, if done with a small percentage (5 or 10 per cent) of funds that you're prepared to lose, can be lucrative and fun. Stocks do double, triple and quadruple in value; 'ten-baggers' — even '20-baggers' — do come along, but not often.

Chapter 9

Working with Brokers

*B*rokers seem always to get pretty bad press. Their huge salaries and flashy Porsches, combined with the latest float fiasco and discredited recommendations, have lowered their standing in the investor community. Following the 2000 tech stock crash, and again following the global financial crisis of 2008 to 2009, a facetious definition of broker was 'poorer than you were last year'.

But no matter how much you may complain about stockbrokers, as an investor, you can't do without them. Stockbrokers are an essential part of the investment process because in most cases you can't buy or sell shares without using a broker. Only a qualified broker can place your order to buy or sell shares via the Australian Securities Exchange (ASX) system.

In this chapter, I show you how to deal with brokers effectively. Finding a broker isn't difficult, but you need to know what brokers do and how they do it before you make your choice.

What a Broker Does

A *stockbroker* is licensed by the Australian Securities and Investments Commission (ASIC) to offer investment advice; a stockbroker also works for a firm that's licensed by the ASX to trade in the sharemarket. The sharemarket is a public marketplace, but only stockbrokers can place orders.

Shares can be transferred outside the market without involving a stockbroker, but the shareholder has to find the other party to the transaction and settle on a price. Shares can also be transferred privately without any payment; for example, you can transfer shares between family members. In all off-market transfers, a standard transfer form must be used to advise the company's share registry. The transferor and the transferee must sign this form. Off-market transfers don't require a broker because technically the shares aren't going through the physical market.

A broker acts as your agent, buying or selling shares on your instructions. Stockbrokers charge a fee for this — called brokerage — and they may also offer other services, such as advice on which shares to buy or sell, portfolio management and financial planning.

Ninety-three broking firms (called ASX market participants) are active in Australia, including Australian branches of global investment companies, such as Deutsche Bank and Morgan Stanley, as well as independent local firms, such as Baker Young, stockbrokers of Adelaide, South Australia. Seventeen of the broking firms are online brokerages.

Many of the large investment bank-owned brokerages deal solely with the institutional investors (managed funds), superannuation funds and insurance companies that own most of the sharemarket. You probably won't deal with this kind of heavy-duty broker; fortunately, the kind of broker that you deal with probably needs you more than you need them.

Stockbroking for Everyone

Stockbroking was once a sellers' market. Stockbrokers held the monopoly on transactions in securities listed on the stock exchange and brokerage rates were fixed. If you wanted to buy shares, you had to use a broker. They knew you needed them and if they didn't like you as a potential customer, you were locked out of the sharemarket. You could go to smaller firms, but if your investment was too small the broker would tell you to use a managed fund. Indirect share ownership was the best you could hope for.

In the past, stockbroking firms charged high prices to cover their transactions as well as their other costs, including opulent offices, well-paid research analysts and client advisers, client newsletters, and a labour-intensive back-office shuffling of the firm's paper. A brokerage rate of 2 to 3 per cent of the value of a transaction was considered justifiable.

That scenario is no longer true. Although stockbrokers still hold the monopoly on transactions, the difference is that, since 1984, they're free to price their charges according to the service offered. Today, you can choose among *full-service* and *execution-only* (or *discount*) brokers, who mostly conduct their business over the internet.

Buying full-service

Full-service brokers offer their clients the whole traditional kit and caboodle — advice on shares to buy and (much rarer) sell, research reports, client newsletters, access to floats, portfolio management and financial planning. Full-service brokers also know how to charge for their services.

If you use a full-service broker, be prepared to pay a brokerage fee of up to 1.2 per cent of the value of the transaction, with a minimum fee of $80–100 — for small purchases. Brokers work on a sliding scale of commission, so by the time you're buying stocks worth more than $30,000, your brokerage costs are probably going to be down to 0.9–1 per cent of the value of the transaction, or lower. This fee is still more expensive than the same purchase costs through an internet broker — about ten times more expensive than average online brokerage rates. You're giving a full-service broker a significant portion of your profit. A full-service broker may also charge you an annual fee of 0.75–1 per cent of the portfolio's value. You may also encounter a minimum account size; $50,000 is common.

However, the benefits of a full-service broker may be worth the cost. Such brokers offer you research and advice on stocks and other investments, and, potentially, access to upcoming floats. Brokerage fees are usually negotiable with advisory brokers; if you're trading frequently enough, you can probably negotiate a better rate.

The rise of online broking has not killed off full-service broking; far from it. If you have a client adviser who's helpful, courteous, interested in you and how your financial knowledge develops, and who becomes a trusted confidant, you're in good shape. If you're happy with the firm's research, newsletter and other services, excellent. Any investor in this position would consider the increased cost of the service cheap. Many investors have the same adviser for years and stick with them as the adviser moves on to different firms.

Online broking certainly suits self-reliant investors, but not everyone can be that. Plenty of investors welcome the help of their stockbroker. Not all investors want to follow the market closely or trade frequently. Some are more interested in a very strategic approach to long-term investment. Investors need to work out what kind of investor they are before they decide which medium — online or full-service — to use.

Using internet broking

Execution-only brokers (often called discount brokers), offer only one service — they place your share order in the system. These days, discount broking means online broking. If you transact your share order with your execution-only broker via the internet, the transaction takes place in seconds. The broker takes your order and completes the job for you.

Most online brokers offer *straight-through* processing, which means that trades are fully automated — you're trading directly into the market yourself. But the brokers also have filters, and if an order looks like an error (for example, it's too far away from the last trade of the stock) or possible market manipulation, it won't be lodged and you'll be asked to check it.

The 39 trading platforms offered by the 15 online brokers give investors open, cheap access to the market, for as little as $9.90 a trade for amounts up to $10,000. As of 2015, online brokers accounted for 10 per cent of all ASX trades. Effectively, that represents more than 70 per cent of retail trading. The average trade size on the online market is $19,000, and this is increasing all the time.

According to financial services research firm Investment Trends, CommSec is the leading online broker, being the main broker of 44 per cent of online investors, and with 59 per cent of online investors holding an account. (CommSec says it has 1.1 million customers, holding 1.9 million accounts.) E*Trade holds about 15 per cent of the market, Westpac Online Investing about 10 per cent and nabtrade about 7 per cent. CommSec's website is the busiest single-purpose website in Australia!

Online broking is much cheaper than full-service broking, but headline brokerage rates can be heavily qualified. The amount of brokerage you pay for an online share trading service depends a lot on the trade size and how often you transact. Some brokers with lower headline charges charge monthly subscription fees; others charge a fee but give a rebate to people who trade frequently. The bank-backed online brokers charge more if you want to settle trades through a cash management account or margin loan that they did not provide. You may also need a minimum account balance.

Online broking allows self-directed investors to have total control over their investment strategy. People now have on their desks the trading capability that an institution would have had ten years ago. Such investors can trade online as much as they like. They can look at where the market is at, look at the buy and sell orders in the market, look at the trend of the market that day, place their order, and instantly see what it went for.

Some online brokers have expanded beyond simply offering cheaper transactions, expanding their offering to include extensive research, information, software, analytical tools and more. These brokers compete with full-service brokers, but, using the internet, offer cut-rate prices. Using the internet to trade is easy and anyone can do it.

In fact, so much functionality is offered in terms of education, information, research and charting that the online brokers have moved well beyond their 'execution-only' beginnings. They may not give direct advice, but they certainly give self-reliant investors the tools and the knowledge base that they need to inform themselves and to be self-directed.

Australian online investors can now place orders directly into the stock market in two seconds. They can place their orders more cheaply than ever before, and using a wide range of pricing arrangements, depending on their level of investing activity and which services they use.

Most online brokers offer different product features to different sectors of the market. For example, customers new to online broking are provided with fundamental and economic research, educational material and portfolio management tools, while active traders — those that meet a minimum level of activity — are offered features such as dynamically updated data, price alerts, upgraded charting packages and the ability to make conditional (or 'stop-loss') orders for free. If a customer has an active trader package, they've probably also got a sophisticated charting package, dynamically updated data and alerts. Customers also have access to tax reporting tools.

Different customers may also have different data requirements. Your data needs largely depend on how frequently you intend to buy and sell. You can access three types of data delivery:

- ✔ **Delayed**, where the data you see is 20 minutes old

- ✔ **Live**, where you click to refresh your browser for market updates

- ✔ **Dynamic**, where the data is streamed live from the market

It may not be necessary for an active investor to pay for dynamic data: It depends on whether you need to react to changes within minutes, over the course of a day, or over a week.

Mobile apps have made it easy to trade, and to track and monitor portfolios, on a smartphone or tablet. Investment Trends says 53 per cent of people with an online trading account access it with a smartphone or tablet, while 59 per cent of 'frequent traders' — those who trade at least four times a month — use a smartphone or tablet for online trading. Australians' use of mobile trading apps for trading online is behind only Singaporean traders (76 per cent) and US traders (60 per cent).

While online brokers don't give advice, they do try to give their customers access to as much information and insight as possible. They help their clients to make better investment decisions by offering educational content that's relevant to first-time investors, economic and company research, news feeds, relevant and timely market information, and scanning and number-crunching tools. Online traders want fundamental and technical research available at the click of a mouse; they want to be able to put in the parameters, filters and indicators that they feel are important to their trading decisions. They want to set stop-losses or 'stop-profit' orders — either on price or percentage moves — so that they can control their entry and exit strategy. These days, online brokers see themselves as one-stop-shops for investment, wealth creation and trading — providing everything short of actual advice.

Online brokers are also moving into social media, with some hosting online 'communities': Where clients can exchange ideas, post real-time news, speak to the firm's analysts, or talk to the firm's trading services team if they have any issues with the trading platform or their account. The next frontiers may be those explored by online foreign exchange (FX) providers (such as automated FX trading systems — or 'robots' — which are software programs designed to analyse the markets and trade automatically on your behalf) and *copy trading*, a form of trading that allows would-be traders to follow and copy automatically the positions opened and managed by selected expert investors, usually through a 'social trading' network.

Choosing the Best Broker for You

To choose the kind of broking service that best meets your needs, you need to answer the following questions:

- ✔ How much are you prepared to pay?
- ✔ How many trades are you likely to make?
- ✔ What services do you need?

If you're new to the sharemarket, and you're investing a relatively large amount of money and want to establish a well-diversified portfolio designed for patient capital appreciation, you can benefit from a consultation with a full-service broker. If you know the sharemarket well and want to use your knowledge to trade your portfolio, you can opt for an execution-only broker.

You don't have to confine your trading activity to one or even two brokers. By all means spread your activity around. If you want to participate in floats, opening and maintaining an account at one of the larger retail brokers makes sense. Large retail brokers have access to the big company floats. The more transactions you put through this firm, the better your chances of getting in on the float action.

Cheaper brokerage means less service, which can lead to poor purchases. If you save 1 per cent in brokerage fees but pay an exorbitant price for the shares, you haven't achieved a saving. You need to know what you want from a broker before making your choice.

Fighting for full-service

After several years of copping the online assault, full-service brokers made a comeback through one of their trump cards — access to floats. The stockbroking industry earns 90 per cent of its revenue from 10 per cent of its clients — that's why full-service brokers get first crack at the floats. A stockbroking firm handling a sought-after float is under no obligation to offer the shares to the wider public, unless the floated company so requests. Most floats are small enough to be handled comfortably by the large full-service brokers.

However, online brokers have built up the distribution ability to challenge for the large floats; after all, CommSec's 1.1 million customers is a pool of potential investors that is very hard to ignore! CommSec and E*Trade were part of the consortium of brokers handling the $15.5 billion Telstra 3 share issue in 2006, and in 2010 CommSec secured a role as co-lead manager of the $6 billion float of freight company QR National.

The brokers fill float issues from their own client base first. If the brokers know they can achieve this without help from another firm, only their clients receive an offer of shares. That's why many internet clients also work with a full-service broker, although larger floats increasingly use the online brokers as a distribution tool.

Doing the research

Research analysts from stockbroking firms produce a huge amount of information. Their newsletters contain a good deal of research for private clients, but this is only a fraction of the paper mountain of analysis sent to institutions. Since the Australian market is one of the most concentrated in the world, the Top 50 companies are the most scrutinised and researched. Stocks that aren't large enough for the ASX/S&P 200 Index are less likely to be researched.

The total bill for research from the top brokerages is more than $15 million a year, not counting computerisation and desktop publishing spending. The bulk of this information is aimed at the institutional buyer. This information can be a problem for the investor who's receiving recycled institutional research, laden with jargon, diagrams and acronyms. What your full-service broker should be doing is advising you when to buy and sell shares.

Unfortunately, brokers rarely tell you when to sell — unless you're one of their best clients; brokers prefer to offer buy recommendations. Only people who already own shares can act on sell recommendations.

Companies don't like to see their shares rated as a 'sell' since they never think they deserve it. In the best broker–client relationship, for example, your broker may recommend selling a particular stock at $5 and buying back in at $4, not because he hates the company, but because his research has shown that at $5, the stock has gone past fair value.

Paying for service

Let's face it, the reason full-service brokers aren't cheap is because they don't want small clients who generate only a small amount of brokerage. They'd rather let small clients go to discount brokers or managed funds.

If you buy $1,000 worth of shares through a full-service broker who charges a minimum brokerage of $80, the brokerage on your purchase is 8 per cent of the total. The share has to rise by more than 8 per cent before you're ahead. The same investment can be made through an online broker for as little as $9.90. According to research house Canstar, in 2015 the average brokerage on a $1,000 share purchase through an online broker was $19.15, while for a $10,000 share buy, the average brokerage was $20.08.

If you're a longstanding or highly active client, you're probably able to negotiate a discount, but if price is your only criterion, clearly you'd be mad to go through a full-service broker. But the story is different if your relationship with the full-service broker is a good one — if you get sound personalised service and good long-term strategic advice, this relationship can pay for itself many times over.

Where are the customers' yachts?

A well-known story relates that a visitor to New York was being shown the wonders of the city. Down on the river, at the New York Yacht Club, his guide said: 'And there are the brokers' and the bankers' yachts.'

Came the reply, 'Where are the customers' yachts?'

This reply also became the title of one of the best books on investment, written by Fred Schwed Jr, called *Where Are the Customers' Yachts? A Good Hard Look at Wall Street.* The story also explains something about the paradox of the sharemarket and sheds light on who benefits most from the broker–client relationship.

Interviewing for a Broker

Always remember — stockbrokers need you more than you need them. The market today is a buyers' market for stockbroking services, particularly if your stockbroker thinks you may defect to an online broker.

A full-service firm assigns an adviser, who asks you how much you have to invest. For a full-service broker, an investment less than $10,000 wouldn't be considered worthwhile. For that amount of money, the broker may argue that achieving proper diversification is difficult and that you're better off with the in-built diversification of a managed fund (refer to Chapter 5 for an explanation of how managed funds diversify).

Although the ASX's trading system could accommodate the purchase of one share in any company, the brokerage fee would be more than the cost of the share. If you pester a broker enough, they'll buy or sell your small parcel — but expect to pay a hefty fee if it's a troublesome transaction.

Your adviser establishes

- ✔ How comfortable you are with risk.
- ✔ How well you understand the sharemarket.
- ✔ Whether you want capital growth or income.
- ✔ Whether you intend to invest in capital for the long term, or whether you want to trade shares.

A good broker may tell you that your $10,000 would probably be better off in a managed fund rather than buying several shares; if one of the stocks purchased doesn't work, the portfolio is in trouble. For the money invested, a managed fund makes more sense.

You don't have to accept that advice, but you then have to do your own research and analysis to make your small portfolio work (refer to Chapters 7 and 8 for details on how to research companies).

If you decide to work with a full-service broker, be ready to ask the broker some questions, such as:

- ✔ Where do they invest?
- ✔ What sort of shares do they prefer?

 ✔ How many floats have they participated in? (Check this against a list of floats that have taken place over the same period.)

 ✔ Are they willing to have a two-way relationship? (Ideally, your adviser will be prepared to listen as well as talk.)

It's not okay if your adviser patronises you or obviously fails to prepare for your consultations. Nor should you accept being badgered to buy or sell stocks. A broker's income comes from commission on transactions. To make money, the broker must be raking in commissions. Repeat this mantra: 'My broker needs transactions to make money. Ergo, he wants transactions to

---

The retail client's glossary of brokers' research terms

If you're going to work with a broker, you're going to have to talk the broker's talk. Here are some important terms — some simple, some more technical — to get your head around:

Accumulate: A nothing call. The broker can't manage to say 'buy'.

Avoid: This share is a dog. The broker has been wavering between fear of upsetting the company and fear of embarrassment at being caught out as the only firm supporting a dog. The latter fear has won.

Buy and sell: These terms explain themselves. You'll hardly ever hear the latter. Some cynics claim that these mean, respectively, 'We've got a load of these we want to get rid of' and 'We're desperate to pick up as many of these as we can for a large client'.

Get on this, it's headed to the stratosphere: As an ordinary retail client, you're never going to hear this. All up, that's not a bad thing.

Hold: After exhaustive study, the broker wants to sit on the fence, because no one else has made a buy or sell order.

Marketweight: A jargon word for 'hold'. (The institutions prefer this word to 'hold'.)

Overweight: You can think of this as, 'We mean buy, but we want to sound more impressive.'

Reduce and lighten: The broker wants to say sell, but doesn't want to upset the company. Let's face it, to reduce or lighten a holding without selling some shares is difficult.

Speculative buy: In other words, 'Some huge gains could be made, but, hey, don't blame me if it goes belly-up.'

Switch: Your broker is saying, 'Sell, and buy the one we want you to buy.'

Underweight: An impressive-sounding technical term that doesn't hurt the company's feelings as much as the word 'sell'.

occur. Ergo, he is happiest when I am transacting.' A broker's business is a sales business. The best clients, who generate the most sales, receive the best service.

If your broker says a company looks good, ask why. Ask the broker for the price/earnings (P/E) ratio, the net asset value, the revenue and earnings track record over the past three years, the consensus forecasts for the next two years, and the proportion of its sales that go to export markets. Put pressure on your broker to provide factual substance to the recommendation, otherwise all you're getting is a tip, and you can get enough of them at dinner parties.

Making the most of full-service

If you decide to take the full-service route, make sure that the broker earns their commission. When your broker commits to maintaining a properly structured investment portfolio, some essential steps must be taken. These steps should

- ✔ Determine your risk profile and the level of risk that you're comfortable with that will meet your investment objectives.

- ✔ Locate the investments that fit your risk profile and meet your investment objectives.

- ✔ Monitor your investment portfolio and your financial situation.

- ✔ Structure your financial affairs in the most tax-efficient manner, to maximise your potential to create wealth and minimise tax.

In a full-service broker–client relationship, you pay for extra services that help to maximise your ability and opportunity to create wealth.

Forging a new relationship

Some brokers, notably the Australian arms of major US and European investment banks, have embraced a deliberate strategy of moving away from transaction-based commission revenue to an annual fee levied on assets under management. Under this model, called *relationship management*, the brokers manage the portfolio of their customers in return for annual fees. In this situation, the broker brings in the services of experts to take care of the client's overall financial needs — in fields such as taxation, banking, property investment, derivatives and futures.

This approach is based on the 80:20 rule, which dictates that 20 per cent of the firm's clients generate 80 per cent of its revenue. This rule is more like a 90:10 rule at the high end of stockbroking, and some firms allocate their resources to the most lucrative area — those with the most to invest. In other words, the firms cull their client list and encourage their advisers to build assets under management rather than generate trades.

Stockbroking is a buyers' market and willing investors can easily find a firm happy to carry their business, although some clients may find it a wrench to leave an adviser they trust. Investors who prefer to conduct high-volume, low-cost business are not suited to relationship management; these investors find that an execution-only broker is the best fit for their needs.

Using broker sponsorship

Shareholders can arrange to be sponsored by a broker in their dealings with the CHESS clearing house (refer to Chapter 6 for a full explanation of CHESS). It doesn't cost anything, but a formal agreement is required. The shareholder is allocated a holder identification number (HIN) that covers the client's shareholdings and acts as an identifying password into CHESS. Your HIN must be quoted when placing orders.

Alternatively, listed companies can sponsor their own shares. Shareholders electing to use this system are allocated a security holder reference number (SRN), which covers only the holding in that particular company. Issuer sponsorship is popular with shareholders who don't want a formal relationship with a broking firm. With broker *sponsorship*, if you want to sell through another broker, you must first transfer your shares into the sponsorship of the other broker, which is unnecessary paperwork. Discount brokers also offer CHESS sponsorship facilities. Your account and paperwork are the same but you're paying a lot less to trade.

Locating the ideal broker

You can try several effective ways to find a good stockbroker. Word-of-mouth is a good starting point. If your friends are happy with their brokers, these brokers may be worth contacting;

it helps if you can contact a broker armed with a referral from an existing client. The ASX also offers a referral service and its website (www.asx.com.au) lists all brokers' contact details. Visit these brokers' websites and assess their offering. For online brokers, Infochoice at www.infochoice.com.au, Canstar at www.canstar.com.au, Trading Room at www.tradingroom.com.au, Finder at www.finder.com.au and RateCity at www.ratecity.com.au provide a summary of all online brokers' fees and charges, and which services they offer.

Chapter 10

Taxing Matters

· ·

In This Chapter

▶ Understanding how franking credits work

▶ Sharing your capital gains with the tax office

▶ Using tax strategies wisely

· ·

Shares generate income for their owners through the flow of dividends paid out of the company's profits. Before you get too excited about this, remember that the Australian Taxation Office (ATO) takes its cut of this income, too. Not only are your dividend payments part of your assessable income, the tax office also claims a cut of any money you make when you sell your shares. Because of this, shares play an important part in managing your tax affairs.

In this chapter, I explain the system of dividend imputation, which gives Australian investors a tax credit for tax paid by the company on its profit. I describe how you can use fully franked dividends for tax-effective investing, particularly in a self-managed superannuation fund (SMSF). I also cover how your capital gains on shares are taxed, and how you can manage capital gains tax (CGT) and try to offset losses against gains.

Benefiting from Dividend Imputation

Dividend imputation allows investors who've been paid a dividend to take a personal tax credit on the tax already paid by the company. The rebate, known as the *franking credit* or *imputation credit*, can be used by a shareholder to reduce their tax liability. In some cases — depending on the marginal tax rate — the franking credit can offset the individual's total tax liability. In certain circumstances, excess franking credits (after the total tax liability has been extinguished) can be claimed as a refund.

For Australian resident investors, franking credits are the third element of total shareholder returns, after capital gains and dividends. Analysis conducted by fund manager Fidelity in 2015 suggests that an average dividend yield of 5 per cent on Australian stocks is actually closer to 7 per cent once you factor in franking credits.

For an investor with a SMSF, dividend imputation is particularly important. First, because it can snuff out the tax liability on the fund, levied at 15 per cent. Properly balanced, a flow of imputation credits can offset the tax on contributions to the fund, which is a practical and legitimate form of tax planning. Second, once the fund begins paying a pension, there's no tax on the income or capital gains from the assets and any unused franking credits can be refunded fully in cash.

Franking credits made easy

Australian companies that are in the 3,000 largest companies by employment (which effectively covers the stock market's dividend-paying companies) pay corporate tax at the full rate of 30 per cent. When one of these companies pays tax, it builds up credits in its *franking account*. The company's ability to frank its dividend depends on the credit balance in this account. With a surplus available in the franking account, the company may declare a fully franked dividend; if the credit balance isn't large enough, a partly franked dividend may be paid.

Unfranked dividends are paid out of company profits that have not been subject to the full Australian corporate tax rate. Such dividends don't have any franking credits associated with them, and are taxable at the shareholders' marginal tax rate. When the company makes a loss, it pays no tax that year, and doesn't receive any franking credits. The only way the company can pay a franked dividend the following year is if it has sufficient franking credits in its franking account from prior periods.

Legally, companies can pay franking credits only by attaching them to cash dividends, whether ordinary, special or the deemed dividend components in off-market share buybacks. On average, 70 per cent of credits are distributed.

According to investment bank Credit Suisse, Australia's top 200 companies will pay more than $80.5 billion in dividends in 2015, not including the benefits of franking credits. The Australia Institute also notes that about $30 billion in franking credits is distributed each year, with $10 billion going to households, $10 billion going to superannuation funds, charities and trusts, and $10 billion going to other companies.

In 2014, Australian companies held a stockpile of franking credits estimated at about $73 billion, which would be worth about $36 billion in shareholders' hands. The stockpile arises because Australian companies generally pay out about two-thirds of profit as dividends, and the excess franking credits go into franking accounts. One way to distribute excess franking credits is to mount an off-market share buyback where part of the buyback price is identified as a *deemed* dividend (see the section 'Biting on a buyback' later in this chapter).

Fully franked dividends

Shareholders who receive fully franked dividends must add the imputation credit on the dividend to the amount of dividend in order to arrive at the taxable income represented by the dividend. This procedure is called *grossing up* the dividend.

With the company tax rate at 30 per cent, dividends are grossed up by $30 for each $70 of dividends received. This means that Australian companies that pay tax at the 30 per cent company tax rate have $428.57 of attached franking credits for every $1,000 of dividends they pay out.

As a shareholder, you have to include the grossed-up dividend amount in your assessable income. You receive a tax credit of $30 for each $100 of grossed-up franked dividend included in your assessable income.

After the tax liability on the grossed-up amount is worked out, the imputation credit is subtracted from the tax liability, to give the actual tax payable. Table 10-1 shows the situation where an investor on the current top marginal tax rate of 47 per cent (plus the 2 per cent Medicare levy) invests $10,000 in shares and receives fully franked dividends of $700. (This tax rate is in place until at least 30 June 2017.)

Table 10-1 Tax Liability ($700 Dividend Fully Franked)	
Investment	$10,000
Fully franked dividend income	$700
Gross yield	7%
Imputation credit $700 × 30/70	$300
Included in taxable income	$1,000
Tax payable at 49%	$490
Less imputation credit	$300
Tax payable	$190
After-tax income	$510
After-tax equivalent yield	5.10%

The franking credit reduces the investor's tax liability on the cash amount of dividend received from 49 per cent to 27.10 per cent ($190 of the $700 received). At the same time, the 7 per cent dividend yield becomes the equivalent of an after-tax yield of 5.10 per cent. If the income came from fixed interest or rent, the 7 per cent yield after tax would reduce to 3.57 per cent.

Partially franked dividends

Depending on its franking account, a company may declare a partially franked dividend or an unfranked dividend. An unfranked dividend carries no tax credit and is simply added to the investor's assessable income. A *partially franked dividend* carries a partial imputation credit. To calculate the tax payable, the franked portion is grossed up by the proportion of tax paid. In the example shown in Table 10-2, it's again assumed that your marginal tax rate is 47 per cent, plus the Medicare levy (2 per cent), and you receive a dividend of $700: But this time, it's 80 per cent franked.

The franking credit reduces the investor's tax liability on the cash amount of dividend received from 49 per cent to 31.5 per cent ($220.60 of the $700 received). At the same time, the 7 per cent dividend yield becomes the equivalent of an after-tax yield of 4.79 per cent.

Table 10-2 Tax Liability ($700 Dividend Partially Franked)	
Investment	$10,000
Dividend income	$700
Franked income = 80% of $700	$560
Gross yield	7%
Imputation credit $560 × 30/70	$240
Included in taxable income	$940
Tax payable at 49%	$460.60
Less imputation credit of	$240
Tax payable	$220.60
After-tax income	$479.40
After-tax equivalent yield	4.79%

Franking credit refund

Taxpayers (including superannuation funds) can claim cash rebates on any excess franking credits. Excess franking credits arise when the shareholder's marginal tax rate is less than the corporate tax rate of 30 per cent.

For investors on the same marginal tax rate as the corporate tax rate (that is, individuals earning up to $70,000), this franking credit rebate makes the fully franked dividends tax-free: They pay only the Medicare levy on this income.

For investors on a marginal tax rate higher than 30 per cent, imputation credits reduce the tax liability on the dividend. For those on a marginal tax rate of less than 30 per cent, excess imputation credits may be offset against tax payable on other income in the year of receipt, or be claimed as a cash rebate if no other tax is payable.

Investors on the 15 per cent tax rate (for example, a SMSF in the 'accumulation' phase) actually get a tax refund of $215 for every $1,000 of fully franked dividends they receive, because this amount is not needed to offset tax on the dividends. For such investors, a dollar of fully franked dividend income is effectively worth more than a dollar.

Even better is when a SMSF moves to 'pension' phase; that is, you can choose to have your fund pay you a pension. In this case, the assets are held in the fund's 'pension account', which means they're being used solely for the purpose of paying out a pension. In this case there's no tax on the income or capital gains from the assets, and the franked dividends can actually be refunded fully by the ATO.

Table 10-3 shows the effect of the franking credit rebate on the tax status of individuals on the four individual marginal tax rates above the tax-free threshold (the 15 per cent rate is also that paid by a SMSF in 'accumulation' phase; once the fund moves to 'pension phase', its tax rate is zero). The workings ignore the Medicare levy of 2 per cent, because super funds don't pay it.

Table 10-3	The Benefits of Dividend Imputation*				
	Nil taxpayer	*19% taxpayer*	*32.5% taxpayer*	*37% taxpayer*	*47% taxpayer*
Dividend	$1,000	$1,000	$1,000	$1,000	$1,000
Grossed-up dividend	$1,429	$1,429	$1,429	$1,429	$1,429
Gross tax payable	Nil	$271	$464	$529	$672
Franking credit rebate	$429	$429	$429	$429	$429
Tax payable	$429 refund	$158 refund	$35	$100	$243

* Amounts rounded

Obeying the 45-day rule

Shareholders who receive more than $5,000 worth of franking credits in a tax year must own each stock in their portfolio for more than 45 days (not counting the day of purchase or sale) before being entitled to a franking tax offset from dividends paid or credited on the shares. For preference shares, the holding period is 90 days. The rule was introduced to prevent tax-driven investors from trading shares merely to gain the imputation credits on fully franked dividends, and so lower their tax liability. (In fact, because the days of purchase and sale aren't counted, the rule could more accurately be called the 47-day rule.)

Watching Your Capital Gains

As part of the tax system, Australia has a *capital gains tax* (CGT), which taxes the gains made on the sale (or disposal) of shares (and other assets), at the individual's marginal tax rate; although you may get a tax discount depending on how long you've held the shares. CGT isn't payable on shares that were bought before 20 September 1985, but if you've bought any shares since then and sold them for a gain, that gain will be taxed.

Calculating your liability

You're liable for CGT if your capital gains exceed your capital losses in any income year. When filling out your annual tax return, you add up your capital gains and capital losses. Your net capital gains (capital gains minus capital losses) figure is added to your taxable income, and taxed at your marginal tax rate.

If you have a net capital loss figure, you can carry the amount forward to help offset future capital gains, but your loss can't be used to offset any other income received for that year. Capital losses can be offset only against capital gains, but can be carried forward indefinitely until fully used up by being offset against future capital gains. Nobody likes to sell a share for a loss, but reducing the tax office's take of your capital gains helps to lessen the pain of buying dud shares.

Reducing the tax office's take

If you hold shares for at least 12 months, you pay CGT on only half of the profit made, which makes receiving a capital gain much more attractive than receiving income. For shares bought and sold within a year, CGT is levied on the entire capital gain at the individual's marginal tax rate.

Say a person is on the top marginal tax rate of 47 per cent, plus the Medicare levy of 2 per cent; this rate cuts in at $180,001 of income plus taxable gains. The person has a capital gain of $50,000 on an asset the person has owned for a year and a day. Thus, the person is eligible for the CGT discount. The gain is halved to $25,000 and the tax rate of 49 per cent is applied, meaning that CGT payable on the gain is $12,250. On the $50,000 capital gain, the tax incurred is 24.5 per cent of the gain. Although the Medicare levy itself isn't halved, in effect the maximum CGT rate for assets held for at least a year is 24.5 per cent, which is half of the top marginal rate plus Medicare levy. But the discount doesn't technically apply to the individual's tax rate; it's a discount on the gain taxed.

If you own shares that you bought between 20 September 1985 and 21 September 1999, you have a choice of methods to calculate your CGT liability.

You can use *inflation indexation* (using the consumer price index or CPI) with indexation frozen at 30 September 1999. This way, you're taxed only on the real, or after-inflation, capital gain that you made. No corresponding inflation adjustment is available for losses. With the other method, you can elect to have half of your net capital gain taxed: But you don't get this concession if you choose the indexation method.

You're within your rights to use the method that gives the tax office the least. Given that asset price inflation was far more dominant in the 2000s than inflation, most people will find that they get a better result using the 50 per cent discount method.

A SMSF that is in 'accumulation' phase, in which its tax rate is 15 per cent, earns a one-third CGT discount if it holds an asset for more than 365 days. Subsequent sale of the asset incurs CGT at 10 per cent, unless the asset has been transferred into the pension account of the fund, at which point the tax rate on income and capital gains from the asset becomes zero. If you have different parcels of a shareholding that have been acquired at different times and for different prices, it's necessary to keep track of these 'tax lots', since the capital gain or loss may be different for each. The shareholder can choose to their advantage: For example, selling a parcel with a capital loss to realise the loss immediately, or keeping particular parcels until they've been held for one year, to qualify for the discounted CGT rate. Some portfolio management software systems can help with this task. Many online brokers offer clients a tax monitoring tool that keeps track of 'tax lots'.

As always, investors should think investment first, and tax considerations second. Shares can change in value very quickly, and with some shares there's no point in waiting until your shareholding is a year old just to qualify for the CGT discount — because the 'CG' part may have disappeared by then!

Having to pay CGT should be viewed as a good thing, because it means you've made a capital gain. That's what sharemarket investing is all about.

Although you don't have to be an accountant to benefit from the tax treatment of shares, talking to an accountant at least once a year helps. Chances are your accountant can help you keep more of your investment gain from the tax office — perfectly legally, of course.

Taxing Tactics

You can use your share portfolio to make strategic tax decisions. You can sell shares before the end of the tax year to crystallise a capital loss and take a tax liability on a capital gain made in the same year. You can also invest in a financial instrument such as a warrant to secure a tax deduction.

Tax can play a big part in your buying and selling decisions, but it should never be the sole reason for buying or selling a share.

Tax-loss selling

Nobody likes making a capital loss on a share, but using it to soak up a capital gain that you've (hopefully) earned elsewhere in your portfolio is a perfect way to ease some of the pain. Rather than moaning about shares that have fallen in value, investors should look to use this situation to reduce the tax office's take of their capital gains.

If you have a $10,000 loss on a stock that has gone down and a $10,000 profit on a stock that has risen, and you sell both, you're square with the ATO. Tax-loss selling is common in June, towards the end of the tax year, when people are looking to crystallise capital losses to offset against gains. You can make good use of the fact that your shares have fallen in value.

When using a capital loss to offset a capital gain, a good idea is to use it to offset a capital gain on a stock that you've held for less than 12 months — where you pay CGT at the full rate — rather than the discounted CGT. That way, you get the full value of the loss offset.

You can always buy a stock back if you really want to hold it for the long term. Selling the stock gives rise to a handy tax loss that can be offset against a capital gain on another share. If you buy it back at a lower price, you've lowered the average buying price of your long-term holding.

However, you can't do this too quickly. People used to sell on a Monday and buy back on the Tuesday; as long as there were two separate trades registered, they had crystallised a tax loss. But this was red-carded by the ATO in 2008. It said that if it considered this kind of *wash sale* (sale and purchase within a short period of time) as being done to obtain a tax benefit, it would deny the loss.

You're allowed to change your mind and buy back into a stock, but to avoid an ATO rejection of your capital loss an investor may need to show that the sale has another purpose, such as restructuring your portfolio, or that the repurchase has been made because the market has changed, or on the basis of new research. If in doubt, consult your accountant.

Another possible strategy is to sell capital loss-making shares to a SMSF or a discretionary master trust that handles direct shareholdings. This is an *in specie* transfer where you as an individual are deemed to have disposed of the shares for a capital loss, which you can use in your tax return for this year; the shares become the property of the super fund or master trust, at the price on the day. Shares can also be transferred in this way to a company, or into a spouse's name.

Using a delisted dog

Generally speaking, shares make a remarkably successful investment asset, but occasionally companies go bust, as shareholders in the likes of high-profile global financial crisis collapses like ABC Learning Centres, Allco Finance Group, Babcock & Brown and MFS/Octaviar know only too well. More recently, timber firm Gunns went into administration in September 2012, engineering company Forge Group went under in February 2014, labour hire firm Bluestone Global Limited collapsed into administration in August 2014 and drug company PharmaNet followed in April 2015. It happens occasionally. Nobody wants to see a share they buy end up in the company graveyard with these stocks, but some benefit can be extracted from the disaster if the capital loss is claimed.

The firm handling the burial of your unbeloved 'dog' — its administrator, receiver or liquidator — has to ascertain how much the company's secured and unsecured creditors are claiming before it declares the shares worthless, allowing you to claim the capital loss. Unfortunately, this can take years.

The problem is that if the company has collapsed, its shares will be suspended and you have no way to sell them in order to gain the capital loss. Normally a capital loss (or a capital gain) for tax purposes only occurs if there's a CGT event. Common CGT events include the sale of shares or units, distribution of a capital gain by a managed fund, declaration by an administrator or liquidator that they have reasonable grounds to believe there's no likelihood that shareholders will receive any further distribution, or the creation of a trust over a CGT asset and deregistration of a company.

The creation of a trust has been used extensively (since an ATO Determination in 2004) to facilitate the crystallisation of losses in companies suspended from ASX quotation and in administration. As shares can no longer be sold on the market, shareholders may enter into an agreement to dispose of their shares and create a trust over those shares until transfer of ownership can be registered: This is the only way to achieve effective change of ownership pending the subsequent registration of an accompanying transfer when and if the company emerges from administration. These transactions have to be at 'arm's length' and should be executed professionally to satisfy taxation and other requirements.

The creation of a trust doesn't help with companies in liquidation but it does with those suspended from quotation and in administration, which covers most of them.

A helpful service is provided by the website www.delisted. com.au, which tracks what's going on with the hundreds of companies trapped in the limbo of administration, receivership or liquidation. Many of these companies eventually return to the stock exchange lists as 'shell' companies, through a 'backdoor' listing. The website keeps in touch with the administrators and posts any news on delisted stocks so that shareholders know whether there's a chance of a recovery — or, at least, the latest developments during an administration.

This website also operates a mechanism whereby shareholders essentially transfer their stocks into a trust, meaning that it acquires the stocks pending the registration of the transfer, which satisfies the ATO that the shareholders can claim a loss. This service comes at a cost, which works out at about $40 after tax, which is a small price to pay if you have a potential capital loss worth thousands to put to work in your tax return.

Biting on a buyback

Although they were prohibited until 1989 — and then heavily regulated until 1995 — share buybacks have become a common feature of the Australian sharemarket. According to investment bank Credit Suisse, in the six years up to the end of 2014, the S&P/ASX 200 companies bought back $30.5 billion worth of shares. Credit Suisse also predicted that another $9.3 billion worth of equity would be bought back in 2015. In February 2016, Credit Suisse gave a final figure of $2.9 billion for buybacks in 2015. They explained the discrepancy ($9.3 billion predicted versus $2.9 billion actual) on the poor conditions in the credit (corporate debt) market - doing a buyback increases the debt on the balance sheet. In it's February 2016 report, Credit Suisse predicts a recovery in buyback activity to $8.6 billion in 2016.

Companies undertake share buybacks as part of their capital management strategy. They may want to improve earnings per share (EPS), return on equity (ROE) for shareholders or return on assets (ROA), or they may want to return surplus capital or franking credits to shareholders.

The company can either buy back its own shares on-market, or conduct an off-market buyback, inviting eligible shareholders to offer to sell their shares within a certain time frame, and usually at a discount to the current market price. The shares bought back are cancelled, reducing the number of shares the company has on issue.

When you sell shares into a buyback, you must work out the capital gain or capital loss on the sale of your shares, to include in your tax return. You may also have to include in your tax return a dividend as part of the buyback: In an off-market buyback, it's common for part of the buyback price to include a fully franked dividend. This is not an actual dividend, but a *deemed dividend* that is the difference between the *capital component* of the buyback price and the actual price. The ability to deem part of the price to be a dividend enables companies to distribute their excess franking credits to shareholders. In an on-market buyback, the proceeds are treated as a return of capital only.

The tax consequences of a share buyback depend on what kind of buyback it is. If you're looking at an off-market buyback where part of the price is treated as a franked dividend at below the prevailing market price, the buyback may be unattractive to a retail shareholder on the highest marginal tax rate, but very attractive to lower taxpaying shareholders (for example, a superannuation fund) receiving a large distribution of franking credits, as well as a capital loss to use in offsetting capital gains.

The company may make special arrangements with the ATO to reduce the amount of tax that shareholders accepting its buyback offer will pay. The ATO often provides fact sheets on its website (www.ato.gov.au) that spell out the consequences for different taxpayers of buyback proposals in the market.

Borrowing a tax deduction

If you borrow to invest in shares or use an instalment warrant, the interest costs are tax deductible because the borrowing is used to produce assessable income. If you negatively gear a share portfolio, meaning that you pay more in interest than you get back in dividends, you can also claim this difference against your other income. The loan product may also allow you to pre-pay interest before the end of the current tax (financial) year, no more than 12 months in advance, and claim the full amount as a tax deduction in the current financial year.

Keeping tax breaks in perspective

Your decision to buy or sell an investment should never be driven by tax considerations. Always use investment factors when you decide to trade shares and let any tax benefits come as a bonus. If you have some poorly performing stocks in your portfolio, and you're convinced that they're not going to recover in the near future, sell them to realise some capital losses to offset your capital gains. However, when you try to create losses by selling shares you don't want to sell, you can encounter problems.

Buying and selling for tax advantages can be complicated. You can sell your shares at a loss and then buy them back afterwards. However, because you're buying the shares again, at a lower price, you now have a lower cost-base for CGT purposes. You have deferred CGT, but any recovery in the share price is taxable when you eventually sell the shares. When you buy the shares again, you have to keep them for at least 12 months to be eligible for the CGT discount of only half your capital gain being taxed (which effectively halves your CGT rate).

Similarly, you don't want to take a share loan or buy a structured product, such as an instalment warrant, just to get a tax deduction. The share portfolio you buy with the loan, or the shares your instalment warrant is based on, may fall in value. In these situations, you can lose money — perhaps more than you saved with the tax deduction the loan gave you.

Trading as a business

The ATO treats individuals who conduct a business of buying and selling shares differently from ordinary investors. If you meet certain criteria set by the tax law and the ATO's guidance, you may be classified as a professional trader and the profit you make from share trading will be treated as ordinary income, not capital gain; and you may be able to claim expenses, such as brokerage, as a tax deduction. You cannot declare yourself a trader: Your level of activity dictates whether the ATO treats you as such.

To be a share trader means that you're in the business of trading shares for gain. As such, you're allowed to use all the provisions that relate to business, one of which is that your shares are treated as trading stock.

Traders are taxed on the income derived in the course of carrying out their business of trading in shares (dividends or profitable sales) and are allowed to offset any losses incurred in their share-trading business against any gains made in that business, any capital gains from other sources and indeed, any other income.

For traders, gains are not actually 'capital' gains because the trader isn't assessed under the CGT regime: Any change booked in the value of a trader's stock is either assessable as income or deductible as a loss. This means that unrealised losses may be claimed in a tax year, but gains don't have to be brought to account until they're realised.

For all other shareholders, capital gains incur CGT and the only losses that can be claimed are realised capital losses, which can be offset only against realised capital gains, in the same year or future years. Net sale value is minus brokerage paid. The cost of buying shares isn't an allowable deduction, and profit from sales isn't assessable income.

Traders are allowed to value their closing stock at the lower of cost — what the shares cost to buy — or net realisable value, which is the market price on the last day of the tax year (the financial year. Say that you own shares that cost you $100 when you bought them on the first day of the year, and the market value of the shares at year-end was $75. You can write down the value of the holding to $75, and claim a loss of $25.

Assume that at the end of year two you still hold the shares, but their market value is $150. You make no stock adjustment at all: The holding remains valued in your books at $75. The stock has doubled to $150, but you have no assessable gain. You don't have to mark up the value, because you hold it at the lower of cost or net realisable value.

At the end of year three, you sell the shares for $125. You then have an assessable gain of $50, but on income, not capital. You incur tax on this income at your full marginal tax rate.

 The introduction in 1999 of the 50 per cent CGT discount applying to assets held for more than 12 months took away much of the perceived advantage of professional trader status. When a trader sells shares, the profit is liable for income tax at up to 49 per cent, whereas for an ordinary investor on the top marginal tax rate, if the shares have been held for longer than 12 months, only half of the capital gain incurs CGT, meaning that the investor pays CGT effectively at a maximum rate of 24.5 per cent.

 Potentially, investors using the CGT regime may fund share purchases through debt, gaining an interest deduction of 49 per cent, yet pay CGT at only 24.5 per cent on any gains — an extremely profitable arrangement! Whether being treated as a share trader is best for you depends on your marginal tax rate and your level of trading activity.

If you want to be classified as a trader, you have to meet various criteria set by tax law and interpreted by the ATO. No specific law on share traders exists, but the ATO publishes a fact sheet with guidelines based on previous court rulings (see www.ato.gov.au). The ATO website says that the following factors have been considered in previous court cases:

- ✔ Amount of capital employed
- ✔ Nature of the activities, particularly whether they have the purpose of making a profit

✔ Organisation in a businesslike manner, the keeping of books or records, and the use of a system

✔ Repetition and regularity of the activities

✔ Volume of the operations

The ATO needs to satisfy itself that you're running a business dealing in shares. You have to show regular activity employing substantial capital. You should possess or have undertaken the following:

✔ A business plan (your trading strategy written down), with profit targets, budgets and records, and details of any software systems used

✔ A detailed trading history of profits and losses, dividend income, bonus issues and changes to capital structure (for example, splits, consolidations, share buybacks and capital returns)

✔ A financial year statement with opening and closing inventory

✔ Relevant educational courses and/or qualifications gained

A possible alternative to seeking trader status is to conduct your share trading activities through a personal super fund. Your share profit within the fund is taxed at a maximum of 15 per cent, regardless of whether the profits are treated by the tax office as income or capital. The drawback in this case is that losses are quarantined within a superannuation fund and can't be used to offset tax on your other income or capital gains.

Keeping a record

For CGT purposes, you need to maintain a share register. Often shares in the same company are purchased at different times. You must maintain separate records in order to calculate correctly the total CGT liability when the shares are eventually sold.

Sufficient records for tax purposes include:

✔ Brokerage charged on each transaction

✔ Company name

✔ Date of transaction

🖝 Incidental expenses

🖝 Number of shares or units bought or sold

🖝 Price per share on buy or sell transactions

🖝 Type of transaction (buy or sell)

You usually include as incidental expenses any expenditure the ATO allows as furthering your investment knowledge, such as the cost of financial books, and subscriptions to magazines and financial websites. Other items may include money spent travelling to annual general meetings of companies whose shares you own, or even visiting your companies' factories and mines, although this will depend on the facts of each case. Always check with your accountant or tax adviser about what to include in your record keeping. At worst, a taxpayer can use the system of private rulings to get an ATO determination on their particular circumstances — or circumstances they're contemplating.

Part IV
The Part of Tens

In this part...

✔ Admire the strategic prowess of some of the world's greatest investors.

✔ Watch out for some share investing pitfalls.

Chapter 11

Ten Great Investors and Their Strategies

● ●

In This Chapter

▶ Trading tips from the masters

▶ Investing for value

▶ Looking for prospects of growth

▶ Doing it with ratios

▶ Becoming an expert in your field

● ●

*I*nvestors come in all shapes and sizes. Here I select nine of the best-known and most successful investors of the past 80 years — and one (Charles Viertel) perhaps not so well known, but no less effective. Each has followed a fairly stringent set of principles to achieve their success — Benjamin Graham was the 'father' of value investing, while Philip Fisher took a different point of view with his strategies for growth investing. These investors had these features in common — each took his task seriously and each has added to our understanding of the investment process.

Warren Buffett and Charles Munger

Much has been written about the investment philosophies of Warren Buffett, who's known as the 'Oracle of Omaha'. He built a US$40 billion fortune from a $50 start in 1956. Warren Buffett is part of a two-man team that manages the legendary investment firm Berkshire Hathaway, and is certainly more famous than his partner, Charlie Munger, vice president of Berkshire Hathaway, who acts as the Dr Watson to Buffett's Sherlock Holmes.

The annual letter to the shareholders of Berkshire Hathaway has become one of the most eagerly awaited investment documents in the world. The stated aim of the company is to

> ... *increase Berkshire's per-share value at a rate that, over time, will modestly exceed the gain from owning the S&P 500. A small annual advantage in our favour can, if sustained, produce an anything-but-small long-term advantage. To reach our goal we will need to add a few good businesses to Berkshire's stable each year, have the businesses we own generally gain in value, and avoid any material increase in our outstanding shares.*

Warren Buffett doesn't dwell on Berkshire Hathaway's share price or its earnings; instead, he examines the company's net tangible asset (NTA) value, or what Americans call 'book value'. Since 1965, Berkshire Hathaway's annual percentage change in book value has beaten the S&P 500 (with dividends reinvested) in 39 of 50 completed years. Over that time Berkshire Hathaway's value has grown at a compound annual growth rate of 19.4 per cent, versus 9.9 per cent a year for the S&P 500 Index. In only 11 years has the index beaten Berkshire Hathaway: The most recent occasion was 2014, when Berkshire's book value grew by 8.3 per cent, while the S&P 500 gained 13.7 per cent in total return. The strategy has consistently outperformed the S&P 500 on a medium-term basis, but just recently, the index has made a comeback: As of the end of 2014, the S&P 500 had bested the Berkshire Hathaway portfolio in five of the most recent six years. (The S&P 500 numbers are pre-tax, whereas the Berkshire numbers are after-tax.) However, a 50-year record of a compound annual growth rate of almost twice that of the market index is successful investing, in anyone's language.

How do Buffett and Munger do it? They look for companies with a track record of financial success. This means the companies have competitive advantage, excellent management and superior products or services with a respected brand name. Buffett and Munger also try to buy these companies at a reasonable price. That's the simple secret of buying a stream of earnings reliable enough to fuel Berkshire Hathaway's growth. The key statistics these fund managers look for in companies are

- ✔ Growth in sales and earnings
- ✔ High return on equity
- ✔ Low gearing (33 per cent or less)

- Rising book value
- Strong and growing profit margins

Buffett and Munger also look for growth in *owner earnings*, which is earnings (per share) minus depreciation (per share) plus capital expenditure (per share). Owner earnings represents the cash that the business has left after its required maintenance spending — cash that it can spend however it wants. This pair also prefers a company with a relatively high price/earnings (P/E) ratio — they're long-term investors and figure that a stock trades on a high P/E ratio because the market is prepared to pay a premium for it.

Buffett and Munger are known for having 'permanent' stock holdings: Buffett says his ideal investment horizon is 'forever'. Berkshire Hathaway is the biggest shareholder of Coca-Cola Co. and American Express Co. and Buffett has held those stocks for almost 25 years. Retail giant Wal-Mart is another 'permanent' holding. At the time of writing, Berkshire Hathaway's top ten holdings were

- Wells Fargo (18.9 per cent of the portfolio)
- Kraft Heinz (18.0 per cent)
- Coca-Cola Co. (12.6 per cent)
- IBM (9.2 per cent)
- American Express (8.8 per cent)
- Phillips 66 (3.7 per cent)
- Procter & Gamble (3.0 per cent)
- Wal-Mart (2.9 per cent)
- US Bancorp (2.7 per cent)
- DaVita HealthCare (2.2 per cent)

Many Australian fund managers say that they follow similar principles to those of Berkshire in terms of valuation precepts. But even managers considered to be Buffett-oriented, like Magellan, Clime and Caledonia, will tell you that using the basic premises that Buffett and Munger espouse is one thing, but putting it into practice on a Berkshire scale is difficult in the Australian market. Our market is both much more limited in terms of high-quality businesses than the US market, and is very highly concentrated in resources investment, where many of those principles do not work.

Buffett and Munger have been able to pick the fundamental eyes out of an industrial-based economy like the US through 'information arbitrage': Learning more about a company than anyone else. Not only is this harder to do these days in the US, but it's very difficult to do in Australia, where the market's resources orientation means that there are tremendous swings in earnings in many of the major Australian companies.

Moreover, no Australian manager can invest in exactly the way that Berkshire does, because Australian fund managers have to service their investors' capital. Since its inception Berkshire has paid only one dividend.

The compounding effect of retaining earnings and retaining dividend flows gives the company its dramatic earnings power. Buffett also has the ability, as he did at the height of the global financial crisis (GFC), to invest in companies through instruments other than shares. In fact, this was Buffett's preferred method of investing after the GFC hit in 2007.

For example, Buffett's US$5 billion investment in Goldman Sachs in 2008 — hailed as a dramatic and confidence-boosting announcement at a time when the global financial system looked to be in danger of collapse — was actually a purchase of perpetual preferred Goldman shares that pay an interest rate of 10 per cent. In addition, Berkshire received warrants giving it the right to buy $5 billion worth of Goldman's common shares at any time up to September 2013, at a price of $115 per share. Goldman Sachs currently trades at $174 on the New York Stock Exchange, making Berkshire's 10.9 million shares worth $1.9 billion.

Quotable Buffettisms abound, such as: 'When a management with a reputation for brilliance tackles a business with a reputation for bad economics, it is the reputation of the business that remains intact'; 'When you combine ignorance and leverage, you get some pretty interesting results'; and 'I don't care if the stock exchange closes down for five years. I've got my stocks and I like them.'

John Neff

John Neff managed Vanguard's Windsor fund for 31 years, from 1964 to his retirement in 1995. The Windsor fund was closed to new investment in 1985 and was, at that time, the largest mutual fund in the USA. Neff beat the market 22 out of 31 years, turning each dollar invested in Windsor in the first year to $56 by 1985.

The total return of the Windsor fund was 5,546 per cent, more than twice as good as that of the S&P 500 Index over the same period. The average return of the Windsor fund was 13.7 per cent a year, versus 10.6 per cent for the S&P 500.

Neff's strategy was to look for stocks trading at a low P/E ratio. Often described as a value investor, the label that Neff thought best described his style was *low P/E investor*. He bought companies that were in line for a re-rating in the medium term, reasoning that a re-rating was more likely to happen to a company whose P/E was about half the market average than to a high P/E growth stock.

He looked for companies with an earnings growth of 7 per cent or better. Above 20 per cent, Neff thought the stock too risky. Neff considered yield a return that investors could pocket. He said that share prices 'nearly always sell on the basis of expected earnings growth rates and shareholders collect the dividend income for free'.

The total return that Windsor was looking for was annual earnings growth plus dividend yield. Because the P/E ratio showed what it paid to achieve that annual return, Windsor divided total return by P/E ratio to give a total return ratio. Neff bought stocks with a total return ratio at 2 or above. He was happy to buy cyclical stocks, but at low P/E ratios based on the earnings that he thought were achievable at better points in the cycle. He looked for solid companies in growing fields.

He also looked for companies with what he called a strong fundamental case, which meant that the trends in cash flow, sales and margins combined to drive earnings growth. Neff would sell when he felt that the fundamental case was deteriorating, or if the price approached his expectations. Typically he held stocks for about three years.

My favourite Neffism is: 'Falling in love with stocks in a portfolio is very easy to do and, I might add, very perilous. Every stock Windsor owned was for sale. When you feel like bragging about a stock, it's probably time to sell.'

Benjamin Graham

Benjamin Graham, who died in 1976, was one of the most influential investors the stock markets have known. He developed his ideas about value investing during the Great

Depression, and co-wrote, with David Dodd, the 1931 classic text *Security Analysis*. He followed this up 18 years later with *The Intelligent Investor*. These two books set out the concept of value investing.

Value investing involves buying stocks that are trading at a low price relative to the company's net worth per share, which is its value as though it were to be sold off tomorrow, or its NTA backing. According to Graham, this is a stock's intrinsic value. He compared this intrinsic value to the current market price to determine a share's true value. The further the share's market price was below what Graham had worked out as its intrinsic value, the bigger he considered his margin of safety.

Benjamin Graham's ten rules for choosing stocks are

- ✓ Current ratio greater than two.

- ✓ Dividend yield of at least two-thirds that of the AAA bond.

- ✓ Earnings growth of at least 7 per cent a year, over the preceding ten years.

- ✓ Earnings-to-price yield of at least twice the yield offered by the best AAA bond. (The earnings-to-price yield is the reciprocal of the P/E ratio. For Australian investors, this yield would be twice the yield of ten-year bonds.)

- ✓ P/E ratio less than 40 per cent of the highest P/E ratio the stock had traded at over the past five years.

- ✓ Share price of less than two-thirds of book value (NTA) per share.

- ✓ Share price of less than two-thirds of net current asset value, which Graham defined as the current assets of a company minus all of its liabilities.

- ✓ Stability of growth of earnings. (No more than two annual falls of 5 per cent or more in profit in the preceding ten years.)

- ✓ Total debt less than book value (NTA).

- ✓ Total debt less than twice net current asset value.

Over four decades, Benjamin Graham honed this set of ten criteria to what he described as a 'practically foolproof way of getting good results out of common stock investments with a minimum of work'.

Philip Fisher

What Benjamin Graham is to value investors, Philip Fisher is to growth investors. His strategy was to identify growth companies early, buy them and hold them for a long time. Fisher was averse to bargain hunting. He wanted to identify the business characteristics of superbly managed growth companies. He felt that great growth stocks show gains in the hundreds of per cent each decade, while a value-oriented investor rarely finds a stock that is more than 50 per cent below its real value.

Fisher did not use economic data to help him decide when to buy stocks because he thought economists were not accountable. He preferred to use what he called 'scuttlebutt', which involved talking to suppliers, customers, company employees, and people knowledgeable in the industry and, eventually, company management. Not all investors can do this, although the internet era makes it a bit easier.

Fisher developed a series of questions you can ask before buying a stock:

- Are there aspects of the business, somewhat peculiar to the industry involved, which will give the investor important clues as to how outstanding the company may be in relation to its competition?
- Does the company have a management of unquestionable integrity?
- Does the company have an above-average sales organisation?
- Does the company have depth to its management?
- Does the company have a short-range or a long-range outlook in regard to profits?
- Does the company have a worthwhile profit margin?
- Does the company have outstanding executive relations?
- Does the company have outstanding labour and personnel relations?
- Does the company have products or services with sufficient market potential to make possible a sizeable increase in sales for at least several years?

✔ Does the management have a determination to continue to develop products or processes that will still further increase total sales potentials when the growth potentials of currently attractive product lines have largely been exploited?

✔ Does the management talk freely to investors about its affairs when things are going well, but 'clam up' when troubles and disappointments occur?

✔ How good are the company's cost analysis and accounting controls?

✔ How effective are the company's research and development efforts in relation to its size?

✔ What is the company doing to maintain or improve profit margins?

✔ Will, in the foreseeable future, the growth of the company require sufficient equity financing so that the larger number of shares then outstanding will largely cancel the existing stockholders' benefit from this anticipated growth?

Fisher is famous for the comment that 'if the job has been correctly done when a common stock is purchased, the time to sell it is — almost never'. However, he would sell in three situations: When he decided he'd made a serious mistake in assessing the company; if the company no longer passed his tests as clearly as it did before; and if he simply decided to take a profit and reinvest the money in another, far more attractive company.

Jim Slater

British investor Jim Slater's theories of share investment centre on the price earnings growth factor, or PEG. The *PEG* is a measure of the relationship between a P/E ratio and the expected rate of earnings per share growth. To calculate the PEG, you divide the P/E ratio by the forecast growth in earnings per share (EPS).

Any company trading on a PEG of 1 or less is generally considered appealing, while those on PEGs of 0.6 are cheap as chips. To qualify for a positive calculation, a company must have displayed solid normalised EPS growth going back at least three years, with no setbacks.

Slater found that PEGs tend to work best for what he called small, dynamic companies. He formulated ten critical points against which a candidate for investment must be assessed:

- ✓ Competitive advantage linked to reliability of earnings growth based on well-known brand names, patents, copyrights, market dominance or a strong position in a niche business.

- ✓ Dividend yield — it doesn't matter how low, as long as dividends paid are growing in line with earnings.

- ✓ High relative strength of the shares compared to the market — when the market's strong, the shares are strong; if it's not, you're on red alert.

- ✓ Low P/E ratio relative to the growth rate (in other words, the PEG).

- ✓ Optimistic chairman's statement (in the annual report).

- ✓ Positive rate of growth in earnings per share in at least four of the past five years. Cyclical stocks not allowed!

- ✓ Reasonable asset position. Very few growth shares in a dynamic phase, said Slater, were priced near to or below asset value. A share price as low as 33 per cent of asset value is 'passable for a growth share'.

- ✓ Shares must have a 'story', that offers potential reasons for growth in earnings.

- ✓ Small market capitalisation — elephants don't gallop! Slater preferred companies valued at £10–50 million, and would not invest above £100 million. Bear in mind, though, that the UK is a larger and deeper sharemarket than Australia.

- ✓ Strong liquidity, low borrowings and high cash flow. Liquidity here means ability to convert assets to cash. Avoid capital-intensive companies; look instead for those generating cash.

Slater also looked for management with significant shareholding in the company because investors wanted to see shareholder-oriented management that would look after their interests with an owner's eye. Slater believes these criteria allow investors to identify smaller growth stocks, which give investors substantial capital and earnings growth.

These days Slater is a big investor in the commodities arena. His investment principles are accessible on the website Company REFS (Really Essential Financial Statistics) at www.companyrefs.com and his personal website at www.jimslater.org.uk — but the stock data pertains to UK stocks only.

Charles Viertel

Charles Viertel was one of the great unsung heroes of the Australian Securities Exchange. From a fairly humble start in life, Viertel left a $60 million charitable foundation when he died in 1992, which has since appreciated to about $160 million — from which about $7.5 million a year flows to charities. He advocated the principle of buying and holding quality shares and picking up more of them after a correction. Viertel was one of the great exponents of the buy-and-hold investment strategy.

Viertel started buying shares and property during the Great Depression but later sold all his property to concentrate on the sharemarket. Reportedly, he was so shamed by the notice written on the blackboard at primary school, 'Viertel owes threepence' (for schoolbooks), that he never again borrowed a cent. Nor did he smoke, drink or own a car. Until he died he lived in the same modest home in Brisbane that he bought in the mid-1950s.

Trained as a cost accountant, Viertel based his sharemarket investment strategy on the forensic study of financial statements. He looked for value, whether it was a company that showed potential to grow its business or be taken over. He liked to buy Queensland companies. Once he decided to concentrate on shares as his investment vehicle, Viertel looked for companies with strong dividend yields that gave him the cash flow to expand his portfolio.

According to an interview that long-time friend George Curphy gave to *Personal Investor* magazine in 2001, the three fundamentals on which Viertel placed most emphasis were:

- ✔ NTA backing
- ✔ P/E ratio
- ✔ Track history

Viertel was a voracious and methodical reader of company financial statements. He was always alert for takeover appeal and was reportedly a large buyer of shares when the market crashed in October 1987. He stuck to his principle of solid long-term investing.

Peter Lynch

Peter Lynch became a household name in investment through his work at the Boston-based international fund Fidelity Magellan. Lynch retired in 1990, handing over to his successor a fund worth $14 billion. In his 13 years at the helm, Lynch managed the fund to an average compound return of 29 per cent a year, a record for funds of that size. This translates to a total return of 2,510 per cent, more than five times the appreciation in the S&P 500 over the same period. Lynch believes that individual investors who know what they're looking for can spot good stocks before professional investors. He says that products or services you deal with in your workplace, buy in the shops, or use in your spare time and on holidays are a great source of ideas for investment in the companies that make or offer them.

He divides companies into these main types:

- **Asset plays:** Companies trading at a discount to their NTA backing.

- **Cyclicals:** Those companies whose earnings closely follow the economic cycle.

- **Fast growers:** Small, aggressive companies growing at more than 20 per cent.

- **Slow growers:** Companies whose earnings growth matches the rate of growth in Gross Domestic Product (GDP).

- **Stalwarts:** Companies with solid growth in earnings of about 10–12 per cent a year.

- **Turnarounds:** Poor performers that have cleaned up their act and are poised for recovery.

Of these types of companies, Lynch is interested only in fast growers, turnarounds and asset plays. Lynch likes companies that have a low PEG ratio (their P/E ratio is below their forecast rate of growth in EPS), a strong cash position, low gearing and a high profit margin.

John Bogle

John Bogle deserves to be considered one of the great investors — for inventing the index fund. An *index fund* owns a portfolio of stocks that is constructed to match the investment returns of a specified market index. The manager of the fund buys and holds that index. He doesn't try to actively manage the portfolio.

Bogle was an economics student at Princeton University in 1949, researching his thesis on mutual funds managers, when he first hit on the idea. He founded the Vanguard Group in 1974 to practise his theories. His approach was that funds managers couldn't consistently beat the market. A bond fund manager can't outguess interest rates; nor can a share fund manager outperform the market, on a cost-adjusted basis. As Bogle put it: 'What's the point of looking for the needle in the haystack? Why not own the haystack?'

John Templeton

John Templeton rose from poor beginnings in Tennessee to found the huge Templeton Mutual Fund group, and was one of the first US fund managers to invest in foreign shares. The Templeton group paved the way for US investment in the Japanese stock market in the 1960s, but by the 1980s, the company felt that the Japanese market was overpriced and sold its holdings. The company looked silly for a few years, but with the Nikkei losing 80 per cent of its value over the period 1989 to 2003, you'd have to say that Templeton was right.

Templeton's investment credo has been set out in ten points:

- **Avoid the popular:** Too many investors can spoil any share selection method or any market timing formula.

- **Buy when the market is most pessimistic:** Conversely, sell when the market is most optimistic.

- **Hunt for value and bargains:** In the sharemarket, the only way to get a bargain is to buy what most investors are selling.

- **Invest for real returns:** The true objective for any long-term investor is to get maximum total real return after taxes and inflation.

✔ **Learn from your mistakes:** 'This time is different' are among the four most costly words in investing history.

✔ **Never adopt any type of asset or selection method permanently:** Stay open-minded, and sceptical.

✔ **Never follow the crowd:** If you buy the same shares as everybody else, you'll get the same results as everybody else. To be a true contrarian, buying when others are selling and vice versa requires the greatest courage, but pays the greatest reward.

✔ **Recognise no one knows everything:** An investor who has all the answers doesn't even understand the questions.

✔ **Search worldwide:** If you do, you'll find more and better bargains than if you confine your investing to only one country.

✔ **Understand everything changes:** Bull or bear markets, they've always been temporary.

Because he was a pioneer in overseas investing, Templeton also had a set of rules to cover his decisions. He avoided countries plagued by socialist policies and/or inflation and favoured those with high long-term growth rates. Templeton especially favoured countries that showed a trend towards economic liberalisation or privatisation, anti-union legislation, and greater openness and transparency in sharemarket dealings.

In Australia, the Templeton Global Growth Fund Limited, a listed investment vehicle, manages funds on Templeton's investment principles. The fund's $390 million in assets is held in 111 companies, spread over 21 countries.

Chapter 12

Ten Things Not To Do, Ever

In This Chapter

▶ Staying patient with your stocks

▶ Understanding volatility

▶ Staying cool and calm

▶ Ignoring dividends at your peril

▶ Knowing what you're buying into

▶ Letting go of lost returns

*W*hen dealing with the sharemarket, you face many dos and don'ts. All the chapters in this book deal with the many dos that can guide you to making the right investments on the sharemarket. Now the time has come to give you a chapter that deals with some of the very important don'ts.

Don't Think You Can Get Rich Quick

The sharemarket is a place to get rich slowly. While the sharemarket offers the best chance for long-term wealth creation, the market can also be used for short-term speculation, which is a form of gambling. Sure, short-term killings can be made on the sharemarket but, in the main, if you try to compress the wealth-growing powers of the sharemarket into months or weeks (even days), you're asking for trouble.

It's very tempting, in boom times, to say, 'Every share that I buy goes up in price. Where has this instant wealth been all my life? I am a genius!' The reality is that the shares you bought are rising in price because the sharemarket is experiencing a boom. The shares are not going up in price because you, 'the genius', chose them. You'd be amazed how hard it is for people to face reality and rid themselves of these insidious thoughts. Conversely, in November 2007 to March 2009, your shares weren't falling because you were a 'bad' investor — the market was falling across the board.

A corollary to this rule is: Don't sign up for an expensive share-trading course (or software program) if the promoters use the term 'millionaire' to get you in, or worse, say you'll be able to quit your day job. The way to wealth on the sharemarket is through diversification, careful stock selection and time, time, time. Investment can't be hurried and anyone who says you can get rich quick is a fraud. Don't waste time talking to them and don't waste money buying their product.

Another corollary to this rule: Don't listen to tips. If you buy shares on a tip, how can you be sure that the tip didn't originate from insiders who want to lock in a profit before the price falls? A fall they most likely know is coming.

Don't Underestimate Volatility

Yes, shares have been the best-performing asset class over long periods of time. Since 1900, according to AMP Capital, Australian shares have earned a return of approximately 11.9 per cent a year, as measured by the S&P/ASX All Ordinaries Accumulation Index — which counts capital growth and dividends — and its predecessor indices.

But shares have also been the most volatile of the asset classes. In any given year, shares could be the worst-performing asset class. Over the long term, however, nothing beats shares as a wealth accumulator. The biggest mistake you can make is to leave shares out of your investment portfolio. You see more rising years than falling years, making shares a great long-term generator of wealth, but statistically, investors can expect a negative year on the sharemarket about every five years. Research firm Andex Charts says that in the last 65 financial years — 1951 to the year ended 30 June 2015 — 51 years out of 65 delivered a positive result in the S&P/ASX All Ordinaries Accumulation Index (and predecessor indices). The best financial-year return was 76.5 per cent, observed in 1967–68, while the worst was a drop of 29 per cent, seen in 1981–82.

The volatility in any given year can be a big problem for investors. A 54 per cent fall in the stock market index — as occurred between November 2007 and March 2009, at the height of the global financial crisis (GFC) — certainly got investors rethinking risk versus return (the Australian index is still below its November 2007 peak, although the US market has surged 35 per cent higher). In particular, investors are far more attuned to volatility and the risk they're taking.

 If you're a long way from retirement, the sharemarket's good long-term track record is working for you. But if you're getting close to retirement and the sharemarket's volatility worries you, maybe look to leaven your share portfolio with some bonds; they give you on average about 75 per cent of the return of the sharemarket, with less than half of the volatility.

Don't Be Panicked Out of Your Shares

You've bought your shares. You like the company's prospects for making money, and paying you a dividend. But all you hear on the evening news is that there seems no end in sight to the bear market. That's what confronted a lot of investors during the GFC, and many 'capitulated' — they sold out and moved to the perceived safety of cash, thinking that they could buy back in later, to participate in the recovery. The problem is that this is a difficult strategy to get right; you need well-timed selling and re-buying decisions.

During the GFC many superannuation investors, for example, switched their accounts to the most conservative options in March 2009, when markets were at their lowest ebb. If these members had remained in their original investment options they would not have missed out on the large gains made after the market hit its bottom. As Paul O'Neill, former US Treasury Secretary, once put it: 'You don't pull up your turnips to see how they're growing.' Nor can you accomplish anything useful by selling your share portfolio during a market downturn. Think of yourself as an investor for the long term and not a trader.

 A loss is only a loss if it's realised. If you don't have a very pressing need for money, you don't have to sell a share that you believe will eventually recover in price. Also, tax and cost considerations are involved in selling out. Finally, remember the paradox of cash; it's the safest investment option, but it won't give you the growth in capital you need over the long term.

Don't Ignore Dividends (Especially Franked Ones)

Since 1900, according to AMP Capital, Australian shares (as represented by the S&P/ASX All Ordinaries Accumulation Index and predecessor indices) have earned a return of approximately 11.9 per cent a year on average — despite wars, recessions, economic crises, full-blown sharemarket crashes and a depression. This return was split fairly evenly between capital growth and dividend income.

That's right: Over the (very) long term, half of the total return came from the humble dividend. The dividends from high-quality stocks are far less volatile than their share prices. If you're picking up the dividend income stream from this kind of stock, you don't have to worry about the share price on a day-to-day basis. Over the long term, the share price will probably benefit you, but you can afford to ignore that.

The really great thing about using shares for income is that over a long holding period, the rising dividend can start to generate almost incredible yields, based on the original purchase price. Due to the benefits of franking credits, tax takes less of the return from Australian shares than from the return of any other asset class. The lower the investor's tax rate, the more the after-tax return exceeds the before-tax return. Franking credits have a value that is part of your total return as a shareholder, and these credits come in very handy at all tax rates, but start to give huge benefits in the superannuation environment. Make sure you understand how helpful franked dividends can be.

Don't Buy a Share You Know Nothing About

I should have known that the technology stock boom was doomed in early 2000 when a work colleague boasted about the gain she'd made on a stock, which she referred to by its three-letter Australian Stock Exchange code. I asked her what the company was and what it did. She didn't know the company's name, let alone its business. There's a saying: 'If you can't explain what a company does, don't invest in it.' When you buy a share, you're supposed to know something about the company's cash flow, how profit is made and whether money is reinvested to fund the development of the business or used to pay you a dividend.

As an investor, you should invest your time getting to know the companies that you're considering for your portfolio. Knowledgeable investing requires you to work out a few basic financial ratios, which helps you understand how well the company's managers are running the business. Being able to quote the stock exchange code won't help you evaluate a company. If you buy shares and don't do your homework, you're only a punter.

Don't Expect Things to Stay the Same

Try to avoid imagining that recent past returns will be repeated in the future — investors do this all the time. Predicting the future based on the past reflects wishful thinking, and an inability to imagine the prevailing sentiment — be it good times or bad times — ever changing. It's why Australian investors have a bad habit of getting into and out of an investment at the wrong time — either into it when it's peaking, and all the headlines make it seem you're a fool for missing out, or out of it when it's bottoming out, and no one wants to touch it with a barge pole.

When you're investing on the sharemarket, it's never 'different this time'. If share prices, price/earnings ratios and investor returns divert from long-term averages for too long, they will revert to that mean. Over the last 50 years the Australian sharemarket generated an average return (capital growth and dividends) of 12.5 per cent a year. But between 2002 and 2008, the market averaged 21 per cent a year. If an investor had decided that she could expect 21 per cent a year from her shares forever, she was in for a rude shock: Since 2008, the local sharemarket has delivered an average return of 5.8 per cent a year.

Don't Delay a Sale to Save Capital Gains Tax

If you own a share for less than 12 months, any capital gains you make on its sale is taxed at your marginal tax rate. When you hold shares for more than 12 months, only half of your capital gain is taxed (which means, in effect, that the rate of capital gains tax (CGT) is halved). Good practice is to cash in a profit if your shares rise sharply in price. In such cases, you may hesitate because you haven't held the shares long enough to qualify for the discounted CGT rate. You may think that if you held on to those shares for just a few more months, you'd save half of the capital gains tax bill.

When you find yourself thinking like this, place your face under a stream of cold water. Let the capital gain you made on the shares drive your decision, not the capital gains tax. If you decide to delay the sale to save on the tax bill, you may well lose out on the entire profit if the share price falls.

Don't Let Tax Drive Your Investment Decisions

Don't invest in a share investment mainly for tax reasons. This is particularly true in the case of a margin loan. A *margin loan* is a long-term wealth accumulation strategy that can be structured to ride out short-term market fluctuations. Margin loans are attractive to traders as leverage vehicles and because they offer a tax deduction, but you should enter into a margin loan with the intention of owning the portfolio outright, just as if you'd taken out a home loan.

With a margin loan, you're making a leveraged investment in the sharemarket, which is one of the most volatile of all asset markets. After you take out a margin loan, the sharemarket will be revaluing, every day, the portfolio that you bought. A margin call for more cash (or shares) can happen to you at the worst of times and be a nasty surprise.

While on the subject of gearing, I want to caution you not to overdo it, particularly with one stock. A portfolio geared to 70 per cent (that is, 70 per cent of the funds are borrowed) can get into a margin call situation very easily (with a fall of only 6 per cent) but a portfolio geared to 40 per cent would need a 45 per cent fall in the market for that to happen. As was seen from 2007 to 2009, such a fall is possible: A margin loan would have had to be geared to 30 per cent to have escaped a margin call in that market rout.

Don't Fret Over Lost Profit

When you sell a share at a profit, don't follow its later progress and worry about the money you could have made. You need great mental discipline to do this, but it does help keep your stress level low.

Investing in the sharemarket is not a competitive sport. The only runner you're trying to beat is inflation; you're not competing against other investors. The extra profit that another investor gets from the sale of a share at a higher exit point than you is not money that you didn't get.

If somebody delays a sale and reaps a better selling price than you did, congratulate them. Their success doesn't detract from your profit, which has been banked, or put towards new entries in promising stocks. You made your profit, which took into account your needs and objectives. You set a target. You had the discipline to sell and move on. If you'd hung on another day, the risk/reward equation could have changed dramatically.

Don't Let Yourself Be Churned

Your broker makes money when he gets you in and out of shares, right? So whose best interest is served by absolutely every trade you make? That's right, your broker's. Some brokers try to take advantage of you by suggesting trades. Your money belongs to you, so don't be afraid to question your broker. Make the broker explain the exact strategy being followed. Above all, don't allow yourself to be patronised with jargon. If you don't want to take your broker's advice, just say 'no'. A good broker should welcome this kind of involvement on your part; if your broker doesn't seem to like it, look elsewhere.

Index

About the Author

Over a 28-year career, James Dunn has built a reputation as one of Australia's leading investment journalists. James was founding editor of *Shares* magazine, and oversaw one of the most successful magazine launches in Australian publishing history. He has also written for *BRW*, *Personal Investor*, *The Age* and *Management Today*, and was subsequently personal investment editor at *The Australian* and editor of financial website investorweb.com.au. He writes for *The Australian*, *The Australian Financial Review*, *Asia Asset Management* and *Listed@ASX* magazine, as well as the *Switzer Super Report* online newsletter and the Share Café website (sharecafe.com.au). He is also a sought-after speaker on investment, economic and leadership issues. James also has a weekly commentary spot on Sky Business.

Born and raised in Ararat, western Victoria, James graduated from the University of Melbourne as Bachelor of Letters and Bachelor of Arts. He is a fellow of the Williamson Community Leadership Program, operated by Leadership Victoria.

In 1984, James won two BMWs on *Sale of the Century*. The sale of the cars financed a year of overseas travel and a substantial share portfolio, which did not survive the crash of 1987 because it was virtually all in speculative stocks. After that event, James decided on a career in financial journalism.

He has never lost his fascination with the sharemarket, and has developed a strong interest in educating people about their investments.

Dedication

Some things have not changed from the first edition of this book, when I wrote: This book simply would not exist without the support of and inspiration from my family. Writing a book is a selfish thing to do, and I can't thank my wife, Jane, enough for her love and support. I dedicate this book to her and to my wonderful children, Eliza and Harry, to whom I apologise for locking myself in the study and worse, hogging the computer. This is for you.

Getting Started in Shares For Dummies is also dedicated to my mother and father, who made books a part of my life from my earliest memory. At long last, I was able to put my own on the other side of the ledger, a feat they never doubted.

All of the preceding still stands in this third edition of *Getting Started in Shares For Dummies* — triply so with regard to Jane, Eliza and Harry. They've got their own computers now, but I still hog the one with all the bells and whistles.

Author's Acknowledgements

Thanks firstly to Ingrid Bond, Kerry Laundon and Alice Berry at John Wiley, who have helped to make this book possible.

I also want to express my appreciation to Matthew Gibbs at ASX, David Reid at Andex Charts, Shane Oliver at AMP Capital Investors, Phillip Gray at Morningstar Australasia, Geoff Wilson at Wilson Asset Management, Richard Morrow at Baillieu Holst, Tim Kelley at Montgomery Investment Management, Alex Dunnin at Rainmaker Information, Stephen Hiscock and Callum Burns at SG Hiscock & Company, Gavin Wendt at MineLife, Max Lin and Mitchell Watson at CANSTAR, Hasan Tefvik at Credit Suisse, Mat Sund at Franklin Templeton, David Grace and Andrew King at Concise Asset Management, Ben Witteveen at the Department of Industry, Craig Morris at Russell Australia, Ken Atchison at Atchison Consultants, Gary Stone at Share Wealth Systems, Peter Strachan at StockAnalysis and Sara Rich at the New York Stock Exchange.

Publisher's Acknowledgements

We're proud of this book; please send us your comments through our online registration form located at dummies.custhelp.com.

Some of the people who helped bring this book to market include the following:

Acquisitions, Editorial and Media Development	Production
Project Editor: Kerry Laundon	**Graphics:** diacriTech
Acquisitions Editor: Kristen Hammond	**Proofreader:** Jenny Scepanovic
Editorial Manager: Ingrid Bond	**Indexer:** Don Jordan, Antipodes Indexing

The author and publisher would like to thank the following copyright holders, organisations and individuals for their permission to reproduce copyright material in this book:

- **Cover image:** © adrian825 / iStockphoto

- **Figure 1-1, Figure 1-2, Table 5-3, Figure 6-1:** © ASX Limited ABN 98 008 624 691 ASX 2015. All rights reserved. This material is reproduced with the permission of ASX. This material should not be reproduced, stored in a retrieval system or transmitted in any form whether in whole or in part without the prior written permission of ASX

- **Table 2-1:** World Federation of Exchanges

- **Figures 4-1, 4-2, 4-3, 4-4, 4-5, 5-1, 5-4:** © IRESS Market Technology

- **Table 5-2:** Reprinted with permission of Standard & Poor's Financial Services LLC, a wholly owned subsidiary of The McGraw-Hill Companies. © 2014. All rights reserved.

- **Table 6-2:** CANSTAR Pty Ltd

- **Table 8-1:** ABS *International Trade* catalogue no. 5465.0

Every effort has been made to trace the ownership of copyright material. Information that enables the publisher to rectify any error or omission in subsequent editions is welcome. In such cases, please contact the Legal Services section of John Wiley & Sons Australia, Ltd.

Printed in Australia
29 Nov 2017
654793